The Child to Come

The Child to Come

Life after the Human Catastrophe

Rebekah Sheldon

UNIVERSITY OF MINNESOTA PRESS
Minneapolis · London

The University of Minnesota Press gratefully acknowledges financial assistance for the publication of this book from the Office of the Vice Provost of Research at Indiana University Bloomington through the Emergency Grant-in-Aid Program as well as the English Department of Indiana University Bloomington.

Portions of chapter 2 were previously published as "Reproductive Futurism and Feminist Rhetoric: Joanna Russ's *We Who Are About To*," *FemSpec* 10, no. 1 (2009): 19–35; and as "Joanna Russ and the Murder of the Female Child," in *Practicing Science Fiction: Critical Essays on Writing, Reading, and Teaching the Genre,* ed. by Karen Hellekson, Patrick B. Sharp, and Lisa Yaszek, 183–96 (Jefferson, N.C.: McFarland, 2010). Portions of chapter 4 were previously published as "Somatic Capitalism: Reproduction, Futurity, and Feminist Science Fiction," *ADA: Journal of Gender, New Media, and Technology* 1, no. 3 (2013), http://www.adanewmedia.org/.

Published by the University of Minnesota Press
111 Third Avenue South, Suite 290
Minneapolis, MN 55401-2520
http://www.upress.umn.edu

Printed in the United States of America on acid-free paper

The University of Minnesota is an equal-opportunity educator and employer.

22 21 20 19 18 17 16   10 9 8 7 6 5 4 3 2 1

Library of Congress Cataloging-in-Publication Data
Names: Sheldon, Rebekah, author.
Title: The child to come : life after the human catastrophe / Rebekah Sheldon.
Description: Minneapolis : University of Minnesota Press, [2016] | Includes bibliographical references and index.
Identifiers: LCCN 2016020064 (print) | ISBN 978-0-8166-8987-3 (hc) | ISBN 978-0-8166-8988-0 (pb)
Subjects: LCSH: Nature—Effect of human beings on. | Children. | Global environmental change. | Human ecology. | Feminist theory.
Classification: LCC GF75 (print) | DDC 304.2083—dc23
LC record available at https://lccn.loc.gov/2016020064

Contents

Preface

This book is animated by a central question: why, when we reach out to grasp the future of the planet, do we find ourselves instead clutching the child? In this age of extinction, the first answer is so obvious it is almost parody: children are the very stuff of survival, of course. Speaking of the ending of his climate apocalypse *Snowpiercer*,[1] director Bong Joon-ho writes that the two surviving children—an African American boy and a teenaged Inuit girl—"will spread the human race." At the conclusion of her apocalyptic MaddAddam trilogy,[2] after leading us through nearly a thousand pages of headless chickens grown in vats, helicopter rescues of trapped polar bears, and diseases vectored through vitamin supplements, Margaret Atwood closes on a strikingly utopian image: a small enclave of survivors, their gardens, and their brood of newborn children, all perfectly alive despite the rudimentary medicine and their status as the first generation of wild hybrids, progeny of the apocalypse's human remnant and their genetically modified lovers. As the screen fades to black on Alfonso Cuarón's sterility apocalypse *Children of Men*,[3] the world's only mother and child head toward a boat called the *Tomorrow* in a wooden dinghy. From the vantage of eco-catastrophe, in other words, the child stands in the place of the species and coordinates its transit into the future.

Life is central to politics today. Michel Foucault's claim that power operates at the level of life-itself can only be reckoned the stronger for the many ways in which life has proliferated in the four decades since the publication of *History of Sexuality 1*.[4] From the artificial reproductive technologies pioneered at the same moment as Foucault was composing his theory of biopolitics to the death in 2003 of Dolly the cloned sheep, late-twentieth-century biotechnologies have made clear the plasticity and mutability of forms-of-life and inspired anxious projections of a posthuman future. Increasingly, however, the biotechnological elicitation and control of life-itself have operated under a different sort of threat: that of life's finitude. Where it was still possible, in Foucault's late seventies, to imagine life as the unmarked partner compared to the problematic of the political, today no such attitude can hold. Life can no longer be taken for granted as the immutable substrate for political manipulation. Exhaustion, sterility, extinction, entropy, desiccation: these are the watchwords for life vitiated by its own waning vigor. Life's enervation, however, is matched at the same time by the animacy of the nonliving. Paradigmatically in the specter of climate disaster, the very industrialization that testified to life's tractability has now begun to massively amplify and extend the productive power of natural systems. Life is at once too feeble and too fertile, equally susceptible to excess production and to perilous passivity. Together these tendencies make apprehensible life's autonomous agency.

Take, as a recent example, the geometric increase in the number of earthquakes in Oklahoma. Between 2009, when oil and gas hydrofracking became commonplace across the state, and the most recent findings for 2015, the number of recorded tremors went from around five a year to around five hundred. The situation in Oklahoma is so dire and so obvious that Mary Fallin, the state's Republican governor, conceded her skeptic's position and acknowledged the role of wastewater injection wells in generating seismic activity.[5] This link between extraction technologies and shifting geological expectation well exemplifies what scholars in the humanities and social sciences have recently theorized under the term *the Anthropocene,* a neologism coined to name the geological epoch during which human activity came to have geoscale impact.[6] What Governor Fallin has admitted is that putting wastewater back into rock at levels below one thousand feet—often called "basement rock"—triggers local seismicity. That the hundreds of earthquakes around Stillwater, Oklahoma, are the result of the state's nearly three thousand fracking sites is now not even disputed by those who have the most invested in maintaining the state's oil and gas industry. Admitting the anthropogenic origin of this crisis, however, shifts emphasis away from what is perhaps most profound about it: the responsiveness of stone. As it turns out, Precambrian basement rock, imagined as a passive substrate, has long-standing relations of its own with the geological layers to which it gives shape—relations made palpable through the addition of pressurized water.

Life is not what it was even a few decades ago, and neither are the children who stand in its place. This book is dedicated to following out the ways these two figurations—life and the child—form and deform around each other. I began work on this book in spring 2008. It is hard to overstate how substantially the conversation has changed since then. From the vantage of 2008—the year that Sarah Palin endorsed a "drill, baby, drill" stance on the Arctic during the vice presidential debates—the idea that the Pope would issue an encyclical on climate change was laughable. But that was before Deepwater Horizon, before Superstorm Sandy, before the routine announcement of another train derailment, or oil tanker explosion, or catastrophic waste container breach, back when Hurricane Katrina could be dismissed as an anomaly. The year 2008 was also the year of the housing crash, two years before the Tea Party congressional takeover and the massive sweep into office of conservative state governors. These changes have not only taken hold in the realm of politics and public culture. In the humanities, constructivism began to slide away under the pressure of resurgent materialisms of all kinds. In 2007, Duke released Karen Barad's landmark *Meeting the Universe Halfway,* Indiana published Stacy Alaimo and Susan Hekman's edited collection *Material Feminisms,* Harvard put out Timothy Morton's *Ecology without Nature.*[7] This was not the beginning of new materialism, of course, but it was certainly something like a tipping point between niche obscurity and widespread recognition.

I have carried this book through these years. The transformations they have engendered undoubtedly show up in this text. What it is possible to say about matter, nature, ecology, extinction, futurity—even queer theory!—is just flatly different now from what it was eight years ago. Yet what is remarkable is how persistent the child has been despite these changes. It is on this premise that I offer *The Child to Come.*

INTRODUCTION

Face

> A face drawn in sand at the edge of the sea . . .
> MICHEL FOUCAULT, *The Order of Things*

It is supposed to be the novel's denouement. Kathy H. and Tommy, the doomed lovers of Kazuo Ishiguro's 2005 novel *Never Let Me Go*, already suspect that there was never any real possibility of attaining a deferral. They hold on, nonetheless, to the rumor they cherished during their childhoods at the boarding school Hailsham that couples in love may be given a reprieve of a few years before beginning their life's work. By the time they succeed in finding and quizzing their former school headmistresses, Miss Emily and Marie-Claude, they are already deep into their lives as caregiver and donor. But Tommy is on his third donation—most donors don't make it past four—and so they risk the illicit trip. Their suspicions are confirmed; there are no deferrals for donors. What they receive instead is their history. Miss Emily narrates for them the story that, though theirs, was excluded from their education:

> After the war, in the early fifties, when the great breakthroughs in science followed one after the other so rapidly, there wasn't time to take stock, to ask the sensible questions. . . . And for a long time, people preferred to believe these organs appeared from nowhere, or at most that they grew in a kind of vacuum. . . . So for a long time you were kept in the shadows, and people did their best not to think about you. And if they did, they tried to convince themselves you weren't really like us. That you were less than human, so it didn't matter.[1]

Tightly focalized through Kathy, the novel gives the reader only as much knowledge as Kathy herself can glean to parse the insinuations, delicate refusals of nomination, and half-explained expectations that halo her life

1

and the lives of her friends. From these sources, we know that the designation "student" (like that of "donor") is a euphemism—that the children are clones, test tube grown and raised in schools for later harvesting. We know, too, that Hailsham students were the privileged recipients of an unusual education—unusual, that is, in its apparent normalcy. Through Miss Emily's reluctant exposition, Kathy and Tommy learn that Hailsham was a taxing but short-lived political experiment. The otherwise inexplicable liberal arts education, the training in painting and sport, and the careful documentation of feeling were all in the service of building an archive of evidence to prove the children's humanity.

Perhaps most salient of all, Kathy and Tommy learn from their visit that, despite their zeal for the mission, the school's headmistresses could not feel the empathy they sought to instill in others. "We're all afraid of you," Miss Emily tells them. "I myself had to fight back my dread of you all almost every day I was at Hailsham" (269). This confession isn't shocking—the children surmise it early in the novel—but its revelation underlines the bankruptcy of Hailsham's premise that humanity derives from the authenticity of the children's sentimental selves. It's no wonder that Kathy and Tommy carry the dream of deferment so far into adulthood, all evidence of their lives speaking to the contrary. It aligns so well with the rhetorical intent of Hailsham's many art shows because both take seriously the notion that humanity comes from interiority. If they love, how can they be sacrificed? But no one at Hailsham sought to rescue the students, not really. No essay or poem or painting, no matter how poignant, would save them from the recovery centers. Hailsham's ambition was the more modest one of giving the children a few years to pretend they might have a future after all. Not even the students would go so far as to fantasize a total reprieve from their obligation to donate.

Kathy and Tommy cannot be saved because they have too much saving of their own to do. Keeping in bifocal view their remembered childhoods and the premature deaths to which they are headed, Ishiguro's novel elegizes the vulnerable child and stages in exemplary fashion the new mutation with which this book will be concerned: the slide from the child in need of saving to the child who saves.[2] *The Child to Come* is about this child—the child as resource—and the figurative and literal uses to which we put her in an age riven between unprecedented technoscientific control and equally unprecedented ecological disaster. Like her antecedents, the child as resource is freighted with expectations and anxieties about the future. Unlike them, however, she is tethered to a future that can no longer be taken for granted. For all the heavy weather of global climate change and all the suffering born of industrialism—extinctions, droughts, melting ice caps, rising sea levels, oil spills, poor air quality, and ocean acidification, to name a few—much of the horror of ecological disaster comes from the projected harm to the future these things portend. And the future is the provenance of the child.

Futurity's Child

We don't need Whitney Houston to tell us; we already believe the children are our future. But the relationship between children and futurity, often naturalized as self-evident, in fact has a distinct path of origination in the long nineteenth century alongside burgeoning theories of life-itself. As Carolyn Steedman argues in *Strange Dislocations,* scientific accounts of physiological growth and development were central to the construction of the child as well as to evolutionary thought, a congruence expressed in recapitulation theory.[3] The link forged between the child and the species helped to shape eugenic historiography, focalized reproduction as a matter of concern for racial nationalism, and made the child a mode of timekeeping. Through a developmental model that linked embryonic growth to the succession of evolutionary forms, the child came to summarize the deep biological past of the species. At the same time, the child's own reproductive potential subsumed her individual growth within the broader story of generational succession and lineage. Thus the child became legible not only as a record of the past but as the recipient of a specific biological inheritance freighted with consequence for the future.

The child exited the nineteenth century as the nexus point coordinating life, species, and reproduction with history, race, and nation. This child persists into the twentieth century as the subject of biopolitical management, but it does so substantially transformed by Freudian psychoanalysis. For Freud, the child is not a blank slate (à la Locke), but neither is he mechanically determined by biological imperatives.

Instead, psychogenesis occurs in predictable stages that nevertheless take shape through the influence of early experience. These experiences, the ones that count, are paradigmatically about sexual knowledge. For it is in psychoanalysis that the child's consequential weight for the future of the species comes to play out in terms of interior life and, more specifically, in the binding of free-floating libidinal energy into subjectivity and thus into what Michel Foucault will call "the perverse implantation of sexuality."[4] Indeed, it is by this route that the operation of power at the level of life-itself (or biopower) comes to center on sexuality as its principal technology. Through the child, concerns over reproduction merge with and emerge through the social reproduction of norms.

That the child requires careful management as he stages toward sexual knowledge is therefore less the result of concern for the child than for the adult he will become. The child, then, is a kind of retronaut, a piece of the future lodged in and under the controlling influence of the present. By the same token, however, the innocence that is worth protecting cannot be preserved indefinitely, and so the child's relationship to the future is defined, in part, by a melancholic anticipation of necessary loss. By way of analogy, the prolepsis that defines the child comes to shade the future of the species grasped along with the child. Through the combined influence of physiology and psychoanalysis, the child as cipher for the future of the adult and the child as cipher for the future of the species intertwined and engendered the vulnerable, innocent child whose rescue from harm appears tantamount to the future safety of us all—a future that is in any case already irremediably harmed.

The Child to Come in many ways situates itself against the imperative to rescue the future through the child and as an analysis of the predictive temporalities that subtend the assumption that the future might be thus saved. It builds on Lee Edelman's invective against the figure of the child and the future he signifies in his *No Future: Queer Theory and the Death Drive.*[5] That said, however, *The Child to Come* also departs from Edelman's conceptualization of reproductive futurism in two important directions. First, where Edelman's conceptualization is largely ahistorical, I look at a specific milieu, American culture from the 1960s to the present.[6] Second, where Edelman's concern is with the significance of the child in the symbolic order, my interest centers on the ways in which the child's figuration of interlocking biological processes stands in the place of the complex systems at work in ecological materiality. The conceptual and the historical claims I've outlined are really one. The development of the atom bomb, of satellite photography of Earth from space, and of the mass implementation of synthetic insecticides and pesticides in the postwar moment, I argue, engendered a burgeoning apprehension of nonhuman animacy. *The Child to Come* takes off from the assertion that the capacity to elicit the vitality of natural systems implicit in these technologies also occasioned a reciprocal recognition of the potential for that vitality to slip its bonds and exceed human control. For this same reason, however, the story I am telling is not of an accomplished turn or even of a well-delineated shift but instead of a kind of torsion between multiple modes, all of which continue to circulate together.

The polemic with which I open the book thus winds up serving the more incisive contention that the child stands in for life-itself in a period of vibrantly (and virulently) resurgent materialisms of all kinds. Since Donna Haraway's "Manifesto for Cyborgs,"[7] scholars working in post-human theory and feminist new materialism have argued that matter is no passive substrate for human design and have called on us to recognize its agency. This isn't just a disciplinary or intellectual contention, however. The urgency of the call comes from the way that industrial production relies on and at the same time misrecognizes the vitality of natural systems, a process that Hannah Arendt named the "unnatural growth of the natural" under conditions of the "constantly accelerated increase in the productivity of labor"[8] both human and nonhuman. As a figure of life-itself that is nonetheless enshrouded in the mantle of plenitude and innocence, the child shores up that misrecognition and is shored up through it. Contiguous to and issue of the reproductive, the child reminds us of the autonomous processes and subindividual capacity of which we are composed and so matches the "vital, self-organizing, and yet non-naturalistic structure of living matter."[9] At the same time, the child binds the realization of nonhuman vitality back into the charmed circle of the human, encircling the future in the promise of generationality. For it is not just the case that the child retro-reproductively forecloses

the future but also that the figuration of the child as the self-similar issue of the present, the safe space of human prosperity and a return to a
manageable nature, forecloses the mutational in the reproductive. And
yet this grafting of the culture of life over the *culturing* of life generates a
queer child-figure whose humanity is always suspiciously intimate with
other-than-human forms-of-life. Through the child-figure, I contend, we
manage and come to terms with the insurgent futures forecast by these
resurgent materialisms.

The first half of the book explores the incision of the planet into the
child–future relationship; the way the child comes to inform the rhetorical figuration of future catastrophe; and the effect of that rhetorical
form on the epistemological and cultural fabrications of nature, matter,
and life-itself. While still looking at widely circulating representational
media, the second half of the book departs from the rhetorical focus of
the first half by taking the child literally as a matter of reproduction and
not just as a disciplinary tool toward social reproduction. What does it
mean to take representations literally? Both halves of the book approach
the child as a dense figuration that threads together diverse domains into
"material-semiotic knots."[10] That is, like Haraway, I understand figuration
as the place "where the biological and literary or artistic come together
with all the force of lived reality."[11] In the book's first two chapters, my
concern with the child centers on the way that he makes sensible the
proleptic temporalities that then justify the preemptive management of
the future. Beginning with an analysis of Cormac McCarthy's 2006 novel
The Road, the second half of the book considers the child whose biological
innocence promises to extend species-survival into the future. In the two
chapters that follow, I take up the ways in which the child, the fetus, and
the reproductive woman became subjects of intense discursive investment
under conditions of planetary threat. This shift in focus from the child
in need of salvation to the child who saves coincides historically with the
first articulation of the concept of the Anthropocene, or the geological
period characterized by human geoscale impact first theorized by Paul
Crutzen and Eugene Stoemer.[12] More generally, it speaks to a burgeoning
apprehension (in both senses of the word) that we are past the threshold
by which we might recover a complacent nature happy to provide a scenic

background for human action. In this sense, the child allows for a cultural and political negotiation of the postnatural or the intuition that "we have never been natural (and neither had nature)."[13]

None of this, however, quite explains why the child is greeted with so much and such intense emotion. Telling that story requires first stepping back to the late nineteenth century to rehearse some of the ways in which the child came not only to signal the future but to sentimentalize a rescue that is, in a profound sense, more important than the child who is its putative subject. In what follows, I argue that the biopolitical regime that Michel Foucault describes as of a piece with the modern production of sexuality also made the child a hermeneutic project capable of catalyzing intense emotion. The artifact of this process is the face.

The Masturbating Child Is All Face

We have seen so far that the story of the child is a story about stories. Signs and symptoms, causes and effects, buried meanings and deciphered clues: saving the child is first and foremost an epistemological task. The vexed dynamic of innocence and experience set out by the romantic inheritances of psychoanalysis and famously analyzed by Foucault hinged the child's salvation on the revelation of his concealed vices. It is for this reason that Foucault includes the masturbating child as one of his four key figures of biopolitics. In his well-known argument, the proliferation of demands to tell the truth of sexuality—the "whole network of varying, specifying, and coercive transpositions into discourse"[14] erected by nineteenth-century science, medicine, jurisprudence, educational theory, and child psychology—engendered what it sought to describe. Sexuality was thus the name given to and the practice of hollowing out the space for interiority, binding libidinal energy to generate a vertical model of subjectivity and casting meaning as a movement from subterranean causes to symptomatic surfaces.

Generically a ghost story, Henry James's 1898 novella *The Turn of the Screw*[15] thematizes the consequences of installing sexual subjectivity by way of the child. The novella concerns the fraught and ultimately fatal struggle for interpretive control between young Miles, his younger sister Flora, and their governess. As the story opens, Miles has been sent home from his boarding school for reasons never made fully clear. Incensed by the school headmaster's refusal to name Miles's crime, the governess seeks first to clear Miles of wrongdoing. This motive, however, soon turns into the conviction that some "secret precocity" (61) lurked beneath his "beautiful face" (53). This in turn gives way to the horrifying certainty that the children have been consorting with ghosts. To save them, the governess must wrangle from them the truth of their secret assignations, but her task is stymied by the "monstrous utterance of names" (51). If Miles and Flora are not concealing anything, then the very suggestion would be a corruption in its own right, bringing with it the poison of self-consciousness. Indeed, even the governess's own knowledge suggests the taint of corruption. And so instead of stating her inquiry outright, the governess circles the children with a web of allusions and half-stated accusations, a sidelong interrogation that ends when she literally reads the older child to death. Even then, however, there is no guarantee of a finally revealed meaning, for the performance of innocence can always be exactly that—a performance.

Throughout, it is the face that records the doings of the soul. The governess returns again and again to compare the evidence she has gathered to the photographic plates of the children's faces to espy the truth. When she finally believes she has caught Flora in the presence of the ghost, it is her face ("her small mask of disaffection" [70]) that provides the final confirmation: "Her incomparable childish beauty had suddenly failed, had quite vanished. . . . She was hideously hard" (70). Ironically, Flora's inability to deceive the governess affirms her as the less corrupted of the two. Miles's face, by contrast, never loses its beauty, instead becoming increasingly "feverish" (84) as it grows increasingly "sealed" (84). That his performance of innocence is so complete and so convincing only indexes the depth of his duplicity and the extent of his canniness. Even at the very last moments before his death, as he says the words the governess has given to him to say, she wonders if he is "perhaps innocent" (83) after all.[16]

Over the course of the narrative, the words that the governess seeks to coax out of her young wards move from the diffuse to the exact as her attention fixes on the children's prior caretakers, both dead at the novella's opening. In a work that is so much about the inability to land on any final meaning, however, the ghosts merely hold a position that could be occupied by any number of things, including the "things" (83) Miles confesses to have said to his friends at school. To take it one step further, the ghost story is itself a kind of sleight of hand, allowing James to tell a tale that modesty would otherwise forbid without it losing its legibility as another version of the story of the sexual secret, that is, the story of the masturbating child.

The Turn of the Screw's drama of reading (to borrow Sheila Teahan's phrase[17]) has made it a favorite tutor text for both deconstructive criticism and queer theory. Yet the novella is also and importantly about feeling. "I was infatuated," the governess reports of her final conversation with Miles. "I was blind with victory."[18] The book's refusal to resolve its central question throws the reader back on the obsession that fueled the governess's epistemological drive and reminds us that the problem of nomination is only partially a matter of preserving innocence. The governess's lust to know also forbids any direct accounting because it would put an end to the pursuit and the circuit of arousal it enables. Citing the repetition of verbs like *to grasp, to seize, to catch,* and *to fix,* Teahan contends that James's novella equates comprehension with capture as a kind of physical seizure and, in this way, makes Miles's death the result of a bathetic fall from potentiality. Eric Savoy, in his reading, formalizes this hermeneutic procedure:

> The governess's spiral of hermeneutic connotation is restrained when it comes too close to nomination; because nomination is simultaneously unbearable and unknowable, it is arrested by aposiopesis, the gap in explanatory syntax in which, as we have seen, the prosopopoeic figure of the ghost is generated.[19]

Aposiopesis, the name for abruptly ended sentences and ascetic refusals of knowledge, produces prosopopoesis, the personification of an abstraction or, literally, the production of a face. The governess may take the face as a surface to be interpreted, but James's novella also demonstrates how her persistent acts of interpretation call the face into being as the trace of obscured interior depths waiting to be deciphered.

The child's face thus brings out the affective dimensions of hermeneutic indeterminacy. The task of managing innocence—contaminated by questioning, forbidding examination—generates a quest that can only spoil what it seeks to verify. What it discovers instead, over and over again, is what Savoy calls "the gap in explanatory syntax"[20] that wings it back for another route around the hermeneutic spiral. For Foucault, the figure of the masturbating child was produced from out of the interlocking discourses of medicine, law, pedagogy, psychiatry, and child-rearing. What backgrounds Foucault's discussion and what James's novella so powerfully reveals is the structural predication of the masturbating child on the panicked adult reader intent on maintaining the innocence of her search to espy the child's vices. Hermeneutics and paranoia not only are fitted to each, as Eve Kosofsky Sedgwick[21] has it, but the shape they form in their juncture is paradigmatically the face of the child in the eye of the adult.

Reading the Child

In two early and sweeping studies,[22] James Kincaid describes this phenomenon (what we might call the "Governess Phenomenon") as "child-loving" and uses that concept to theorize the panicked response to ascriptions of childhood innocence that he argues are likewise responsible for the (prosopopoeic?) figure of the pedophile. In Kincaid's reading, the child's definitional emptiness—her lack of sexual knowledge and adult rationality—makes the child the perfect figure for figuration as such.[23] With some notable exceptions, this is the version of the child most often taken up by scholars: "innocent, malleable and fragile" in Steven Mintz's words, "immured in an innocence seen as continuously under siege" in Edelman's.[24] The child is made of narrative: "literally, these children—the ones I know from life and the ones I know from reading—lead fictional lives," writes Kathryn Bond Stockton.[25] The child heads a narrative whose sentimentality issues from the "cultural process of 'sacralization,'" in Viviana Zelizar's analysis, but that can also veer from the melodramatic to the gothic, as Steedman shows.[26] The fictions that they inhabit, Stockton continues, allow a too often unacknowledged lateral spread, what she calls the "suspensions and shadows of growth"[27] and which, for Natasha Hurley and Steven Bruhm, complicate the "simple stories, euphemisms, and platitudes"[28] often assumed of narratives for children, narratives about children, and the interpretations we draw from them. For Edelman, by contrast, the child-figure's narrative cogency merely fleshes out the dynamic set down by the double logic of the sign, that is, the tension between the apparent fullness of signification and its threatening "collapse into the letter's cadaverous materiality."[29]

If the child is made of stories, then the face is its inscriptive surface. Many scholars have theorized the relationship between the face, subjectification, and significance. For Giorgio Agamben, the face emerges through invagination, an introjection of the outside that creates depth via folding. "There is a face whenever something reaches the level of exposition and tries to grasp its own being exposed,"[30] he writes. For Michael Taussig, the face is an allegory and, like allegory, all shuffling surfaces and illusory depths. "How masklike all faces are," Taussig writes. "Sets of meaningful features, like pictures or texts, trading in apparent permanence or realness for a mobile façade, not unlike writing itself."[31] For Gilles Deleuze and Félix Guattari, facialization precedes significance and subjectification and coordinates their concurrence as face. The face is a kind of replication machine, both an artifact of the process and the process that gives rise to it. "The faciality machine is not an annex to the signifier and the subject; rather, it is subjacent to them and is their condition of possibility."[32] For Emmanuel Levinas, finally, the face is the wellspring of ethical comportment that provokes an "awakening to the precariousness of the other,"[33] which reminds us of our own vulnerability and mutual responsibility. Levinas's sense of the face is less far afield than it may at first appear, for the responsibility inaugurated by the face requires a human subject able to meaningfully respond, as Jacques Derrida discusses at length in *The Animal That Therefore I Am*.[34]

Spur to ethics, abstract machine, allegory, or invagination—for as differently situated as these accounts may be, they all present the face as an ontological predicate. Even Deleuze and Guattari, for whom the critical imperative is to "know your faces; it is the only way you will be able to dismantle them,"[35] even they title their chapter on faciality "Year Zero." Where other topics in *A Thousand Plateaus* receive at least minimal historical contextualization (as in the title of their chapter on psychoanalysis, "1914: One or Several Wolves"), the face precedes calendar time. In her reading of the child, Claudia Castañeda makes a congruent point about the child in poststructural theories. Looking specifically at the use of the child by critical theorists as figure for an ahistorical desubjectivization, Castañeda criticizes Foucault, Deleuze and Guattari, and Jean-François Lyotard for their abstracting appropriations of the child. Each of them constitutes the child as "a site or space through which an alternative, implicitly adult subjectivity can be imagined."[36] The drama of subjectivization and its escape is tied to the Lacanian logic of the law of the father, itself deeply invested in thinking with and through the structure of the linguistic. There is good reason, then, to wonder if these theories (of the face, of the child, of the child-as-face) aren't in fact vestiges of the linguistic turn even as they (some of them) are critical of it, itself a response to the biopolitics of sexuality we have been lengthily discussing. Such a periodization would put the waning of faciality alongside the turn against symptomatic reading in the first decade of the twenty-first century.

The evidence, however, suggests that the child's face remains pivotal to the affective adhesiveness of biopolitics in the twenty-first century. The story of the face is complicated because it is composed of a series of differences and laminations, as indeed the child-figure's variety of meanings have also been de- and reactivated over the course of its two centuries. On one hand, the form that the child's affective adhesion takes differs from its hermeneutic counterpart in ways we shortly encounter. And yet, and on the other hand, it is given significant propulsion from the structure of panic inculcated by the child's late Victorian iteration. Another pair: while the modulations in the meanings of the child's face (as a widely circulating figuration) became distinctively legible in light of the last three decades of feminist posthumanist theory,[37] its divergence from the readable child predates the unraveling of the semiotic consensus and indeed predates the full instantiation of neoliberal economic policies that provides the primary context for much of my analysis.

I'd like to discuss two instances of the child's new affectivities, both from the atomic 1960s, before turning back to Ishiguro. Both visual narratives[38] have been understood as ushering in new practices in their respective spheres. The first, Lyndon Johnson's infamous reelection campaign advertisement (originally titled "Peace, Little Girl" but subsequently referred to as "Daisy Girl") ran for only a single day, September 7, 1964.[39] By the time it was pulled for being too incendiary, it had been seen by an estimated 50 million television viewers.[40] Despite the brevity of its run, it was discussed at length in a *New York Times* story authored by Pete Hamill that ran the following month and, the following year, was honored with a Distinctive Merit Award from the Art Director's Club. Since then, the ad has been analyzed as a turning point in American campaigning, the beginning of the modern synthesis of marketing and presidential politics.[41] The second, *2001: A Space Odyssey,* was screened to audiences nationwide in spring 1968 and earned $138 million over its several months in the theaters. A collaboration between the American-born filmmaker Stanley Kubrick and the British science fiction author Arthur C. Clarke, *2001* has been acclaimed since its release for its innovations in cinematography and cinematic storytelling and is often used to mark the renaissance in Hollywood filmmaking that was to come (though *2001* itself was shot outside of London). Science fiction critic David Higgins uses Clarke's novelization to pinpoint the turn from the imperial Golden Age to the inner exploration of the New Wave.[42] The fact that neither text was in any real sense about children, childhood, or reproduction (unlike, for example, the Roman Polanski film *Rosemary's Baby,* released the same year as *2001*) makes them all the more powerfully indicative of the child's continuing rhetorical and affective salience.

The Star Child

"Daisy Girl" was a product of atomic anxiety. Produced at the height of the Cold War, in the aftermath of the Cuban Missile Crisis and in the wake of John F. Kennedy's assassination, "Daisy" sought to paint Republican nominee Barry Goldwater as a warmonger who could not be relied on to use America's nuclear armament judiciously. To do so, the design team of Doyle Dane Bernbach brought together three elements: stock footage of an atomic bomb testing blast, the voice of a mission control officer counting down from ten, and three-year-old actress Monique Corzilius. Shot in black and white, the sixty-second spot opens with Daisy (Corzilius) kneeling in a field of flowers that arch over her heard. While a sound track of birdcall accompanies her, she plays a counting game, picking the petals off a flower, the titular daisy (though it is in fact a daffodil). She lisps endearingly, skips over some numbers and stutters through others, until, as she approaches ten, her voice is overridden by an unmistakable mission control countdown. She stops counting and looks up into the camera. The camera zooms in on her face. "These are the stakes," Johnson intones as a nuclear mushroom cloud fills the screen. "To make a world in which all of God's children can live or to go into the dark. We must either love each other," he continues, "or we must die."[43]

In many ways, Daisy herself is perfectly familiar. Chosen for her youth and plunked down on a field of flowers on the banks of the Hudson, she is the legatee of Wordsworth's Lucy Gray, the romantic death-bound child of nature, and of her melodramatic nineteenth-century inheritor, the child in need of saving. Cannily, the ad never punctures Daisy's innocence with knowledge of the future harm it prophecies, all of which takes places outside of her cognitive grasp. While it happens beyond her comprehension, however, it doesn't happen outside of her.[44] What makes the advertisement not just *compelling* but also *telling* is its formal choice to frame the bomb through the proscenium of Daisy's gaze. As the count ticks down, the camera moves closer and closer to Daisy, her upturned face becoming an indistinct blur around a single eye until her cornea fills the whole screen. Even then the camera keeps moving inward, the dark of her iris morphing into the darkness of the sky against the false sun of the mushroom cloud and its expanding coronas of fire. And it never leaves. In the next moments, the ad cuts to the title card. The bomb hangs there, in the future signaled by the child, forever exploding inside of Daisy's eye.

Narratively opposed but visually symmetrical, the innocent child's body and the virulent materiality of the bomb are rendered formally equivalent by "Daisy Girl." This is a relation less of analogy than of flat identity as the explosion takes place inside of the child. In Stanley Kubrick's *2001: A Space Odyssey,*[45] it is the child and the planet that are locked in tropic correspondence. As is well known, the sequence occurs at the end of the film. Dave, the far-traveling astronaut, finds himself saved from certain death (after his onboard AI HAL kills off his companions) by the mysterious alien Monolith. To save him, the Monolith sends him traveling into its interior. During these scenes, the camera cuts between geometric neon lights seen from Dave's perspective and a third-person point-of-view shot of Dave's increasingly gaping and lidless eye until he and his escape pod come to rest in an empty, perfect, and perfectly impossible neoclassical bedroom. He wanders, growing rapidly older as he moves through the rooms, until he winds up an old man under the covers.

At this point, the clock flicks over: Dave is replaced by the Star Child and the eighteenth-century bedroom by a twentieth-century starscape. It is Earth. Wrapped in his amniotic sac, the Star Child pulses blue light into the depths of space as he falls into the camera's frame. This is the film's conclusion. It's as slow as the rest of the film—the shot lasts for over a minute—but for fully half of that time, the child drifts slowly into the frame, his glow reaching out toward the peaks of Earth's atmosphere. The child and Earth appear on-screen together for only a single frame before the torque pulls the child around to face us. Something no longer human flickers in his gaze. His regard lingers for several long seconds, and then it is over.

Despite the brevity of their encounter, the formal symmetry between the child and Earth is hard to miss. They are visually parallel, taking up nearly the same space on the screen: rounded, glowing objects falling away from each other in the void. Unlike the merger of child and bomb that we witnessed in Daisy, however, their symmetry does not signal an identity. If anything, they appear superimposed against each other, contiguous metonyms that nevertheless fail to touch. Released in 1968, *2001: A Space Odyssey* thematizes emerging technologies of space flight, deep-sensing photography, and human–computer interactions. The first lunar orbital images showing the whole Earth rising over the moon (and the deep space fields in the background) preceded the film by two years, and the iconic Blue Marble NASA images were still eight years in the future. At this ductile moment—sharing a decade with Rachel Carson's *Silent Spring*[46] and the burgeoning environmental movement—*2001*'s final scene welds together a particularly compacted and contradictory set of meanings. On one hand, the child and the planet recapitulate and supplement each other, the child humanizing Earth. At the same time and by the same logic, Earth planetizes the species, rendering palpable again and in a new way the contingency of biological form and the co-composition of biological and ecological matters that had been plaguing human exceptionalism since the evolutionary theories of the long nineteenth century.

Child as Resource

It was in a crucible of new findings in the life sciences that the child took on its modern form, and it is by way of the child that we continue to adjudicate the boundaries around the natural, to interrogate the essential features of life-itself, and to draw conclusions about the future. For the questions opened by nineteenth-century materialists and vitalists about the causalities immanent to organic and inorganic life are by no means dead-letter in the twenty-first century. In many ways, the new sense of the malignancy of the future results from and exists in torsion around the impact of contemporary biosciences and their artifactualization of the processes of life-itself. While evolution theorists imagined the mutability of species long before the last fin de siècle, contemporary advances in tissue engineering, nanotechnology, 3D organ printing, in vitro meat, synthetic biology, genetically modified food, cloning, and stem cells have demonstrated the plasticity of form in a way previously unimaginable. In a different domain, data modeling—both fine grained and large scale, intimate and impersonal—has rendered experience as information flow and netted the future in chains of cause and effect. From the U.S. National Security Agency's PRISM warrantless surveillance program to the ubiquity of password protection, from personal biometrics to the algorithms used by federal agents and large-box retailers alike, we live in an age of predictive control.

In a recent interview, Elizabeth Povinelli[47] suggests that these and other similar changes have shifted the cultural dominant far enough from its twentieth-century moorings to justify reconsidering the salience of the biopolitical. Under conditions of planetary threat, she argues, when the preeminent partition is no longer the one maintained between human populations but rather that between the living and the nonliving, biopolitics necessarily shifts away from Foucault's four figures: the masturbating child, the perverse adult, the Malthusian couple, and the hysterical woman. I agree. And yet, as we have seen, the child continues. As I will argue throughout, the new context within which the child circulates continues the management of life-itself characteristic of biopolitics, but with a wider and less stable sense of what counts as life.

This book considers the centrifugal relations between the child as a figure for life-itself and the burgeoning of forms-of-life made apprehensible in this period. For it has become increasingly clear that something both subtle and monumental came to a head in these decades. At the same time that the future has turned malignant, the organizing logic through which the child took shape—racial biopolitics—has likewise shifted. These changes redound on the child. The amplification of natural systems under industrial production has put into crisis the border that kept the agential subject conceptually distinct from his passive objects and made apprehensible the autonomy and vitality of the nonhuman and the non-living, just as increasingly minute and emergent forms-of-life have been captured by regimes of technicization and financialization. Under these conditions, the grand thematics of twentieth-century biopolitics do not fall away, but sexuality is no longer the most crucial nexus of power, and thus they no longer take shape through reflexive anthropocentrism. Foucault's four figures, reflexively anthropocentric, bind bodies and pleasures to sexuality as the principal regulatory mechanism governing the reproduction of future populations. By contrast, contemporary biopolitics is no longer channeled through the desiring subject because power today is no longer a matter of norms and tendencies but of thresholds and captures. To modify a phrase from Foucault, we are no longer a society of sex but a society of soma.

Which, in a literal sense, is what happens to the children of Hailsham as they are marshaled from the schoolyard to the operating table. For the meeting with Marie-Claude and Miss Emily is not the end of the novel. In the wake of their dream of conjugal reprieve, in what is otherwise a gentle unraveling toward death and loss, the novel proffers one more unsolved and perhaps unsolvable rumor. It comes as Tommy and Kathy are preparing for his fourth organ donation. "You know why it is, Kath," Tommy says, "why everyone worries so much about the fourth? It's because they're not sure they'll really complete."[48] Kathy reassures him but narrates a different story to the reader:

> But Tommy would have known I had nothing to back up my words. He'd have known, too, he was raising questions to which even the doctors had no certain answers. You'll have heard the same talk. How maybe, after the

> fourth donation, even if you're technically completed, you're still conscious in some sort of way; how then you find there are more donations, plenty of them, on the other side of that line; how there are no more recovery centres, no carers, no friends; how there's nothing to do except watch your remaining donations until they switch you off. (279)

"Completed" is a euphemism for death, of course, that is used because donors were never understood as alive in the sense that would allow for the dignity of death so named. The rumor of a life after completion, however, intimates another set of meanings informing the euphemism. On one hand, as Kathy tells us, completed donors no longer participate in the social world of other donors, carers, and recovery centers. They are completed in the sense that their psychological interiority no longer matters compared to the bodily interior whose contents are slowly donated away. The loss of that world, however, enables their completion in the other sense of that word: without the guise of a social identity, they are now exclusively the biomedical tools they always really were. In turn, it is because donors straddle the line between living being and biomedical tool that life "on the other side of that line" can be extended indefinitely. Indeed, the image of surgeons "switch[ing] you off" evokes the technical in technical completion: fourth-donation donors have crossed a threshold beyond which their biological livingness and the technical apparatus that supports it have become inseparable. Like the cloned ovum, the harvested body of the donor is an artifact of the laboratory.

And yet, for all of its artifactuality, something stares back. In his discussion of the ontological status of the coma victim, Giorgio Agamben writes,

> The hospital room in which the neomort, the overcomatose person, and the *faux vivant* waver between life and death delimits a space of exception in which a purely bare life, entirely controlled by man and his technology, appears for the first time.[49]

In passing beyond biological citizenship, technically complete donors embody what this book will analyze as the movement from a biopolitics of population reliant on aggregates of whole persons to a new biopolitics of subindividual, modular, and extractable parts. Within this context,

the child's figuration as controlled metamorphosis—derived from con-
temporaneous nineteenth-century developments in cell biology, evolutionary morphology, and historiography and formalized by Freudian
psychoanalysis—inverts. The children of Hailsham literalize the contemporary child's metonymic substitutability for complex human and
nonhuman material systems and ecological infrastructures.

In cloning, lineage comes to bear a very different set of meanings.
Where sexual reproduction allows descent to be graphed as a branching
tree, the clone confuses verticality and horizontality. Like the stem cell,
the clone inverts the movement from birth to death and thus the normative rules of increasing differentiation and decreasing potency.[50] The clone
confuses part–whole relations and thus elides the distinction between
synecdoche and metonymy by making apparently distant things kin to
each other. Finally, the clone results from the technical mediation of the
laboratory. Instead of the heteroreproductive dyad, the clone generates
from one (the same from which she is a copy) and from many (the technicians and their apparatuses) at the same time. For these reasons, Sarah
Franklin calls the clone "a kind of mutational space in which cultural and
biological categories, presumptions, and expectations are warped."[51] While
this scene of swarming life may trigger disgust, however, it is also an artifact
of a highly controlled process of elicitation, capture, and redirection that,
among other things, allows for its instrumentalization and financialization.
"Nature known and remade as Life," Haraway writes, "through cultural
practice figured as technique within specific proprietary circulations."[52]

Neoliberal capital is an important part of this story of the biopolitics
of reproduction, or what I call *somatic capitalism*. That said, however, the
techniques that engender patentable forms-of-life are themselves reliant
on the willingness of life to express its vitality. Life-itself, then, subtends
and transcends any particular form-of-life no matter how proprietary its
technical–legal modes of capture. In *After Life,* Eugene Thacker demonstrates that life-itself is strictly uncategorizable.[53] Embodied by individual
lives but not exhausted by them, immaterial yet entirely real, life-itself
supports instrumentalization while also receding from it. Pace Povinelli,
then, while the figure of the masturbating child and the medical–juridical
apparatuses that maintained it no longer correspond to the deployments

of power today, the same cannot be said for the child in toto. On the contrary, the child serves as the switch gate for somatic capitalism, giving smooth flow, shape, and circuit to several knotty problematics. As I outline in chapters 1, 2, and 3 ("Future," "Life," and "Planet"), the child joins the security of generational succession and proper development to the promise of human futurity. By the same token, however, the child's assurance of human vitality slides metonymically into an assurance of life-itself. Thus the child and the reproductive woman become sources of figurative and literal value, as I discuss in chapters 4 and 5 ("Birth" and "Labor").

In the famous conclusion to *The Order of Things,* Michel Foucault dates the emergence of the figure of man as the primary object of the human sciences to the beginning of the nineteenth century and then prophesies its inevitable end. He writes,

> [Man] was the effect of a change in the fundamental arrangement of knowledge. As the archaeology of our thought easily shows, man is an invention of recent date. And one perhaps nearing its end.
>
> If those arrangements were to disappear as they appeared, if some event of which we can at the moment do no more than sense the possibility—without knowing either what its form will be or what it promises—were to cause them to crumble, as the ground of Classical thought did, at the end of the eighteenth century, then one can certainly wager that man would be erased, like a face drawn in sand at the edge of the sea.[54]

To extend his metaphor, we might say that the shape of the face remains in the topography of the beach. For a long moment before the face forms a part of a new geography, it mingles with the sand and tide. The child is such a boundary-figure cast up by the apprehension of man's disappearance and the persistence of the interpretive projects that subtended his emergence. Its presence points to the drag of the retreating *epistēmē* but also to the pull of the one approaching. This book works within the boundaries of their mingled territory.

Whereas the great project of modernity concerned the scientific description of the human and thus generated "a being whose nature . . . is to know nature, and itself, in consequence, as a natural being,"[55] the present formation shifts from knowledge to *technē,* from the human as the subject and object of knowledge to the human as a biologically vulnerable, biologically exploitable resource, from totality to systematicity. As a corporeal form-of-life-itself, one of a spectrum of forms-of-life whose value resides in the presence of a definite number of usable material capacities, the human no longer gains his value from his unique ability to synthesize knowledge to form a unified picture of totality. By the same token, however, the human—in her double role as subject and object—persists. As technicians of life, we intervene into mobile, manipulable, autocatalyzing systems. Under these conditions, the child comes to signify life in its contemporary triplex denotations as soul (the child as transcendent value), as interacting biological processes (the child as unstable autoaffective system), and as germ of life-itself (the child as stem cell, as protean germ of materiality's potential to give rise to new forms, still bearing the marks of generation). The child-figure thus takes part in both epistemological formations, reinscribing the face while enclosing behind it the potentialities of life-itself.

In other words, it is not sufficient to renounce or to denounce the child. If we turn our backs, we risk missing that which the child is fitted to capture: the emergent energies of posthumanity. For the same reason, though, our task cannot end with the child, either in celebration or in denunciation. Its nodes describe one pathway through that which it seeks to prevent; its peregrinations describe a part of the machine that will someday cease to sustain it. Throughout this work, I seek out representations of the child-figure to see the vital and virulent materialisms held in oroborous orbit in the child's face, to get so close to the face of the child that we can see through it to the sand beneath. I do this not because I think it is opposed to power but because it is where power operates today. By tracing the epistemologies from which the child-figure arises and to which it gives face, I chart the new topographies distending our familiar forms even as I write.

1

Future

An absolute missile does not abolish chance.

JACQUES DERRIDA, "No Apocalypse, Not Now (Full
Speed Ahead, Seven Missiles, Seven Missives)"

The 2009 United Nations Climate Change Conference (COP15),[1] held in
Copenhagen, Denmark, began with a showing of *Please Help the World.*[2]
Created by Danish director Mikkel Blaabjerg Poulsen, the four-minute
video advertised the Raise Your Voice campaign, a joint venture of the
Danish government and YouTube created to encourage young people to
make climate change awareness videos. The video narrates how a young
girl came to make a video of her own for the campaign. The opening
sequence shows her watching raindrops collect in a puddle on a grassy
playground. The location then cuts to her home, where we find her watching television coverage of climate disasters, a different image of destruction
on each of the channels her father flips between. These images bleed into
her dreams. In the next sequence, the girl dreams that she has awoken
alone in a desert. As she looks around the parched plains, storm clouds
roll in, rapidly breaking into floodwaters, hurricane winds, and tornado
funnels. She is whipped off her feet and barely manages to grab onto a tree
limb. She wakes up screaming, and the sound elicits the help of her father,
who calms her fears by showing her a live feed from COP15. Inspired by
what she has seen, the girl grabs a video camera and races to the roof.
The sequence then breaks off as the point of view switches from a third-
person image of the girl holding the camera to the girl recording herself.
In this new frame, the girl, speaking directly to the audience, says clearly
in English, "Please help the world!" Her image detaches from the frame
and, in falling away from the camera, starts a cascade of tiny screens, each

disclosing a child who yells, "Please help save the world!" as violin music soars in the background. Finally the thousands of tiny video screens of pleading children fall together to form the COP15 logo—a meshwork globe whose soft blue glow is as suggestive of images of an ovum in utero as it is of pictures of Earth from space. After flashing the conference information, the image stabilizes around the words "We have the power to save the world." A second later, the single word "Now" joins the sentence.

The COP15 logo and the didactic narrative that precedes it bind the visual rhetoric of complexity in the meshwork globe, the laboratory elicitation of biotechnical life in the ovum, and the allegedly prediscursive familiarity of the planet and the child as if each were an apt and intuitive metonym for the other. This figural flexibility, Donna Haraway argues, emerged at a particular moment in technoscience coincident with a newly pressing need to give imaginative scope to the idea of life-itself. "The fetus and the planet Earth are sibling seed worlds," she writes in a phrase that highlights the fecundity (the seed) that it doesn't quite name. She continues,

> If NASA photographs of the blue, cloud-swathed whole Earth are icons for the emergence of global, national, and local struggles over a recent natural-technical object of knowledge called the environment, then the ubiquitous image of glowing, free-floating human fetuses condone and intensify struggles over an equally new and disruptive technoscientific object of knowledge, namely "life-itself." . . . The fetus and the whole Earth concentrate the elixir of life as a complex system.[3]

Together, the child and the globe give face and figure to the abstraction "life-itself." Haraway's reading, however, contains a telling tension. The apparent (though actually highly mediated) stillness of the fetus and the planet not only "concentrate[s] the elixir of life," as Haraway puts it, but also shutters the intuition of life "as a complex system" behind the sensuous colors and forms of the planet and the child, which seem to "signify the immediately natural and embodied."[4] The blue-green, cloud-swathed Blue Marble Earth recognizably iterates the landscape tradition of the pastoral, while the face of the fetus in the womb repeats the many faces that make up the history of the child, as we saw in the introduction to this volume. These metonymic figures, in other words, proffer the apprehension of complexity that they then immediately disguise behind the singularity and isolation of the human child and the human world. And yet, as figures for life-itself, the fetus and the globe circulate alongside and lend their new significations to the child and the pastoral in an expanding, mutually inflecting and reversible metonymic chain: child–fetus–ovum–womb; planet–ecology–land–place.

The flexibility of the metonymic chain suggests that the child is not only the premier rhetorical spur to changed policies, not only the subject of future protection, but also a technology in the endeavor to save the future. Saving the child, in other words, appears tantamount to saving the future, just as saving the future is done in the service of protecting the children of the future. Thus the persistence of the hurt, pleading child-figure. Another Raise Your Voice submission, *Le Temps est Venu!* (The time is now!),[5] uses face-morphing technology to create seamless transitions between the faces of children representing diverse nations. Each face is accompanied by the equivalent of the English word "Please." Like *Please Help the World*, *Le Temps* begins with the child and ends with the planet. As the faces of children flick by, each making its plea, they slowly merge with the face of the planet as seen from space. Revealed as two iterations of the same face, the metonymic child–Earth dyad stares back as a single entity.

This singularity is crucial. Both videos make some gesture toward the notion of humanity as a local–global population, but both do so by multiplying the single child. Each child, in his unique individuality, as if alone, stands in the same metonymic relationship with the planet. A swarm of children might call to mind humanity's animality, its species-being. Despite the gesture toward global inclusion, however, these videos do not focus on populations of children but instead emphasize the individual life contained in the single child. They repeat that singularity across many frames and, in the case of the official film, in the conference logo. The planet, too, crests alone. As metonymic icons, the child and the planet singularize life-itself. They enclose the complex movements and swarming multiplicities of biological and ecological systems within the unitary and unified visages of the blue-green Earth and the child's face. The famous NASA photo that captures the face of the globe surrounded by darkness, which came to be the slogan of the Whole Earth movement, singularized for the first time what had before been unencompassable within one frame: Earth as system. At the same time, it produced a deceptively still image. In the same way, ultrasound images disembody and singularize the fetus, opening access to the fetus as process at the same time as and by the same movement that it is captured at a single point.

That freeze-frame stillness casts a different sort of telling tension when framed against the urgency urged by these videos. Despite its advertisement of the Raise Your Voice campaign, the real audience for *Please Help the World* were the diplomats and politicians who attended the two-week-long conference. The child's plea to them, like Daisy's plea to voters in 1964,[6] was to implement stronger policies in the service of reversing climatological and ecological trends. In other words, her rhetorical efficacy (which would seem to stem from her dyadic relationship with the planet) in fact relies on an unstated but necessary third term. The child advocates for the planet because she stands in metonymic figuration not only of the ecologically precarious world but also of all of the children who will come to live in it and in whose name we should pursue environmental action. The child, then, advocates for a particular kind of action with regard to the life-itself for which she is a potent metonymy: specifically, management over the future to protect the future's children. Biopolitical management is not far at all from the history of environmental advocacy. The Earth Summit, Haraway writes, has its roots and objectives in worldwide security, management of resources and populations, mitigation strategies, and diplomatic negotiations.[7] For as much as it takes an oppositional stance toward modern industrial practices, environmentalism is one result of the technoscientific, governmental, and managerial processes of the twentieth century that together produced the idea of a threatened ecology that requires human engineering.

Extending Haraway's incisive description of the globe and the child within the contemporary biotechnical politics of life-itself, this chapter argues that these narratives enclose complexity within performative images that privilege stillness, unity, and isolation and that make life-itself appear vulnerable, unique, and in need of protection. Thus the child and the planet envisage a politics whose recognition of complexity is folded into the rhetoric of protection. Locked in tropic correspondence, the planet inflects and deepens the child's association with nature, the child lends its humanity to the planet, and the vulnerable innocence historically associated with the child enshrouds Earth. Beyond the technical elicitation that renders them visible, the images of the planet in space and the child in the womb circulate as discursive technologies that labor to collapse life-itself, defined as the potentially catastrophic mobility of systemic complexity, back into life, defined as static or progressively developing forms-of-life. As the speaker for future generations, the child encompasses a temporal narrative that grafts present-moment urgency *(Le Temps est Venu!)* onto distant futurities. At the same time, the rhetoric of urgency serves the end of delay. As performative figurations, the child and the planet sentimentalize stasis in the service of life. This chapter explores the consequences of that figural arrangement as a sentimental economy, a temporal rhetoric, and a causal logic evocable in a plurality of contexts through the same highly wrought iconic figure.

The Queer Matter of the Future

What makes this alignment of security and environmental activism the more troubling is how important environmentalism has been, even (especially) in the popular form I have been discussing so far. Since environmentalism's inception in the 1960s, it has been successfully demonstrating the intersecting oppressions of women, animals, the environment, and those lives raced and classed as not worth living. Environmental activists have rightly insisted on the dignity and autonomy of other-than-human lives and decried the myopia that makes environmental costs into so-called business externalities. In these ways, popular environmentalism has helped to rejoin the conceptually severed relations between human and natural productions and fostered awareness of the effects of current industrial practices.[8]

Popular environmentalism shares with other social justice movements a commitment to wide-scale social and political transformation. Though sometimes this is accomplished via direct action, the more common route has been to engage in persuasion campaigns like Raise Your Voice. And this has meant telling a story about the future and about the possibility of change: changed expectations, changed relations, changed configurations.

The Global Warming Mug, for example, shows the coastlines of Earth's continents disappearing as the mug heats up and reappearing as it cools down. As this small instance exemplifies, thinking environmentally requires reckoning with the complex mobility of all forms-of-life. Yet the backward and forward temporality of the global warming mug suggests that the only possibilities are future destruction or present stasis. More potently, the positing of a clear and knowable end point to ecological change pulls against the central insight that matter is mobile. Finally, linking environmental policy to an undesirable eventuality (in this case, rising sea levels and coastline loss) dovetails with a pervasive belief in the need for security against a harmed and harming future in the name of future generations.

In this way, the indeterminacy built into popular environmentalism becomes a source of threat. The future engaged by popular environmental hortatory relies on and activates a series of epistemological certainties that subtend narratives ostensibly about uncertainty: that we understand the effects of present actions; that we may extrapolate from that understanding to see the coming future; that most things will remain unchanged enough to provide a stable background against which to chart the changes whose ramifications we can then call the future. Together, these assumptions cast the movements of time as the reorganization of space. It is as a plot, grid, or landscape that the already present future may retain certain topographical features, while other features remain indeterminate and thus open to the shaping effects of the present.

Keith Ansell-Pearson, in his book-length treatment of Henri Bergson's philosophy of time, makes an important distinction between time imagined as discrete blocks and time imagined as mixed flows of virtual and actual duration:

> The distinction between a discrete or actual multiplicity and a continuous or virtual one marks a difference between thinking objects and things discretely, whereby the relations between them are ones of juxtaposition and exteriority and thinking the components of a system in terms of fusion and interpenetration.[9]

Elizabeth Grosz, in her work on Bergson, refers to Ansell-Pearson's discrete multiplicities as "mechanisms,"[10] a term that has the advantage of evoking a system subjected to and extrapolated from laws that govern each aspect of its functioning as if it were separable from the whole. By contrast, a virtual multiplicity "changes in kind in the very process of getting divided up."[11] In popular environmentalism, the future is a discrete multiplicity. Like the global warming mug's appearing and disappearing coastlines and their single mechanism of sea level rise, the future known in advance presumes no changes in kind. What Grosz and Ansell-Pearson suggest is that causality has no such discrete boundary lines, such obdurate stabilities. Instead, as Karen Barad writes, causality is always in process: "changing patterns of difference are neither pure cause nor pure effect; indeed, they are that which effects, or rather enacts, a causal structure, differentiating cause and effect."[12]

By asserting an already known future, popular environmentalism discounts the very capacity for change that its rhetoric propounds. By overestimating the strength of discrete multiplicities (e.g., subsystems like species populations) while underestimating the mutability of virtual multiplicities (e.g., ramifying ecologies), popular environmentalism reifies the causal structure it promotes, locates itself outside of those causalities, and hypostatizes the environment as the passive victim of the very dynamism whose recognition it demands. The landscapification of the future organizes the present around the need for security. The future, however, cannot be truly opposed; it may only be guided such that it might reproduce the fragile safety housed by the present. It is on behalf of, but also through, the child that the present may be safely reproduced as the future, forming a closed loop via generation.[13] The threat to the future, in this sense, emanates from the notion, inherent in the idea of the future, that tomorrow may not resemble today, that is, that radical change is not only possible but also continuously operating within the logic of self-similarity and as the condition of reproducibility. Like the child (and her cognate fetus, ovum, seed, womb), the future has two faces: discrete on one side, multiple on the other; linear and chaotic; generational and mutational; closed and open. Janus-like, they are grafted together. Let this double enunciation stand as a definition of futurity. As I argue in the following pages, attempts to fix the future—to heal it and to immobilize it—rely on closed, determinate systems.

It is against this reproduction of fixity that I seek to situate the queerness of matter.[14] Whereas popular environmentalism has taken up the sustainable cultivation of nature, a nature impacted by human action, as its primary topos, philosophers of ontology have turned to matter, both organic and inorganic, to dismantle the boundaries of nature–culture. In *A Thousand Plateaus,* Gilles Deleuze and Félix Guattari use the term *matter* as an analog for "the plane of consistency or the Body without Organs, in other words, the unformed, unorganized, nonstratified, or destratified body with all its flows: subatomic and submolecular particles, pure intensities, prevital and prephysical free singularities."[15] Barad defines matter as itself the agent whose force acts as the crosscutting flows across the plane of consistency. As Barad describes it, matter cannot be located in the form or the movement, the contingent conditions of living or the animating principle. Matter is all iteration and permutation. Thus, although both radical materialists and popular environmentalists advocate for the apprehension of nature's activity, the idea of matter importantly differs from that of nature because it does not economize individuals or evaluate more or less desirable states against a transcendent index.[16] Gilles Deleuze writes, for instance, that "an animal, a thing, is never separable from its relations with the world. The interior is only a selected exterior, and the exterior, a projected interior."[17] Interiority and exteriority gain their distinctiveness through a process of incorporation and projection; they aren't immanently separate, and they won't always occupy the same relations. In their shared analytic engagement with affectivity—the capacity to affect or to be affected in a nature without boundary lines—environmentalism and philosophies of ontology alike deconstruct liberal humanist anthropocentricism.[18] When environmentalism proceeds from affectivity to efficacy, however, the two fields split.

For Deleuze, the creativity of matter resides in its indeterminacy: "No one knows ahead of time the affects one is capable of . . . you do not know beforehand what a body or a mind can do, in a given encounter, a given arrangement, a given combination."[19] This insistence on openness and indeterminacy is a consequence of rethinking the boundaries between individuals, indeed, of rethinking individuals, in terms of immanent relations of impingement. In other words, where popular environmentalism advocates change toward averting catastrophe, philosophies of ontology understand change and its speeds as the constitutive condition of the world. This does not mean there are no tendencies, limits, or captures to mattering but that these are unpredictable, nonteleological, and complex: neither acausal nor deterministic. Why call this indeterminacy the "queerness" of matter? I choose this term against linear causality structured by filiation and patrimony, against the conflation of futurity with reproduction, and toward mutations and nonorganic becomings.[20]

Landscaping the Future

An aristocratic couple gazes out from the parapet of their castle at the rolling hills of their estate, their eyes fixed on the horizon. No sight mars the equanimity of their land, but disturbing sounds distantly echo to them: clamorous and agitated. As they watch, the tips of uncountable pitchforks breach the mount of the farthest hills. A mob of peasants is on the march. Together, they descend to the garden and pick from the glass flowers that still bloom among many stalks. The snapped bud glows and then fades; the noise increases suddenly and then dissipates. Resignedly, the couple review the few remaining flowers and return to the castle.

This, in brief, is the plot of J. G. Ballard's allegory "The Garden of Time."[21] As the title implies, these are "time flowers" imbued with the magical ability to slow time. Whereas the story's organizing axis is time, its allegorical analog is space. The future is right over the horizon, as the colloquial expression has it, fully formed, immutable, and already present in the present. Rather than requiring a striding forward to meet it, this future must be held in check, prevented from engulfing the seemingly monolithic but truly fragile stasis of the present. By the tale's end, the flowers have all been picked and the distant mob has overrun the castle, revealed by their passage as the ruin it was prevented from being long past its historical moment by the powerful magic harvested in its garden. The future strips the present of its vitality, cannibalizing and entombing it, exposing it as history.

The vitality of the future is the threat the flowers protect against. Yet, change here is an illusion: the future is what it is, the past too, the present merely the elastic interval between them. It is as allegory that this story can balance on such a strict economy of symbols: the aristocrats, the mob, and the flowers articulate a closed system composed of three points, or rather, two points and a fulcrum. The allegory of the future as spatially located in the same frame as the present actively delimits the contours of change, reducing it to a preestablished certainty. If the tone of this tale is resignation, it is because the threatening future has already been domesticated. The poise of the opening scene is an effect of the inevitability of the terminal scene. Rather than cusping revolution, these three elements labor together to perpetuate self-similarity. The future is already present in the present because the future is known. Ballard's allegory, like the Global Warming Mug, gives us time as a closed system.

As a scientific term, closed systems designate those systems that have limited interface with their environment, usually via one determining factor (heat, say, or information) that does not change the nature of the system. Ansell-Pearson explains how closed systems reduce "all change, all qualitative change, . . . to spatial movement" and all movement to "a mere rearrangement"[22] of already existing parts, thus the possibility of a simultaneous present and future.[23] This reductive determinism has several consequences. It allows designation of a particular threat, which can then be calculated, regularized, anticipated, and managed. At the same time, however, it suspends duration, collapsing future threat into a present configuration and cutting them both away from their moorings in the multiplicity of flowing relationships that constitute the open systems of the world. Processes are then envisioned as a series of points adjacent to one another but discrete from each other, "a series of juxtaposed and successive immobilities"[24] that can be counted, placed on a grid, and assessed. The determining factor in Ballard's story is the constriction of time figured as a specific technology, the time flowers. As the flowers run out, so too does the time allotted to the present. This constriction is homologous to the restriction of elements: the closed system and its two points.

I turn to Ballard's short story because its restricted symbolic economy brings into relief the structure that subtends the rhetoric of urgency in popular environmentalism. The determinism that renders the threatening future safe even while retaining the rhetoric of threat likewise structures the "Fable for Tomorrow" that opens Rachel Carson's *Silent Spring,* released the same year as Ballard's short story. In many ways, Carson's book pioneered the temporal rhetoric of popular environmentalism by joining American nature writing to techniques of scientific extrapolation. The resulting hybrid genre, a type of speculative nonfiction that easily segues into the fictional, takes the future as its primary topos.[25] "A Fable for Tomorrow" uses the fable form to achieve the same closed system as Ballard's allegory. "There once was a town in the heart of America where all life seemed to live in harmony," Carson writes.[26] It is threatened by an "evil spell": "children . . . would be stricken suddenly while at play and die within a few hours" (2), along with birds, bees, and animals. Carson leaves this scenario without conclusion, shifting instead to her moral: "No witchcraft, no enemy action had silenced the rebirth of new life in this stricken world. The people had done it to themselves" (3). She concludes the fable with a direct address to the reader: "A grim specter has crept upon us almost unnoticed, and this imagined tragedy may easily become a stark reality we all shall know" (3). We shall know it, that is, unless we write the missing cathartic ending.

The fable is far more vivacious than a statistical table. Yet the rhetorical efficacy of this speculative fantasy is tempered by its sense of causality. The fable requires both a rigid and a fluid conception of the future. The future must be fixed and thereby knowable *and also* responsive and therefore alterable. Carson, and many others after her, effect this feat by drawing on past crises. In the suspension between past harms that analogize, foretell, and contribute to the harmed future, the present is constituted as the privileged space of safety. It is from the safety of the present that the future may be managed. We can see, for instance, in Frederick Buell's approving citation of Ulrich Beck the way that popular environmentalism recognizes matter's mobility while, at the same time, citing that mobility as the source of threat. He writes, in *The Future of Environmental Criticism,*

> Underlying the advance [of eco-consciousness] has been a growing malaise about modern industrial society's inability to *manage* its unintended environmental consequences that Ulrich Beck . . . calls "reflexive modernization," meaning in particular that even the privileged classes of the world inhabit

a global "risk society" whose *hazards cannot be anticipated, calculated and controlled, much less escaped* [emphasis added].[27]

As goals, anticipation, calculation, and control curiously recapitulate the logic of modern industrial society to the benefit of human civilization. The resulting temporality trends toward stasis despite the rhetoric of futurity.

In this context, then, it is not unimportant that the source of refuge in Ballard's story is contained in a beloved but failing garden. The rhetorical emphasis on rapidly approaching ecological collapse is a mainstay of hortatory environmental writing, and the constriction of time functions as the motive for management and regulation. Carson urges her readers to recognize that "there is no time" remaining for adaptive behaviors to emerge given "the impetuous and heedless pace of man rather than the deliberate pace of nature";[28] Arne Naess's fifth point toward a deep ecology platform concerns the recognition that "present human interference with the non-human world is excessive, and the situation is rapidly worsening." Garrett Hardin cajoles, "Ruin is the destination toward which all men rush." James Lovelock urges us to see that "we are now approaching one of those tipping points, and our future is like that of the passengers on a small pleasure boat sailing quietly above the Niagara Falls, not knowing that the engines are about to fail."[29] Note the spatialization of temporality in Hardin's metaphor of the "destination" and Lovelock's analogy to the falls; the way Carson and Naess position humanity as disorderly occupants of a space not their own: nature's pace against man's; interference in a nonhuman world. This spatialization and division reflect a closed, finite world. This urgency reifies the future as an already known immobility whose arrival must be delayed.

If the future is already decided, it is because the elements impinging on that future are restricted to a closed set of causes. In E. O. Wilson's words, "the changes occurring now will visit harm on all generations to come." For Murray Bookchin, it is institutions of domination and exploitation that will "inevitably lead our planet to ecological extinction." Andrew Dobson writes that "it is within the wit of humanity to rescue itself from the abyss towards which it is plunging." The wit of humanity Dobson cites can be motivated through a dissemination of fear of the abyss: "Green politics seeks to transcend fear by feeding off it." The important point here is that this "ruin," this "rapid worsening," this "harm," this "extinction," this "abyss," is already determined—the "writing is on the wall," in Winona LaDuke's phrase.[30] Just as the peasant army is restrained by the time flowers of Ballard's story, it is the health of our earthly garden that can slow down and reverse our flight toward inevitable doom. While the rhetorical persuasion is aimed at transformative practice, lodging the future in a closed system limits the ends of that change to an artificially delayed present.

Reproductive Futurism

Protection here is protection against harmed futurity, future DOA. Like the mob, it is right over the horizon and getting closer. This empty future is the subject of Lee Edelman's attack on "reproductive futurism." This phrase has several valences for Edelman: the conjunction of the figure of the child with the trope of the future; the promise—infinitely deferred—that there will be a time in time that won't be the present; the imperative to replicate the present into the future in the hope that the future won't come. Reproductive futurism, then, is a two-sided salvation narrative: someday the future will be redeemed of the mess our present actions foretell; until then, we must keep the messy future from coming by replicating the present through our children. In *No Future,* Edelman argues for a "derealization of the order of meaning that futurism produces,"[31] because the future envisioned by reproductive patrimony (the fantasized and actual extension of the humanist human into the future) is no future at all. By this he means that the fantasy of a clean future actively seeks to thwart (protect against) contingency against the coming of a future that is neither a descendant nor a salvific redemption of the present. The clean future of descent, ostensibly the object of protection that necessitates weapons like the nuclear bomb, shares with the dead future a refusal of those disorienting flows that characterize open systems.

The conjunction of the child with the future is never clean, however, because the child is not a guarantee of replication. Rather, the figure of the child "enacts a logic of repetition that fixes identity through identification with the future of the social order."[32] The child never more fully fulfills his function as emblem of reproduction than when his innocence is threatened and is open to protection and management. Thus the implicit doubling of the book's title: yes, Edelman is positioned toward what his critics call "the antisocial thesis" in queer theory, but "no future" also refers to the death drive he sees operating within, and tearing apart, a heteronormative futurity in thrall to reproduction.[33] The figure of the child stands in for a futurity that strips the future of everything but repetition and yet insists that repetition is progress. No future, indeed. The blank face of the child, the blank face of decimation, perfect health or perfect destruction, are preferable to—and modes of controlling—nonrepetitive futures.

Ranged against the figure of the child is the *sinthomosexual,* a word Edelman derives and neologizes from Lacan. The sinthome is fantasy's catachresis, its areferential aporia, which "determines the exchange of signifiers . . . admits of no translation of its singularity and therefore carries nothing of meaning, recalling in this the letter as the site at which meaning comes undone" (35). The force of the bomb is the paradigmatic sinthome, utterly resistant to meaning in its capacities but incessantly the target of figurative labor. The sinthome must be brought back into futurism's fold by becoming a part of its "generational succession, temporality and narrative sequence, not toward the end of enabling change, but, instead, of perpetuating sameness, of turning back time to assure repetition" (60). Internal to futurism but of a different order, capable of turning the seams of reality inside out, apocalyptic end games are the volte-face of protection. In the name of the future, we must be protected from the future. For Edelman, recognizing the function of the sinthome as the basis on which narrative coherence is possible is the revolutionary instant. I'd like to posit as well that the child and the sinthome, ostensibly antagonistic, are the twin poles of catastrophic narratives. Ricocheting between absolute meaning and the threat of nonmeaning provides coherence of a particularly overwrought style that actively shapes the future as neither salvific nor decimated but threatened.

Sianne Ngai defines the cute as "a way of aestheticizing powerlessness."[34] For this reason, the child as the prototypically cute object is most fully itself when weak, hurt, and in need of protection. It calls to us to protect it by possessing it. Yet its to-be-rescuedness is without limit. Cuteness speaks, sadistically, of a future relief it can never inaugurate and still be itself. Like the child, it points toward a future formally foreclosed by its very constitution, because the future the child points to is the adult who stands where the child no longer is. But unlike the child's temporal disjointedness, the cute builds and builds and builds on its own inability to be saved from itself. The cute and the child have no future. Thus also the menacing potential for violence in the cute child: vitality under too much constraint eventually explodes.

The Child in Environmentalism

> A small boy runs in front of an oncoming truck. You watch in horror as you realize the truck can't slow down in time. You think you should save the boy but you are unsure. Still, the moment compels you to act: you rush into the street and grab the boy.[35]

The truck is global warming, the road is the present, the boy is the future. This tiny allegory introduces a new element into the speculative nonfictional narratives we have seen so far. It, too, turns time into space in the service of immobilizing the future, but it does so through the ethical urgency of the child. Over and over, Tim Morton's narrative puts the child in danger. Once he is rescued; twice he dies, and the afterimage of the dead child seems to speak to us from that harmed future, to blame us for its, and his, harm.

The closing paragraphs of the introduction to Al Gore's *An Inconvenient Truth* ask us to imagine that very scenario. He begins by relating the story of his son's near-fatal childhood accident as a parable to explain his subsequent involvement in the environmental movement. "During that painful period," he writes, "I gained an ability I hadn't had before to feel the preciousness of our connection to our children and the solemnity of our obligation to safeguard their future and protect the Earth we are bequeathing to them."[36] Our obligation to Earth's future is coextensive with our obligation as parents to value the "preciousness" of children. Gore then asks us to indulge him in a thought experiment. "Time has stopped," he writes. In its suspension, we may speak to our children "as they are living their lives in the year 2023." Gore provides their end of the conversation: "Imagine now that they are asking us: 'What were you thinking? Didn't you care about our future? Were you really so self-absorbed that you couldn't—or wouldn't—stop the destruction of Earth's environment?'"[37] The opening photo in Gore's book of himself and his heavily pregnant wife Tipper seated in a canoe on the Caney Fork River circa 1973 encapsulates the equations between nature, heteronormative family structure, reproductive futurism, and the landscapification of the future whose consequences are the subject of this work.

This formulation is common in political speeches on the environment. In his speech to the 1993 Earth Summit, Bill Clinton urged listeners to act with urgency: "Unless we act now, we face a future . . . where our children's children will inherit a planet far less hospitable than the world in which we came of age."[38] Newt Gingrich, a prominent Republican during Gore's vice presidency, dedicated his climate change book *A Contract with the Earth* "to our wives, Callista and Addie, our daughters, Jackie, Kathy, Molly, Emily, and Sally, and our grandchildren, who will surely enjoy a lifetime of peace and prosperity on a cleaner, greener, and thoroughly renewed Earth."[39] Obviously his vision is differently pitched, but it is still strikingly structurally homologous with Gore's and Clinton's. In a section of Pope Francis's recently issued encyclical on climate change, *On Care for Our Common Home,* titled "Justice between the Generations," the Pope asks, "What kind of world do we want to leave to those who come after us, to children who are now growing up?"[40]

Nor are politicians any more susceptible to the enchantments of the child-figure than are environmentalists. James Hansen begins the final chapter of *Storms of My Grandchildren* (which also bears that title) with a picture of his eleven-month-old grandson Jake that stands in metonymic relation to the "concept of responsibility to future generations" Hansen encourages us to adopt. Placed without comment next to a further suggestion that lowered fertility rates will help secure a "bright future," we are left to conclude that life, too, even the life of future generations, had best be managed so that each individual life may be preserved and celebrated.[41] Though the immoderate production of population threatens our future, the child's redemptive association with the natural dissevers him from the question of population. As Scott Russell Sanders writes in the conclusion to his *A Conservationist Manifesto,* the integrity we perceive in nature is our own birthright. We swim in the one and only stream of life. By recognizing that we are part of this vast, subtle, ancient order, we are restored to wholeness. A sense of communion with other organisms, with the energies and patterns of nature, is instinctive in children, and it is available to every adult who has ever watched a bird or cloud.[42]

Sanders's rhetoric makes us children of Earth and actual children the exemplars of a primitive and unsullied relationship with nature.

Not only does the child signify originary wholeness but her presence marks the continued vitality of the human. In *The Coming Global Superstorm,* Art Bell, a reporter, and Whitley Strieber, a novelist, combine their two genres to form a hybrid work that intersperses factual chapters on climate change with sections from a novella about climate disaster. The novella, an action-adventure tale, ends with the discovery in the snow-buried public library on decimated New York's Fifth Avenue of a group of schoolchildren shepherded by a nun:

When Bob looked down, he saw what was without question the most amazing sight he had beheld during the storm or at any time in his life. Sitting on the wide marble floor below were about twenty children.[43]

As if their discovery betokened the continuation of life, the final scene in the novella shows the lighting of candles in the apartment towers surrounding their camp: "We're here, they [the candles] said, more of us than you thought possible, many more. We're still here" (240). This sentiment is echoed in the final factual chapter, in which Bell writes in summary, "Mankind wants to survive. We want to prosper" (210), and we will do so by rationally limiting childbirth and developing techniques for predicting and thus managing climate disasters. The child signifies the future we (adults) threaten, the connection to nature we (adults) have corrupted and the human spirit whose ingenuity will overcome the (adult-made) disasters of the present.

The story is the same in visual media. Speculative nonfictional environmental documentaries produced over the past two decades—future histories like *After Armageddon* and *The Last Hours of Humanity* that narrate the present proleptically from the space of the future; environmental forecast films that extrapolate future consequences according to metrics like

Six Degrees Could Change the World or *Arctic Death Spiral*; environmental jeremiads that frame climate change as the result of moral bankruptcy or disordered behavior like *Addicted to Plastic* and *GMO OMG*[44]—all deploy the suffering face of the child as a metonym for the harm already done to the future by present practices, harm for which the child demands redress in the form of preservation. Whether he speaks to us from that harmed future to demand that we account for ourselves and the world we created or inhabits the diegetic present, the child serves as a shard of the future. I am already your future, the child says. I am already in the future. Save me from the future. Make this a different future. Only you can prevent future harm. The plaintive child recodes mobility from the basis of the world-as-system to the specter of harm haunting the future. This tack has become so familiar that there's even an *Onion* story about it with the headline "We Must Preserve the Earth's Dwindling Resources for My Five Children."[45]

Catastrophe and Ecology

Of course, the child is not *actually* the future. Any one child may live another ten decades, but she may equally well not make it past this one. Perhaps we could say that children, though not literally the future, *are* literally the stuff of survival, that is, that reproduction is the only thing standing between us and extinction. (I'll have more to say about this umbilical promise of one last, one more, generation in the next chapter.) The face of the suffering child carries such a strong rhetorical force, I am arguing, not because of the child per se but because of the way the child contours ideas about the future. The child gives us back a future stripped of the very conditions that make urgent action necessary to begin with: the unpredictability of amplifying fields of force. The threat to the future, in this sense, emanates from a notion inherent in the idea of the future that tomorrow may not resemble today, that is, that radical change is not only possible but is also continuously operating within the logic of self-similarity and as the condition of reproducibility. In urging us to rethink environmental narratives, my purpose is not to deny or negate the biospheric changes currently occurring but to put pressure on a causal structure that seeks to secure the self-same as safety. By the same token, however, these narrative forms reveal the burgeoning awareness of systemic agency. Indeed, what is striking is how closely catastrophe and ecology are bound to each other, co-constitutive elements whose mutual implication threatens popular environmentalism's reparative mandate to make the future safe for our children. Thus, my goal here is to show not only how environmentalism constructs a heteroreproductive narrative against the catastrophic but also how catastrophe as the excluded other comes back to queer environmentalism.

Traditionally, popular environmentalism has described nature's proper economy as balanced and harmonious. Such ideas imply the interconnectedness of mobile forces and their voluntary self-moderation into what is sometimes called the "Goldilocks Zone." Catastrophe, then, names the release of the dynamism that subtends and maintains meta-stability.[46] Like its cousin revolution, catastrophe designates a system-wide transformation, a tremor in the web of force relations that breaks up stable nodes and sets them moving again. As such, both revolution and catastrophe are ways of talking about temporality, about the speedy or sluggish flows that are always operating on and as even the most mute and immovable objects. Unlike apocalypse, with which it is often associated, thinking the catastrophic requires the apprehension that all systems are unstable and groundless, without necessity and with no truth other than their own capacity to continue operating. By contrast, apocalypse, which also labors in the temporal register, designates that which has always already been awaiting our discovery, now at the end of the quest literally unveiled.[47] So, apocalypse requires a self-similarity beyond duration, lurking within all the ephemera of the passing hours. The balanced harmony indexed as the health of the environment, then, designates the slowness of time, the delay or deterrence of its capacity to generate turbulence and the manipulation of consequence toward that end.

In other words, ecology already implies catastrophe understood as the effects of time made visible by their escape from balance. Catastrophe is not just the necessary supplement that makes the notion of balance coherent but ecology's very self, its apocalypse. Serving as the ground rather than the opposition, catastrophe rewrites ecology as a refusal of the finality of an end and the metaphysics of health or sickness that accompanies such an ending and that is always implicitly tied to some criterion, some desirable outcome. Unacknowledged, however, catastrophe queers ecology by turning it straight. Eve Kosofsky Sedgwick has most forcefully described the double bind that allows systemic misrecognition to function as a virulently unstable structural principle.[48] By binarizing stability and movement, by laboring toward the perpetuation of one over the other, environmentalism must ignore the centrality of temporality even to a theory of stability. This willed unknowingness unfolds as self-division: on one hand, the repetitious association of environmental goals with human children and, on the other, the specter of wayward movements that threaten the safety or even the likelihood of those children. The resulting heteronormative bias intimates that the criterion used to stabilize what has always been understood to be an unstable system is the continuation of the present, a continuation explicitly at odds with environmental activist argumentation and strangely akin to corporate mitigation strategies intent on subsuming green goals into capitalist production.

The heteronormative peril that attends the division of catastrophe from ecology sacralizes the same present that is also construed as the source of that harm and labors to produce sites of immobility. These sites, however, are located within open systems. In the following section, I argue that open systems engender a complementary fantasy of preemptive security.

Future Harm

An underground neo-Marxist revolutionary network, operating in an alternate United States that has suffered a nuclear explosion and is now at war with Iran, Iraq, Pakistan, and North Korea and that has implemented a series of security measures including closed borders and privatized twenty-four-hour full-access surveillance, schemes to upset the election of a right-wing governor by exposing his son-in-law as an adulterer. The neo-Marxists are helped by a former adult movie starlet turned talk show host, a fitness maven with unsavory motives, a team of hackers, and an eccentric scientist who may or may not be connected to the politician they seek to unseat and who has recently implemented an ocean-based power station whose source of power is inscrutable to everyone but may have tipped Earth off its axis, thereby sending the aforementioned son-in-law through a rift in the space-time continuum and leaving him amnesiac, thus allowing the neo-Marxists to exploit him. Meanwhile, soldiers are returning from the front lines addicted to a new drug that may be the source of power fueling the new station, and one of them may have been put through the space-time rift with the son-in-law. In addition, everyone is armed. Furthermore, any display of unauthorized hostility will result in immediate deadly force, usually via high-powered automatic rifles operated by veterans now employed as private security guards and installed on every rooftop. Lastly, the city is about to riot. Also, everyone has access to real-time mapping technology, spy satellite images, closed-broadcast security cameras, and powerful underground broadcast capacity.

Here we have an open system without points but with innumerable variables. The movie I am describing, Richard Kelly's *Southland Tales,* is not paranoiac.[49] It is not true that each group holds a clue to a larger truth. There is no larger truth. There are only multifarious goals, misunderstood allegiances, and manifold consequences. Nor is there a cathartic revolution: the explosions that close the film catalyze a phase transition, but they do not establish power in one quadrant. To adapt Foucault's phrase, "power is [still] everywhere."[50] Rather, the (singular) "truth" is exactly what each group competes to establish to effect local alterations in what everyone in the film acknowledges is a messy, tangled, distributed, populous, and speedy assemblage of forces. Things move—fast. Politics happens in the future, so control over the future means knowing how that assemblage will redistribute before it redistributes, which in turn means taking a hand in its redistribution. And predication, in this centrifugal environment, is apt to be wrong. Against the closed system characteristic of harmed futurity in which parts may be rearranged or delayed but never fully extricated or transformed, this open system is incessantly trading parts in and out, fluctuating, de-forming, and re-forming. Its behavior is emergent rather than determined. Brian Massumi succinctly summarizes Gilbert Simondon's conception of the emergent or germinal: "A germinal or 'implicit' form cannot be understood as a shape or structure. It is more a bundle of potential functions localized, as a differentiated region, within a larger field of potential. In each region a shape or structure begins to form, but no sooner dissolves as its region shifts in relation to the others with which it is in tension."[51] Seen through the amnesiac consciousness of Kelly's protagonist, this dispersion of causality makes each player seem capable of infinite, slippery movement. Untethered in a field of force with no center, he is literally buffeted from one "home" to another, unable to regain any sense of the shape or stability of his world.

The radiant complexity, promiscuous causality, and speedy mutations that characterize Kelly's alternate United States are frightening and disorienting. Future harm is a reaction to this fright, which still shares in its logic and contributes to its assemblage. I mean those gun turrets, and the apparatus of security they are. What I am labeling future harm is actually a multiplicity of tactics and enunciations centered on the production and perpetuation of threat that allows for the enclosure of stable centers deserving of protection and carved out from the chaos of the larger milieu. But these centers are peripatetic, located only in relation to immediate threat. Foucault describes security as distinct from disciplinary technologies of isolation, concentration, enclosure, and protection. On the contrary, the function of security is to "allow the development of ever-wider circuits" to "let things happen" as they are naturally inclined and, through careful study of things as they really are, to "carve out in reality, as a field of reality, [a] population and its specific phenomena."[52] More recently, Massumi has complicated this description of security through his historicizing account of the Bush-era preemption model as a postmodern discursive-material simulation machine. By locating preemption on a continuum with prevention and deterrence, Massumi makes clear their interlocking mechanisms. He begins this article with an eerily appropriate quotation from President George W. Bush, one that might as well have titled Kelly's film:

> If we wait for threats to fully materialize, we will have waited too long. We must take the battle to the enemy, disrupt his plans and confront the worst threats before they emerge. In the world we have entered, the only path to safety is the path to action. And this nation will act.[53]

As is clear in this quotation, deterrence doesn't give way to preemption in a historical surpassing. Rather, as Massumi argues, preemption begins with full epistemological certainty of future events, the deterrence model we've seen in Ballard's story, but, rather than creating bulwarks, subsumes threat as its own rationality and attempts to intervene in its emergence. In this preemption model, certainty of future events slides across metonymic registers to become certainty of some uncertain future event, for which apprehension will equal both enunciation of a particular threat or population and redistribution of that threat or that population. So, "carving out of reality," as Foucault puts it, collapses the two-stage operation of deterrence (locating the threat, defending against it) into the simultaneous creation and dispersion of a threatening emergent possibility, not to destroy or contain it but to keep it germinal, supple, and moving. This "threat-o-genic"[54] politics, as Massumi calls it, relies on movement as the ground of protection.

Given all this, we might reasonably ask how an environmental politics intent on deterring catastrophe can have any traction against an operative politics that already includes catastrophe as one of a host of techniques. In other words, and more baldly stated, environmental deterrence casts a world of limited operational freedom, such as Ballard's, as its preferred form of sociality—thus the pastoral impulse of environmentalism. Even when that impulse does not predominate, as in E. O. Wilson's elegant description of Earth as an open system in *The Future of Life,* the rhetoric works to celebrate the present operations of that open system. Wilson writes,

> Earth, unlike the other solar planets, is not in physical equilibrium. It depends on its living shell to create the special conditions on which life is sustainable. The soil, water, and atmosphere of its surface have evolved over hundreds of millions of years to their present conditions by the activity of the biosphere, a stupendously complex layer of living creatures whose activities are locked together in precise but tenuous global cycles of energy and transformed organic matter. The biosphere creates our special world anew every day, every minute and holds it in unique, shimmering physical disequilibrium.[55]

In Wilson's account, disequilibrium, rather than balance, provides the harmonious conditions that "create our special world" (39). Most explicitly, this phrase refers to the biosphere and its unique ability to foster life. Lovelock provides us with another sense of what might be special about the world the biosphere provides when he writes, "As individual animals we are not so special, and in some ways the human species is like a planetary disease, but through civilization we redeem ourselves and have become a precious asset for the Earth."[56] Civilization in the form of modernity may be the agent whose actions have triggered the catastrophic future, but human civilization also redeems itself as the path to "stewardship": "Because all organisms have descended from a common ancestor, it is correct to say that the biosphere as a whole began to think when humanity was born."[57] Current environmental norms allow for the human prosperity that enables civilization. Thus, despite the hostility toward anthropocentrism, popular environmentalism recapitulates the central tenet of Western humanist and imperialist discourses: the value of civilization. In this light, it comes as less of a surprise that environmental juridical–legal claims should function in the service of the installation of more gun turrets to forge within the open field of preemption pockets of pastoral protection. Yet, mercury-like, the catastrophic seeps under the fences of deterrence and mutates the forms of preemption.

What, then, does the rhetoric of protection mean when used to justify security? As Foucault defines it, security develops from combining protection's mandate to create bounded immobilities (for instance, the walled city) with strategic interventions into a moving and changing assemblage of forces. In the regimes of protection, the production of threat delimits the protected zone. Threats are productive of and produced through the bodies they threaten. Nation, health, safety, are never more singular, more stolid, more unvarying, than when under threat, because solidity is precisely the attribute that catastrophe threatens. Protection, then, continues to refer to bounded entities in whose name security is deployed. By contrast, the apparatuses of security intervene in crowded, indeterminate fields. In this palimpsest, catastrophe is both the inevitable result and the justifying scourge, because protection only functions alongside the apprehension of complexity characteristic of security systems. The important point here is that there is no such thing as a bounded entity, except as a fantasmatic mandate for protection. The nation, the body, Earth, are open systems with innumerable variables, no matter how many walls sport gun turrets. Indeed, those gun turrets testify to the ineradicable openness of those systems. Not even a dead system is closed. Catastrophe-as-protection leveraged against catastrophe-as-threat will engender further catastrophes.

Catastrophe-as-protection: this counterintuitive formulation bears the name *apocalypse,* the ultimate unveiling of the future's potential for harm that both military plans and cultural productions elaborately routinize, telegraph, and enjoin. Although rigorously material, apocalyptic scenarios are fantasies. In his address on "nuclear criticism," Jacques Derrida urges us to keep the discursive, fictional, and fantastical production of doomsday scenarios in mind (because doomsday as such "does not exist"[58] outside these forms): "The nuclear strategy can never do without a sophistry of belief and the rhetorical simulation of a text" (24). Text, here, references all the disciplinary and governmental technologies that inform simulation, such as statistical extrapolations of test explosions, contamination maps, educational films, nuclear exchange contingency plans, fallout shelters, even the famous red button with its series of irreversible protocols, as well as the fictional texts that give these technologies flesh. All these anxious attempts to imagine the ramifications of the unimaginable point to the supplementary work of future harm against harmed futurity. Against the possibility of a harmed future, these technologies carve out specific sites of future harm and provide the plans for the gun turrets. Chance, change, catastrophe as overturning, are exactly what protection protects against through the fantasy of a fully formed future already present in the present. However, chance, change, and catastrophe are also the repurposed tools of that protection.

In "The Evening and the Morning and the Night,"[59] Octavia Butler gives us one way into this paradox. The teenagers in her short story live with foreshortened expectations of the future because they have Duryea-Gode disease (DGD), a hereditary illness that strikes in mid-life and causes its sufferers to try to skin themselves and those around them. Clinics, on the grounds of old mental wards and functioning in much the same way, rely on physical restraint to keep the patients from mutilating themselves. This tactic works only so long. This earlier treatment of DGD, reminiscent of Foucault's discussions of the disciplinary regimes around madness, has in the present of the story been supplemented by the discovery that dietary restrictions can control some aspects of the illness.

Unlike the carceral wards, the diet is self-administered and self-selecting; only those whose time has not yet come benefit from it. It is a kind of management of the body through the chemical processes of digestion that counters the DGD-body's wayward self-regard by addressing that body as a dynamic process.

The origins of the disease aptly match this solution. Two generations before the story's present, Hedeon Laboratories had developed a drug, Hedeonco,

> the magic bullet, the cure for a large percentage of the world's cancer and a number of serious viral diseases—and the cause of Duryea-Gode disease. If one of your parents was treated with Hedeonco and you were conceived after the treatment, you had DGD. (406)

DGD is a designer disease, then, built into the germ line of its carriers; or rather, the aftereffect of the attempt to create immobilities within mobile systems was the creation of another sort of mobile system. Arresting the body's capacity to produce mutations reframed the body itself as a mutation, a hostile imprisonment. The story narrates the discovery of yet a third complex system working outside of the agency of the subject. At the Dilg Center, an endowed hospital for DGD patients and a research laboratory for a cure for the cure, they stumble upon the realization that male DGDs respond strongly to the pheromonal signatures of certain female DGDs, ones who inherited their DGD-linked gene from both parents. Dilg specializes in instrumentalizing pheromone links as a form of control. Rather than disciplining their patients, Dilg doctors control their patients simply by being there and lacing their instructions and commands with the pheromones they cannot help but produce.

Butler's story makes poignantly clear the identity of protection and harm, both of which discursively enshroud the same material force. Their tangency, however, does not mean that they are equivalent. Instead, Butler's story, like Derrida's example of the bomb, dramatizes the stakes of mobilizing strategic harm to carve out zones of protection within mobile systems. Perhaps this is less apparent in the case of ecological ruin. We are willing, though, to admit that the violence of state power is used to protect against violence to the body politic or that discourses around catastrophic illness are contained through discourses of protective illness via pathologization of risk behaviors, both of which are easily turned into apocalyptic end games of their own. Can the same be said of what Derrida calls "the destruction of survivance"[60] that is the apocalyptic end game of ecological crisis? Does popular environmentalism also conjoin harm and protection? Recent U.S. policy documents suggest that this is not very far-fetched. The purpose of Peter Schwartz and Doug Randall's 2003 Pentagon report "An Abrupt Climate Change Scenario and Its Implications for United States Security" is to protect the United States from the instability that abrupt climate change portends. To do so, however, they suggest that climate change "should be elevated beyond a scientific debate to a U.S. national security concern."[61] They conclude with the following recommendations:

> It is quite plausible that within a decade the evidence of an imminent abrupt climate shift may become clear and reliable. . . . Learning how to manage populations, border tensions that arise and the resulting refugees will be critical. . . . New forms of security agreements dealing specifically with energy, food and water will also be needed. In short, while the U.S. itself will be relatively better off and with more adaptive capacity, it will find itself in a world where Europe will be struggling internally, large numbers of refugees washing up on its shores and Asia in serious crisis over food and water. Disruption and conflict will be endemic features of life. (22)

The emergency predicted by Schwartz and Randall resembles the emergent conditions of Kelly's film far more than the freeze-frame present of Ballard's story, and yet the closure of closed systems remains central to security strategies. From the protected zone, it's always possible to reframe violent preemption as necessary precaution and expropriation as management. Harmed futurity makes dead the future; future harm carries out the material work of its execution.

No Future

Is there, then, as Edelman suggests, no viable way to consider the future? Is futurity always of a piece with patrimony? On the contrary, the prevalence of the fantasy of a harmed future is indicative of our intense awareness of continuing mutations and movements, of material futurity.

The ostensible obsolescence of evolution, which structures ecological doomsday scenarios, is a reaction to its continuing operation. Denying the continuing effect of evolution is a strategic component of harmed futurity's narrative arc, because it asserts that *these forms, these relationships,* are the only ones we have. Get out of the scale of the human, project outward and forward toward the interpenetration and coevolution of all planetary life, organic and inorganic, or inward and forward to our messy, permeable, and permeated interiors, fast-forward past functionalist definitions (eyes are formed for seeing, hands for grasping) or blur together individuals so they look like one crazy-quilt organism, and the results seem less like the blank emptiness of total death and more like the abundance of potential.

Sexual reproduction is the motor of evolution, or so Charles Darwin is often understood to be arguing. *The Origin of Species,* however, is a strangely divided text, full of irreconcilable tendencies. His infamous use of words like *competition, extinction,* and *superiority,* which accorded so well with the prevailing zeitgeist of laissez-faire capitalism, combined with the legacy of social Darwinism, has made Darwin seem like an apologist for the status quo. His assertion that progress in speciation can be charted according to "the standard of high organization, the amount of differentiation and specialization of the several organs in each being when adult,"[62] certainly seems to privilege the human as the largest, most robust, most dominant, and most highly organized of animals. However, a careful reading reveals a series of fissures radiating outward from Darwin's appreciation of the fluidity of form.

"We have good reason to believe," he writes, "that changes in the conditions of life give a tendency to increased variability, and . . . this would manifestly be favorable to natural selection, by affording a better chance of the occurrence of profitable variations" (122). By "changes in the conditions of life," Darwin offers examples like increased competition, climate fluctuations, human intervention (such as domestication), geographic isolation, and food decrease or increase. What is remarkable about this list is its lack of moral judgment. Loss and gain, isolation and competition, make for favorable conditions for the emergence of muta-tion.[63] Where, though, does emergence emerge from? Here we encounter a foundational schism. Darwin emphatically denies "the continued creation of any new organic beings, or of any great and sudden modification in their structure" (132). The first part of this claim is obviously intended to underscore his theory of descent, which claims that the production of new species is a process of incremental and preserved variation. Accordingly, the part responsible for variation must be present, but without relevance, in the originating individuals. For instance, the honeybees with the longest proboscises will flourish if changes in the plant require a new method of penetration. That variation will be preserved through natural selection and inherited through sexual selection. Alternatively, he asserts "the ordinary belief that the amount of possible variation is a strictly limited quantity is likewise a simple assumption" (123). How do these two positions articulate? Through "the law of correlation, [which states that] when one part varies, and the variations are accumulated through natural selection, other modifications, often of the most unexpected nature, will ensue" (124). These variations are not amplifications of existing possibilities but wholly new structures and capacities. If we expand this to relationships from individuals, it becomes clear that the pressures of modification are everywhere at work. In this close coupling of organic and inorganic life, form and species are just the momentary expressions of a potentially inexhaustible mutation. As Grosz writes,

> what evolves are not individuals or even species, which are forms of relative fixity or stability, but oscillations of differences (which underlie and make possible individuals and species) that can consolidate themselves, more or less temporarily, into cohesive groupings only to disperse and disappear or else reappear in other terms at different times.[64]

These dispersions of form are, of course, catastrophic; they are also the movements of life from out of which coalesce new relationships.

The insistence on a rapidly collapsing future favors fixity of form. The future that environmental policies aim to preserve is a future fit for life as it is presently lived against the emergence of the new. Grosz defines Darwin's contribution in terms of *events,* a word closely aligned with my use of the term *catastrophe*:

> In recognizing the surprising, unpredictable, and mobile force of time on the emergence and development of the multitude of forms of life, Darwin brings

the concept of the *event* to the sciences. Events are ruptures, nicks, which flow from causal connections in the past but which, in their unique combinations and consequences, generate unpredictability and effect sometimes subtle but wide-ranging, unforeseeable transformations in the present and future. (8)

The human may be the most highly developed animal, but Darwin is always careful to recognize that strength, utility, and dominance are relative to the contingent demands of the broader ecological context. What will count as strong and useful in the future "no man can predict, for we know that many groups formerly most extensively developed have now become extinct" (148). Life is not a thing but rather a relational force. Autopoetic or allopoetic, organic or nonorganic, human or animal or posthuman or neoanimal, all are forms life takes up in its movement.

Ecological suicide is a doomsday scenario whose maintenance requires the production of simulations. Its corollary rhetoric of protection requires the production of statistical extrapolations, disciplinary techniques of self-governance and juridico-legal intervention. It is a discourse of harmed futurity with its attendant technologies of future harm. It renders the future dead via prognostication. Doomsday scenarios preserve the dead future against what Nietzsche would call overcoming.

The Future Now

So what are we to make of the crop of recent books and articles that begin from the presumption that the future is now? These pieces don't give up on urging radical change, but they do so less in the name of prevention than of survival. (And still very much in the predictive mood.) Roy Scranton's recent thought piece in the *New York Times,* "Learning How to Die in the Anthropocene," exemplifies this new mood.[65] As he phrases it, "the question is no longer whether global warming exists or how we might stop it, but how we are going to deal with it."

Rephrased without the future tense, this is also the central question of *The Child to Come.* For as this chapter has endeavored to demonstrate, the revelation of climate change is not that we may be subject to unpredictable futures but that the predictable future was always a just-so story of humanist hubris. Complex systems, in other words, always contain catastrophe as their necessary corollary. The question, then, is not how to live in catastrophe as if it were a landscape awaiting us in the future but how to live with catastrophic causalities without attempting to reseal them behind the containment walls of management systems and predictive models—how to live, in other words, without the demand for safety and the pleading face of the child that is its warrant. The examples I take up in the following chapters are set in the catastrophic future. Each *fronts* the child, but each also and to varying degrees *confronts* the narrative causalities voiced through the child. In the following chapters, I take up both sides of this dynamic to consider more closely why the child arises with such insistence and what approach to catastrophe opens out from the child. I begin to do so, in the next chapter, with feminist science fiction writer Joanna Russ and the problem made clear by Morton's philosophical puzzle of the truck, the child, and the able-bodied bystander. What would it mean, Russ asks, to refuse rescue? What is the content of child rescue, and to what does it commit us?

2

Life

Rhetoric is the ash of discourse.

SAMUEL R. DELANY, *Longer Views*

"Maybe it would be better *not* to survive."[1] So poses first officer and computer expert Camilla Del Ray in Marion Zimmer Bradley's 1972 *Darkover Landfall.* The novel, the beginning of the Darkover series, narrates the first few months of life for the crew of a downed starship as they come to terms with the idea that they are trapped on an unknown planet. The survival that Officer Del Ray questions, however, does not concern their immediate need for food, shelter, medicine, and safety from predators, all of which the ship's surviving crew and passengers—being, as they are, part of a well-established colonization plan to relieve Earth's overpopulation—handle with aplomb. No, the survival in question is generational. They discover a few weeks into their colonization that the birth control they employ has failed. Camilla is one of the many women who becomes pregnant during a drug-induced orgy. Following crew protocol, she seeks out the medical officer to register for an abortion, but she is rebuffed. "Are you trying to tell me that I've got to have this baby?" she asks.

> "I sure as hell am," Ewan said, and suddenly his voice went hard, "and others too, provided you can carry them to term. There's a one in two chance that you'll have a miscarriage." . . . "If we're lucky, Camilla, we have fifty-nine fertile women now. Even if they all became pregnant this year, we'll be lucky to have twelve living children . . . and the viable level for this colony to survive means we've got to bring our numbers up to about four hundred before the oldest women start losing their fertility. It's going to be touch and go, and I have a feeling that any woman who refuses to have as many children as she can physically manage, is going to be awfully damned unpopular." (113)

Camilla continues to protest, but Ewan and a nurse grab her and jab her with a sedative. "How can she be so selfish?" the nurse asks. In fact, Camilla's resistance is short-lived; she comes to peace with the pregnancy and, we are told in the epilogue, goes on to bear another six children. The final scene is one of happy domestic tranquility: "How lightly fourteen years of childbearing lay on their mother's shoulders!" (159).

Published in the year prior to the U.S. Supreme Court's *Roe v. Wade* decision, the novel is difficult not to read in terms of feminist struggles for reproductive rights and the virulent pro-life backlash to that struggle. In this context in particular, what could induce feminist utopian and fantasy writer Marion Zimmer Bradley, a writer whose novels insist on the importance of depicting women's lives, to write a novel so fully and ardently in praise of enforced birth? This chapter answers that question by turning to Joanna Russ's vitriolic 1977 rebuttal *We Who Are About To...*[2] and its narrator's refusal to succumb to enforced reproduction to save her tiny, accidental colony. That answer is, simply, LIFE, a word that occurs as frequently in the titles of anti-abortion tracts as it does in the speculative environmental nonfiction with which the last chapter was concerned. For what these two lost-colony science fiction narratives share with popular environmentalism is the specter of extinction. Zimmer Bradley's novel reveals that the children who so obviously need to be saved from the onrushing truck of planetary toxification (in Morton's[3] example) need also to be born. The rhetorical equation of the child with the future, that is, is a deeply and inextricably gendered discourse. For women, saving the world through childbirth has specific and all too immediate consequences. When it comes to species-survival, the child always also points to the woman who bears him. In narratives of species-survival, it is the natural givenness of extinction that makes enforced birth appear to be a biological inevitability, indeed, the very limit case of politically motivated disagreements. The burden of Ewan's remarks seems to suggest that a species must have a future to worry about what will happen in it. Women's control over their reproductive capacity, in other words, is a luxury that cannot be sustained in the state of emergency that attends the specter of extinction.

Feminist theorists have extensively cataloged how the apparent naturalness of reproductive destiny upholds compulsory heterosexuality.[4]

They have argued that this view of reproduction is ideologically affixed to physiological procreation for specific political effects in the present. In the epistemology of reproduction, child-rearing names the imagined site of fulfillment.[5] An odd temporality, however, makes reproduction the permanent deferral of fulfillment. As Russ puts it in *The Female Man,*

> besides, what about the children? Mothers have to sacrifice themselves to their children, both male and female, so that the children will be happy when they grow up; though the mothers themselves were once children and were sacrificed to in order that they might grow up and sacrifice themselves for their children, so you begin to wonder whether the whole thing isn't a plot to make the world safe for (male) children. But motherhood is sacred and mustn't be talked about.[6]

The founding assertion that the present must endlessly attend to the future interpellates women into sacred and sacrificial reproduction. Rhetorical figures like safe children and sacred mothers evoke a nostalgic past that each person must labor to restore in the future through childbirth. In this sense, reproduction is a form of repetition. So reproduction has two valences: it suggests first that procreation will guarantee reproduction of the past into the future and second that reproduction-via-procreation is the sovereign task of each individual. For all its ostensible biological underpinnings, procreation becomes the sign of reproduction—the endless labor for fulfillment in the future.

As we have already seen in Zimmer Bradley, the apparently apolitical identity of children and futurity unify even apparently opposed political positions. Indeed, Camilla's assertion—"Maybe it would be better not to survive"—resembles Lee Edelman's argument that we should embrace the homophobic accusation that queer sexuality promotes deathliness through its refusal of the reproductive mandate. His answer has also engendered much critical hostility, and the rancor of this debate suggests the broad appeal of futurity and its cognates. In this chapter's first half, I read Russ's novel for the way it exposes the binding work performed by reproduction. The second half of the chapter turns away from reproduction, a problem effectively closed less than half of the way through the book, to consider textual reproductions. Taking the novel as a whole, I argue, the question of procreation merges with and is overshadowed by the novel's structural rejection of reproduction as a narrative demand and its more subtle interest in transmission and dissemination. Finally, then, I suggest that the novel gives us an intuition of what we might mean by futurity outside of reproduction and, indeed, outside of human agency.

In urging her readers to consider the consequences of heterosexual gendering, Adrienne Rich poses the following question: "Why [have] species-survival, the means of impregnation and emotional-erotic relationships . . . become so rigidly identified with each other?"[7] Though many scholars writing in the thirty years since her article's publication have interrogated compulsory heterosexuality, the supreme value of species-survival as a discursive technology of compulsory heterosexuality has not received the same attention.[8] Although many scholars have written about fetal representation in abortion politics, few of them directly interrogate anxieties around human futurity as a tactic in abortion rhetoric.[9] Rich's question intimates that species-survival designates an individual obligation to a collective human and nonhuman future. As I argue later in this chapter, the critical reception of *We Who Are About To . . .*, like the debate around Edelman's polemic, warns that this individualized obligation to survival sits uneasily alongside a critique of patriarchy.

Death

We Who Are About To . . . centers on a small group of interstellar commuters stranded on an uncharted planet with no hope of rescue. Meaningless in itself, this crash violently negates the futures they had imagined for themselves, jolting them into dizzying epistemological uncertainty. Against this uncertainty, the commuters attempt to fence in the future by invoking the familiar narrative tradition of the frontier settlement where human civilization might take root and their lost futures be, if not quite restored, at least redeemed. This rooting of civilization, they decide, seemingly without discussion, must happen through childbirth. Reproduction functions as a metonymy for a restored future as well as a mechanism for reinstituting patriarchal hierarchy. Remarkably, the breeding plan is not a covert attempt by the male passengers to secure the sexual services of the female passengers. Administered by committee, and endorsed by everyone except the novel's narrator, this compulsory heterosexuality construes the future as the imperative of the present and turns procreation into an instrument of reproduction.

This consensus forms outside of the narrator's observation, and because we have access to their story through her tape-recorded diary entries, we at first know only that the commuters quickly begin to see themselves as colonizers. Successful colonization, their primary goal, does not mean successful survival, as might be expected, but survival for the sake of reproducing civilization through childbirth. Before they even step from their landing module, the narrator begins to list the reasons why they will fail. She notes that they have no foundation on which to base their actions: "A few weeks observation and perhaps we can guess if we're approaching the summer solstice or going the other way around, which could give us some idea of how long the seasons will be: could be ten years of summer" (14). This cynical empiricism marks her as an outsider and troublemaker. Yet the others cannot simply ignore her or allow her to die by herself as she wishes to do. Instead, they try to force her to join them in their breeding plan. And so she kills them and—some seventy pages later—herself.

The narrator's refusal to participate in the breeding plan would seem to make her a heroic figure, or at least a figure espousing a political position recognizable to feminist readers. Even apart from this register, the novel's topos is political in the most rigorous sense, concerned with the establishment of governance, the right to bodily autonomy, the legitimacy of violent struggle, and the relationship of human life to future human life. In its historical context, too, the novel's premise bears directly on second-wave feminist demands for meaningful work and reproductive rights. Even the generic context of the novel indicates political engagement, as the novel refuses the triumphal tonality traditionally associated with science fictional colonization narrative. Taken together, these three registers ask the reader to consider whether the establishment of social order via women's procreative capacity has been a foundational condition of human sociality. Equally important, the equation of procreation with the reproduction of social order asks us to consider whether one of the ideological mechanisms of compulsory heterosexuality resides in the shared belief that civilization must be preserved.

Some critics have indeed embraced the narrator's refusal of the reproductive mandate. Yet Samuel R. Delany is right to call *We Who Are About To . . .* a "dangerous book."[10] This danger, I argue, lies in the novel's apparent polarization of reactions: life and death, the first associated with reproduction and the second with suicide and murder. In attempting to read the novel against the grain, several critics have reversed these values. Brooks Landon[11] situates the novel in terms of conventional depictions of motherhood in formula literature, in which individualized species-survival trumps even the collective survival it signifies. In this analysis, Russ's stranded passengers, for whom the reality that rescue will not come acts as a clarion call to colonization, represent standard formula fare against the nameless narrator's queer deathliness. Landon then rereads this deathliness as refusal to conform to the expectations of sacrificial motherhood. Marleen S. Barr argues that the narrator, in choosing death, really chooses life. "Music, books, friends and love"[12] are absent from the uncharted and uninhabited planet they seek to colonize, and these, not bare survival, are the source of life. Delany implicitly locates the narrator as the novel's subversive element: "Russ suggests that the quality of life is the purpose of living, and reproduction only a reparative process to extend that quality—and not the point of life at all."[13] Of all the characters, only the narrator ever evokes quality of life as a standard for behavior.

Many more critics, however, have found the novel troubling. Whereas Barr, Landon, and Delany laud the book for subverting narrative formulas and epistemological expectations based on allegedly natural maternal instinct, other critics have found the novel hopeless, apolitical, or nihilistic. While praising the book, Marilyn Hacker, in an early article, describes Russ as compelled to write a novel about death "as a statement of what is, in our time, the ultimate alternative to political commitment."[14] Thelma Shinn, in her article on women in science fiction, argues that the novel fails to attain an authentic politics because the narrator stubbornly asserts her individual preferences over the needs of the community, thus "forcing her to become the instrument of destruction"[15] and indicating that the real murder in this novel is the murder of the colony's future. Barbara Garland, in her brief review article, similarly disparages the novel for rejecting "even the laws of biological survival and of society."[16] According to the logic of these readings, the colonizers would appear to value life, specifically future human life, regardless of the incongruities of their position and the suffering procreation might entail. In comparison, the narrator's insistence that their position is terminal appears at best juvenile and at worst homicidal. For these scholars, the novel represents a retreat from political engagement because the narrator's choice violates the ground of political action itself: the commitment to survival.

The disjunction between the contents of the novel and the mixed reception of this work intimates that something discomforts this camp of readers. Their disturbing reaction seems to force the conclusion that the future does depend on reproduction, which in turn depends on restricting women's autonomy. Sherry Ortner's essay "Is Female to Male as Nature Is to Culture?," published contemporaneously with Russ's novel, corroborates just such a conclusion. In her anthropological review of traits common to all human social organization, Ortner includes acculturation to "a society of other individuals," "an interest in personal survival," and a commitment to "continuity and survival, which transcends the lives and deaths of particular individuals."[17] In this definition, to be human is to desire survival and reproduction above all else. Russ asks us to consider whether a woman's life, given these universal conditions, is worth living. Indeed, this acceptance of universal, natural oppression might foster the reading of this novel as a failure of feminist politics.[18] Yet, the recurrent concern for community in these readings points to a different conclusion, namely, that it is exactly the violation of the commitment to survival and continuity, which transcends the lives and deaths of particular individuals, as Ortner puts it, that informs the monstrous character of this novel. When confronted with the moral choice between a return to a patriarchal order and violent resistance to that order's establishment, these scholars balk at the novel's implication that annihilation is preferable to degradation.

The important point here is that the novel's "pocket genocide" (152), as the narrator titles her actions, is ultimately less upsetting than that she murders her companions as a means of resisting future life. By killing off the colonists, by refusing to participate in their breeding plan, the narrator rejects the assertion that human life acquires meaning only by producing future human lives. The validation of the colonists' embrace of the future seems less like enthusiasm and more like a desperate attempt to secure the future despite the oppressive consequences of that position. Ironically, then, the discomfort induced by this novel looks quite a lot like an endorsement of reproductive futurism and the supposed biological laws that structure women's oppression.

More Death

Although this conclusion is disturbing, I'd like to suggest that embracing the narrator's argument does not take us away from reproductive futurism. Rather, where the antagonism between the two groups should render them structurally opposed, and would therefore lead us to expect that the narrator's concern resides with the present, we find symmetrical concern with the future. This is so, I argue, because the two positions maintain their coherence through each other. The narrator says, "But they won't be able to leave me alone. I know. Not because of the child-bearing, because of the disagreement. The disagreement is what matters" (47). Officially, the group won't let her go because of her procreative value; however, she performs a different and perhaps even more valuable service as scapegoat. Because she has so volubly aligned herself with death, failure, and chaos, with the extrahuman agency of the alien planet, she comes to stand in for it. The violence the group threatens, like tying her to a tree, aims at marking her difference from them and then incorporating it. Writing in a slightly different context, Robert Reid-Pharr defines the scapegoat in particularly apposite terms for this discussion: "The scapegoat, then, would be the figure who reproduces this undifferentiation, this chaos, this boundarylessness. The violence directed against the goat would mitigate against prior violence, the erosion of borders that has beset the entire community."[19] Displacing the trauma of the crash onto the narrator consolidates and gives form to their anxiety, but it doesn't mean that she is complacent. While she scoffs at their procreative fantasy, she builds her own vision of reproduction, one equally attuned to preserving a civilized future.

In one of the few explanations for the breeding plan that the novel offers, for instance, John Ude, the burgeoning patriarch, explains that the narrator can't go searching for water because she, like the other four women, is "too valuable to put in danger" (31). In response to the narrator's evasive answer, he reminds her sententiously, "Civilization must be preserved" (31). This commonplace implies that civilization has been threatened and that they must take action to secure its preservation from that threat. "Civilization," she replies, "is doing just fine. We just don't happen to be where it is" (31). Her rejoinder underscores the distance between a biological explanation for the breeding plan and its function as a political or ideological fantasy. Humanity will not be jeopardized if they choose to die or to value their own lives over the lives of future generations. Loading the obligation of civilization onto the eight stranded strangers puts in place a new goal, the only one with enough force to mitigate their loss, and at the same time replicates at the level of the collective the individual romance narrative that similarly concludes with childbirth and the hope of perpetuation. On the other hand, any civilization they might build would not be civilization in the sense they recognize, as the narrator reminds them through a series of rhetorical questions: "Do you want your children to live in the Old Stone Age? Do you want them to forget how to read? Do you want to lose your teeth? Do you want your great-grandchildren to die at thirty?" (25). At which point, Cassie, who wants to bear children, hits her. Where Cassie and the others imagine childbearing as an abstract good, a disembodied method for resuscitating civilization, the narrator insists on its material consequences. Yet, her version similarly delimits and reifies the future. Rather than actual material consequences, the possibilities she lists stand in metonymically for a harmed life, one that, like losing civilization, must be prevented at any cost.

Of all the colonists, Ude most represents reproductive futurism's investment in repetition. In attempting to tempt the others onto the planet, he crafts a figure of Earth as both a sacrificing mother and a justification for further sacrifice:

> Come on now, come on dearies. . . . It's like Earth. And we know Earth. Most of us were born on it. So what's there to be afraid of, hey? We're just colonizing a little early, that's all. You wouldn't be afraid of Earth, would you? (20)

The narrator sees clearly that Ude's encouraging speech invokes "Earth" not as a physical place but as a social and symbolic space, as a mother ("born on it") who cares for her children. The only "Earth," however, that the colonists know how to survive in is the one they left, where food is purchased, energy comes out of a wall socket, and medical technology is at least minimally available. In other words, on their Earth, survival denotes something beyond livingness. As our narrator tartly replies, another vision of Earth might serve as a more apt analogy:

> Oh, sure. Think of Earth. Kind old home. Think of the Arctic. Think of Labrador. Of Southern India in June. Think of smallpox and plague and earthquakes and ringworms and pit vipers. Think of a nice case of poison ivy all over you, including your eyes. Status asthmaticus. Amoebic dysentery. The Minnesota pioneers who tied a rope from the house to the barn in winter because you could lose your way in a blizzard and die three feet from the house. Think (while you're at it) of tsunamis, liver fluke, the Asian brown bear. Kind old home. The sweetheart. The darling place. Think of Death Valley . . . in August. (20)

In attempting to undermine the frontier fantasy she sees coalescing around her, the narrator deploys a congruent discourse of futurity. The accuracy of her description, and its bitter majesty against Ude's clearly symbolic use of Earth, obfuscates its directive: think only of what might go wrong. She might have included autumn leaves, sunsets, and beaches in her list and still have had an accurate description of Earth. Instead, the narrator's sense that they are already dead collapses harm that may or may not be in the future into the present. In effect, the planet has already killed them, because she perceives the only life it offers as guaranteed to harm them. No less than for the colonizers, the present serves only as a measure of the future. She doesn't oppose civilizational discourse; in fact, she repeats it in the form of its other: nature's malignity.

Moreover, the narrator has no immunity to the symbolic power of their home planet. Meditating on her decision to die, she compares her reaction to the current situation to how she might feel were she on Earth:

> If Earth had been hit by plague, by fire, by war, by radiation, sterility, a thousand things, you name it, I'd still stand by her; I love her; I would fight every inch of the way there because my whole life is knit to her. And she'd need mourners. To die on a dying Earth—I'd live, if only to weep. (27)

Like Ude, the narrator personifies Earth. In so doing, she replaces his Oedipal scene with the quite different and specifically nonreproductive metaphor of female lovers. This shift, however, obscures the work of personification: to turn the planet into a person. While her earlier characterization of Earth presents nature as a fierce antagonist to human survival, here the narrator conflates human and nonhuman nature and makes "Earth" a synecdoche for social order and human futurity, especially via procreation. Fire, war, radiation, sterility—these are human troubles, civilizational troubles. In this description, the narrator identifies Earth's death with its sudden hostility to human futurity.[20] In effect, dying on a dying Earth is just what she is doing, because her opposition to procreation is an attempt to preserve the reproduction of civilization. To make this fantasy work, she must insist on the virulence of the future.

One particularly provocative moment in the novel occurs at the pinnacle of the group's attempt to convert the narrator to their breeding plan, when Ude rhetorically questions the narrator's desire for death: "Really," he says, "I cannot understand why you want to die" (46). She has, at this point in the novel, not yet announced her plan for suicide. Rather, Ude's statement assumes that her refusal to allow the possibility of survival and the desirability of colonization amounts to suicide. Her reply reverses the terms of this assumption by asserting that life lived for the future is not life at all:

> John Donne, John-John-with-your-britches-on, John Whittington-turn-again-lord-mayor-of-London-town, we *are* dead. We died the minute we crashed. Plague, toxic food, deficiency diseases, broken bones, infection, gangrene, cold, heat, and just plain starvation.... My God, you're the ones who want to suffer: conquer and control, conquer and control, when you haven't even got stone spears. You're dead.... Galvanism, Corpse jerking. Planning. Power. Inheritance. You know, survival. My genes shall conquer the world. That's death. (46)

Here the narrator makes her critique of reproduction explicit. She does not oppose childbirth as much as what it means: "Planning. Power. Inheritance." Yet her own list of potential harms hinges on planning and power. She, too, has plans that she will enforce, likewise premised on survival, though with a different object in mind. This collapse of probability into certainty, no less a reaction to epistemological disorientation than the other colonists,' ultimately leads to her murders.[21] Certain that the future has already been harmed, she attempts to control the damage. Thus the murders merely complete what the crash began.

Even her syntax reflects this slippage. For instance, she describes Nathalie digging a latrine like this: "Nathalie's digging experimental sanitation pits with a collapsible shovel. And every once in a while it does" (21). She records these events after they happen, at night so the others won't hear her; she is already in command of the plot. The reader, conversely, reads as if it were the present. The ambiguity of the second sentence in the preceding quotation sends the reader back to the first sentence to establish what thing she is referring to and what it does. This return puts in the past of the reading time an event (the collapse) that hasn't happened yet in the sentence, though it has in the narrator's experience. This recursive style structures the narrative. Yet, I would argue that this particular usage by no means accidentally involves a literal and temporal collapse. This syntactic reversal intimates a more pivotal reversal: she who predicts harm becomes the harm she predicts.

This is a shocking novel, but it isn't nihilistic or apolitical. Rather, this shock aims to reveal the shared commitment to human futurity that binds together political movements of all kinds and couples resistance to oppression through a common, but commonly unstated, boundary. On one side, potential catastrophe marks the limit of political resistance. No matter how oppressive its organization, survival of the social body remains paramount. On the other side, the height of political power resides in futurity and the triumphal revivification of the body politic in that future. Both positions sacralize future life for its own sake and not for the particular lives that might be led in that future. For all that the narrator appears to reject futurity, ultimately through suicide, her obsessive cataloging of possible future harms reveals her shared commitment to the future. For all her insistence that civilization will be fine without their help, she sacrifices her life to prevent the degradation of civilization. Russ's critics are right to see in this novel a pessimistic evaluation of political struggle: movement between these two poles isn't movement at all.

The homology between the novel's own apparent polarization and the critical bifurcation I have mapped should therefore give us pause. As

Delany implies, in the same essay cited earlier, the narrator only appears to offer an opposing position. He names her "the most 'civilized' person among the passengers," but then clarifies the definition of civility through Walter Benjamin's aphorism that "every act of civilization is also an act of barbarism."[22] While the novel does challenge the ease with which procreation becomes synonymous with reproduction and its attendant metaphysics of futurity, progress, and life, I contend that that critique comes to us not through the narrator's defection from the group, or her fatalism toward their survival, but through the novel's own organization. Rejecting the ostensible choice the novel offers allows a third possibility to emerge.

Consider the novel's title: *We Who Are About To . . .*[23] The novel's first line—"About to die, and so on" (7)—appears to conclude the anticipatory temporality of the title, to fulfill the death already intimated by the allusion to the Latin salute. The structure these two lines create together, however, is not linear but chiasmic. By replacing the specificity of a verb with the ellipses, the title enunciates not an act but a condition: the awaiting of the future as the infinitely delayed time of conclusion. The first phrase of the first line offers a false resolution of this condition, one that the second phrase immediately undermines. By the time we read these words, the crisis that precipitated them has been averted; they are not "about to die," and so they must "so on." The polarized critical positions map onto the tension between these two originary phrases but ignore the critique inherent in the title. For the title is playing with the temporality of reproductive futurism. It appears to offer imminent fulfillment but mischievously replaces it with a condition. Neither part of the first line signifies real resolution. Death, the narrator's answer to threatened civilization, attempts to evade, but complies with, the "so on," that is, repetition. In both parts, the present becomes the time of wounded openness against which the future must be made to mean fulfillment.

I'd like to suggest a different way to read this "so on." Importantly, the colonists are lost not only in space but also in time. Genealogical succession, the "so on" of reproduction, derives its meaning-making force from conceiving of time as unfolding in a straight line running out to meet the horizon. Space travel is already a perversion of this conception of time. As the narrator ruminates, "the light of our dying will reach you (whoever you are) only after you yourselves are long dead, after your own Sun has engulfed you and then shrunk to a collapsed cinder with no more light in it than what we saw that night" (19). Sarah LeFanu, in her article on the role of readership in Russ's work, sees this temporal delay as part of the strategic function of the narrator's diary: "In the preservation of the journal, however, there is implied a future community with a reader *inside* language that alleviates her despair to some extent by situating her own perspective as the discursive past of some even more remote future."[24] In what follows, I'd like to suggest that this recuperative reading of a future internal to readership—one that ostensibly escapes from the reproductive mandate I've been tracking thus far—is likewise tied to control over the future. In this case, however, rescuing the future depends on the transmission of proper narrative to the child. I'd like to unfold this phase of my argument by turning first to one of Russ's earlier and more highly acclaimed works, *The Adventures of Alyx,* and especially to the tale that closes that story sequence.

Rescue

The final story in *The Adventures of Alyx*[25] posits in fictional terms the politics of representation prevalent throughout Russ's work. In a story sequence that spans traditional boys' genres, from pirate adventures to wizards and warriors, "The Second Inquisition" is unique for its setting, an American suburb in the 1920s, and for its layering of realism and science fiction. The story begins by describing a suburban parlor. This deceptively realist introduction serves as a reminder of Russ's concern with genre throughout the collection. Here the sudden inclusion of "our" world, of a recognizable version of consensus reality, highlights the conventional status of both realism and science fiction. At the same time, this choice signals that the terminal address of the book is the quotidian world of its readers. Alyx the adventurer does not appear in this final story. Instead, "The Second Inquisition" brings an Alyx-like character, the Visitor, into the world of an average sixteen-year-old girl. In other words, the book ends by revealing the fantasy to have been an allegory for the life lived by the reader, for whom the girl serves as representative and into whose suburban parlor Russ's Alyx has come in the form of the book. In the person of the Visitor and in her relationship with the teenage narrator, the story thematizes the relationship of science fiction to consensus reality and, more broadly, of writing to reading.

The story narrates a teenage girl's fascination with the exotic Visitor who has come to stay in her family's home. At first, the Visitor's race, height, strength, and shamelessness mark her exoticism. She befriends the wrong type of people, has little regard for pleasant lies, and reads voraciously, including banned books. Indeed, it is over a proscribed romance novel that the teenage girl finds in the Visitor an ally. A reader herself, the girl peers at the Visitor from perspectives given to her by novels. Their relationship begins by mimicking a bildungsroman, with the Visitor cast in the role of the worldly, and secretly beloved, older man.[26] After a series of skirmishes with strangers the Visitor apparently knows, this model acquires a science fictional gloss. This, too, is introduced through a novel. The girl and the Visitor both read H. G. Wells's *The Time Machine,* and the girl asks her in jest if she isn't really a Morlock, which the Visitor concedes is true. After acknowledging that she comes from the future, through the Trans-Temporal Military Authority, the Visitor explains that the girl is her ancestor, the founder of the Authority, and that she has come to talk with her, perhaps to rescue her, but that now she must leave.

More than a template for their relationship, then, the Visitor embodies not only the kinds of stories the girl reads but also the stories Russ writes. The tale, however, takes one more turn. In the very last movement, the Visitor returns through a mirror in the girl's bedroom to have a final talk with her. After the Visitor leaves, the girl looks down at the outfit she has been wearing and recognizes it as a theater costume version of the Visitor's interstellar gear, with pieces of her wardrobe reconditioned to serve as bodysuit, laser gun, and cape. In other words, the story's final moment collapses its science fictional elements back into the realist frame and makes the girl the source of the story's fantasy elements. In fact, one more step mediates the return to realism. In the midst of confessing that the figure in the mirror is herself, the girl splits into two: "I put one foot up in the air, as if on the threshold of the mirror, and a girl in ragged black stared back at me. . . . She said to me, 'You look idiotic'" (192). "The Second Inquisition" ends with the ambiguous line "no more stories" (192). While this line may refer to the Visitor's departure in failure and the girl's solitude, its presence at the end of the collection seems to me to issue a double warning: on one hand, it functions as an admonishment to stay on this side of the mirror where are found the conditions that make fantasy necessary at all. On the other hand, the resignation in this ending seems to me to demand anger at the failure of stories to provide role models for young girls. Thus the ending urges the book's readers to risk looking idiotic, to don the Visitor's clothes and to be as a stranger in their own living rooms.

The politics of representation that makes the reader and the story cohorts in rescue finds nonfictional expression in Russ's "Recent Feminist Utopias,"[27] which observes a new thematic element in women's science fiction and utopian writing of the 1970s: "The rescue of the female child" (79).[28] Russ defines this as a two-stage operation: first, the rescue of the girl from the oppressive conditions of patriarchy, but second, and crucially, her guidance toward a fully autonomous and meaningful public life. This second stage underscores the importance of age to Russ's formulation. Rescue comes when the relative benignity of childhood play gives way to the serious labor of reproduction:

> Puberty is an awakening into sexual adulthood for both sexes. According to Simone de Beauvoir in *The Second Sex,* it is also the time when the prison bars of "femininity," enforced by law and custom, shut the girl in for good. . . .
> This is one aspect of puberty missing in the above examples [of rescue]: the children therein are sexual beings, certainly, but the last thing (say the tales) that matters for the adolescent girl is that she be awakened by a kiss; what is crucial is that she be free.[29] (80)

Russ's critics have been even more ardently attached to the rescue theme. Kathleen L. Spencer's "Rescuing the Female Child: The Fictions of Joanna Russ" argues that this theme might best characterize Russ's own corpus. In revising and expanding this category, Spencer highlights the representational work Russ's narratives perform: "What Russ has done . . . is to create narratives . . . which go beyond the moment of revelation into the imaging of freedom."[30] Spencer uses the example of female students' reactions to the stories they read in a class taught by Carolyn Heilbrun to demonstrate the necessity of such new narrative performances. In calling on the example of women enrolled in a college course, Spencer makes clear that the rescue thematic applies to readers rather than to characters. By "imaging" freedom, these narratives act: they perform a rescue. Lurking here, then, is an aesthetic theory and a moral imperative, which Jean Cortiel describes succinctly as the choice to compose stories that "authorize or empower women as writers, narrators, readers and characters."[31] The verb *authorize* in this sentence underscores the identity Cortiel establishes between authored characters and authorized readers, both composed by the narrative. As in "The Second Inquisition," the story may come over for a visit.

Even with this explanation, we might wonder why the theme of rescue so insistently designates a child as the recipient of protection rather than women more generally, all of whom are presumably "shut . . . in for good."[32] Moreover, by what logic can girls be saved by virtue of narrative when for women it is already too late?[33] What relationship does this suggest adheres between children and storytelling? I would argue that the restriction of rescue to young girls takes part in the historical construction of the child as (a) being-in-danger. This danger has been most often understood as the danger of sexual knowledge. James R. Kincaid locates the cut that separates children from adults this way: "The child is that species which is free of sexual feeling or response; the adult is that species which has crossed over into sexuality."[34] Construed as empty of sexuality and ignorant of sexual secrets, though destined to be filled up with and initiated into both, the child must properly negotiate the entrance into sexuality. The child inaugurates a process, a kind of adventure story, for which adulthood is both terminal exit and impossible vanishing point. Bound to the future, the child anticipates the injuries that will befall her own adult self. Danger, as Leo Bersani writes, "becomes intelligible as the sickness of uncompleted narratives"[35] or, we might add, of other forms of wayward storytelling, uncompleted or improperly prolonged.

In the rescue theme, the (female) child's vulnerability to sexual danger warrants feminist intervention. Far from radical, this conjunction of narrative pedagogy, sexualized danger to the child, and political investment in future social organization has traditionally made the child the site of public anxiety and juridical control. Edelman has persuasively argued that the child-figure performs as the primary disciplinary technology of heteronormativity. Though Russ cites patriarchal oppression in its most extreme forms—"imprisonment, madness, rape and beatings, or being chained for life"[36]—both sides of this encounter might very well espouse protectionist motives. Clearly establishing proper binary value systems composes a large part of the politics of rescue narratives. But in this tug-of-war for the child, the fact of danger in some form, rather than receiving scrutiny, acts as the ballast around which binary terms might be established.

In this context, the literal crossing-over of the rescuing heroine into the world of the child appears as a rescue into proper narrativity, one so important that it must be modeled and overseen. The occasion for this importance has to do with the mirroring between the children situated at the thresholds of textual narrative and social narrative, mimicking each other as the teenage girl mimics the Visitor. The child inside the narrative figures the child outside of the narrative, the "real" child set-tling into the book while sitting in her parents' parlor. But because the text already projects and incorporates that external child, she stands in synecdochic relation to all potential child-readers. Both children receive instruction: the internal child through the auspices of the older woman and the external child through the model of the story. LeFanu describes this dynamic in Russ's writing as "author, text and reader mov[ing] around the paradigm of mother and child in complex and at times contradic-tory ways."[37] LeFanu's triadic "author, text and reader" later succumbs to reduction as "mother and child," implying, as I am arguing, that a second child haunts this pedagogic scene. Or, rather, an infinite chain of children taking up the place of the reader, who functions as a metonym of all future social organization. And as this dyad also makes clear, the child's status as reproductive issue begins a reversible, metonymic chain that makes the child-figure stand in for the future and its proper produc-tion. Thus worries over the child express anxiety about or management of that future. Even if the influence exerted over the child exemplifies the specter of "bad influence," the game remains the same: figuring the child as "nothing more than what it is constructed to be, nothing in itself at all."[38] While far subtler than her conservative counterparts, the pedagogic impulse of Russ's rescue thematic redeems the future by instructing its representatives.[39]

That words do things in the world is a familiar literary critical conten- tion. These analytic modes, however, assume deep chasms within signifi- cation and complex iterations distorting the homology between significa- tion and enactment, iterations that vibrate with historical contingency, polyvalency, and intersecting forces. At the same time, the economy of correspondence that Spencer and Cortiel find in Russ's writing incorpo- rates mediation to engender it and render it singular. Just as the rescuer in Russ's stories sweeps into a girl child's life from the outside and remakes her, so the story itself, figured as a powerful older woman, will rescue the girl-reader by opening new ingresses and egresses for flows of desire and imagination, allowing her to become the rescuer and the teller of tales that will someday rescue more girl-readers. Or, in other words, they are performative locutions, instituting and constituting a new subjectivity in and through the act of announcing that subject.

Of course, the stories are not women and the readers are likely not children, girl-children or otherwise. In the figural logic that makes children representative, however, a simple slide across metonymic registers engen- ders the story as a speaker addressing the child who lurks inside the adult reader, the self trapped behind the prison bars of femininity, the woman reader's past returned as potential future through the auspices of the ap- propriately named *transtemporal* authority. Gathered all together—the fictional child, the pedagogic older women, the didactic story, the actual woman reader, her spectral inner child, the inner child's figuration of a reborn future likewise figured as child—this interpretive parable forms what Jacques Derrida, in his critique of J. L. Austin, calls a "unity": "this conscious presence of the speakers or receivers who participate in the effecting of a performative, their conscious and intentional presence in the totality of the operation, implies teleologically that *no remainder* escapes the present totalization."[40] As in Austin's most famous example of the felicitous performative, the marriage act, the vitality of the word– story–older woman transforms the strangely passive receiver–reader–girl child, in a closed circle with no remainder and no mistakes. Yet, unlike the marriage example, in which the official and the participants maintain different functions throughout the transformation, here the reader becomes the storyteller in a closed loop.

If the content of the narrative acts mimetically in the world in a strict one-to-one economy, then the story's effects must be carefully calibrated. It is therefore all the more shocking to find, in a novel written before the publication of "Recent Feminist Utopias" and after *The Adventures of Alyx,* a story that culminates in the death of the rescuer and the murder of the female child. What are we to make of the killing of the female child in *We Who Are About To . . . ,* an element I've conspicuously withheld until this point in our analysis? How are we to understand Russ's materializing words when they are homicidal and suicidal? How are we to understand a novel that self-consciously materializes death? Or, as Judith Butler asks of the Austinian performative, "what would it mean for a thing to be 'done by' a word or, for that matter, for a thing to be 'done in by' a word? When and where, in such a case, would such a thing become disentangled from the word by which it is done or done in?"[41] In particular, how are we to understand this materializing word when it represents and comes to bear on the child, in whose name the harming word has been relentlessly interrogated? Although Russ's work images the child's redemption through the auspices of the wise, older woman, their bond might easily be construed as corrupting and endangering in its engendering, even apart from the ultimate panic-inducing tableau of the unruly woman turned child-murderer we will see in the narrator.

"The Second Inquisition" provides a way through this dilemma. By layering science fictional devices over the realist setting, it performs a kind of generic slippage never fully resolved at the level of plot because this slippage concerns impossible knowledge. The Visitor comes from another time in both the realist and the science fictional frames. As an adult uninterested in children's innocence, she passes to the girl untimely knowledge in the form of the banned romance novel, unexplained jokes, and disdain for parental authority. In a reenactment of the Freudian primal scene, the girl spies through the bushes as the Visitor and her lover have sex on a backyard swing. The science fictional elements, however, impose an interpretative dilemma for this traditional bildungsroman topos. As a time traveler, the Visitor knows that the Good War will follow the Great

War, that flapper styles will give way to curvier silhouettes, that aluminum pans and microwave ovens will replace iron pots. If the Visitor is the girl's mirrored self, then the girl must already know all of this, which she can't know and still be the girl. Finally, then, the story's knowledge structure reverses the play of real and imagined. The girl and her suburb acquire the two-dimensionality of a studio set and the Visitor retreats behind the mirror, leaving the vitality to the story and its telling. Far from an engendering word, this final story disentangles textuality from any of its representational truth-claims.

The inquisition of the "Second Inquisition," with its reference to the unreliable oaths of heretics who pose as believers, gives weight to this interpretation. Yet the story can be and has been read as an allegory of "self-rescue"[42] in Spencer's phrase, the ultimate example of the closed loop of the engendering word. If this story nestles both possible interpretations, then perhaps the violence of *We Who Are About To . . .* can be read as a provocation, a kind of interpretive violence aimed at rending open the closed circle of rescuer and rescued to allow for more dispersed transmissions, less calculable effects, and a less strident aesthetic morality. The novel is, after all, about the impossibility of rescue.

Murder

Before her murders, before her suicide, when the narrator still at least pretends willingness to get along, she has an exchange with Lori, the only child in the novel, which provides an opportunity for the sort of future-oriented, engendering word we've seen in "The Second Inquisition." Like the narrator, a musicologist by profession, Lori wants to be a musician when she grows up. This link between them forms the ground on which the narrator might serve as a model for Lori's future self. The narrator asks to read Lori's palms, though she tells the reader in an aside that she fabricates the whole thing. Palm reading supplies a cover for pedagogic instruction. In many ways, the narrator's reading contains all the central elements of the rescue thematic. She tells Lori that she will have a long life and attain much worldly success, riches, and fame, that she will pursue her dreams and find love but never marry, and, most importantly, that they will be saved. This story encapsulates what the novel denies to its readers: a happy ending, certainly, a sympathetic hero as well, but more importantly what I am calling narrative reproductions, or the terminus of the story in the reader's identification.

"Science fiction," writes LeFanu, "enjoys remarkable freedom from rigid rules about what constitutes a novel."[43] While certainly true, most science fiction conforms to the narrative stipulation that the length of the novel and its dramatic action equal each other. Of the many startling departures not only from novelistic conventions generally but from Russ's own established thematics specifically, the most striking in *We Who Are About To* . . . is its violation of the law of dramatic action. Her murders are shocking enough, but the real violence here comes not in the content but in the structure. As we've already had occasion to note, the novel doesn't end with her murders, even though the only actions possibly remaining to the novel would be rescue (an alternative ending the narrator relates as a grimly ironic joke) or her promised suicide. By killing the other characters, the narrator kills off both the future of the colony and the future of the novel. Nothing else can happen, and indeed nothing else does happen. The novel's structure does not so much refuse climax as it prolongs the consequences of that climax. It moves through and beyond what Roland Barthes calls "the pleasure of the corporeal striptease or of narrative suspense,"[44] tapering off into sterility and death. If, as I am arguing, Lori's death must be interpreted within the conventions it violates, then the killing of the narrative's future seems a direct assault on the pedagogic text and an invitation to nonreproductive textual perversions.

Indeed, the novel might have taken a very different turn. One could imagine a third Whileaway, the utopian gender-separatist future of "When It Changed"[45] and *The Female Man,* rising on top of the destruction of the colony's burgeoning patriarchal civilization, just the narrator and twelve-year-old Lori. Of course, such a scenario threatens to turn back into the futureless sterility of the narrator's long suicide in the novel's conclusion without the introduction of some of the parthenogenetic magic that makes Whileaway a place readers want to return to. Even in a lesbian commune, the only future is in reproduction—which makes reproduction and narrative as structurally akin as childhood and narrative. And so Russ has no compassion for her readers, just as her narrator has no compassion for

Lori. Instead, she shoots Lori in the back of the head. By breaking this narrative covenant, compassion's concern, to borrow a phrase from Edelman, with the "communal relations, collective identities, the very realm of the social itself"[46] is shown to hinge on the child who is both hope and issue of those relations. Though LeFanu and Cortiel both praise Russ for her embrace of fragmentary, nonlinear prose and for her hailing of the reader into complicated relationships with fragmenting narrators, neither deals directly with this profound murder of the reader's expectation that rescue will first of all mean compassion for the child.

Given all this, it seems less than coincidental that Lori's murder comes last, for she serves as a vehicle, as her name, an aural analog for the British "lorry," echoes.[47] She maintains the social structure even as she is posted as its outer limits by serving as its ride into the future. In the novel's first phase, Lori's age and virginity keep her from the list of reproductive women assigned to "donate their genetic material."[48] Despite this apparent compassion for the tenderness of her youth, the whole scheme relies on Lori's capacity to breed farther into the future than any of her substantially older companions. As a child, Lori need not contribute to the group's building effort. Despite the limitations of their situation, they accommodate her physical fragility whenever possible. Indeed, their sententious displays of concern for her hardly mortal allergic reaction to their fire—forcing everyone to "memorize the kind of tree whose burning had made Lori sick" while her father monitors them, repeating, "This is very important" (37)—only heightens the general infantilization that quickly enshrouds all of the women. Their protectionist rhetoric, as the narrator points out, has little do with any actual danger, foremost among these the danger of childbirth, but instead works to establish what Lauren Berlant calls "dead citizenship": "identities not live, or in play, but dead, frozen, fixed, or at rest,"[49] surrounded by the disciplinary technologies of protection. As in Russ's more typical rescue thematic, the oppression from which Lori must be saved claims to have her protection at heart.

In one reading of her choice to murder Lori, the narrator might be understood as releasing Lori from the confines of this death-in-life. This explanation, however, does not account for the oddly abstracting denomination of Lori as "a Lori,"[50] which implies that she kills her not as an individual but as a type. In fact, the past given to Lori in the novel troubles the question of personhood. As her mother explains, she was adopted as an infant and chosen because "she needed money like mine" (92). Only barely embodied, Lori underwent seven years of surgical intervention: "They said the only thing that really worked were her central nervous system and her skeletal muscles" (92). Pastiched together from borrowed parts, not even her mind was her own. While her body was assembled, her mind was "on P.D. [psychic displacement] so she wouldn't have to be there while they were doing it to her" (92). The sexual overtones of this phrasing mingle with the literalization of the constructed body of the child to produce a kind of hyperinvested blankness in which the content of the child equals the expertise of technicians, the sentimental regard of parents, and the soft-focus idealization of the never-never land of child-hood fantasy. Lori the vehicle never really lives at all.[51]

Rehearsing Lori's murder in her mind, the narrator once again ab-stracts her into a type, one of an army of "little twelve-year-old girls walking about with billons of dollars of improvements inside them. Like dolls with tape decks in a slot in the back" (132). The vaguely cyborgian evocation of the first line finds equivocal extension in the second. In fact, they have almost no logical relationship. Nothing about a kidney replacement indicates the automaton repetition of scripted loops that the narrator's image conjures. But Lori's speech does. Almost the first thing the narrator reports her doing is lecturing—the narrator terms it a "disquisition" (17)—on the physical reproducibility of sound, a topic she learned about in school, though whether she attended this school in her body or as a part of her psychic displacement goes unnoted. The latter possibility, however, merely exaggerates the mechanical repetition of schooling. In either case, Lori plugs into prerecorded information and then plays it back. In fact, the only tape deck in the novel is the one the narrator speaks into. This strong association of Lori with the narra-tor's means of transmission figures Lori as a kind of repeating machine through which narratives can be perfectly stored and reproduced. If Lori engines the future, she does so as a narrative vehicle freighting the present.

Why does the narrator kill Lori when she might have redeemed her murders by justifying them as for Lori, in Lori's name, as salvation from a future that would have turned them both into breed animals without their consent? She doesn't kill Lori. She kills the means by which she might have turned her unsalvageable life into a memento mori, an error-free transcription. And with her, the narrator kills the possibility of instruction that all of her metaphors collude to expose as the very basis of our figurations of the child.

Dissemination

Lori's disquisition on sound is the third such discussion to arise in the novel's opening pages. Not just sound but questions of material transmissions in many forms surround the novel. Searching for comparisons to explain the plot of Russ's *We Who Are About To . . .*, critics have continually reverted to television show titles. Spencer calls the novel "a grotesque parody of the Swiss Family Robinson,"[52] a television version of which was aired in the same year as the book's release. Landon describes the eight survivors of the spaceship crash as "a somewhat curdled version of the characters in *Gilligan's Island*."[53] Tess Williams points to *Lost in Space,* another popular 1960s television show. The novel warrants these allusions through its own references to popular culture. Soon after the group leaves the safety of the passenger compartment for the alien planet on which they've landed, the narrator quips that their medicine box contains "Benzedrine and bobby-pins!"[54] a joke the others fail to find funny because it's "too vulgar, base and popular" (21) for them to have ever heard it. Much later in the novel, after she has killed everyone else, the narrator compares herself to a character on a situation comedy: "Elaine on Desert Island—of which there are none on Earth that do not contain resort hotels—her 3-D viewer, her burning-glass, her resourcefulness, ages eight to twelve" (105). The interjected comment about resort hotels recalls young Lori's retort when the narrator complains that their planet resembles the Australian Outback and might be just as deadly: "She'd been there, in a special hotel, and it was very, very nice" (37).

The novel signs its own interest in television through the use of the typical situation comedy conceit of ill-matched strangers and through the narrator's repeated comparison of their camp to a "stage-set" (26).[55] More importantly, the novel's explanation of its material composition brings questions of transmission to the fore. The pocket voice recorder requires specific technologies for retrieval and replay, a problem confronted twice in the novel's opening sequences. In the first instance, Cassie finds that her tape deck is out of batteries. Annoyed, she asks if there is any way to recharge the batteries, to which the narrator responds, "There's nothing we can do—our gadgets are all sealed and shielded. It's a different kind of energy; we can't transform the one to the other" (17). Moments later, Alan-Bobby asks if the narrator has any of her music with her. "Tapes," she says. "Want to use them for ribbons? I have the amplifier and the recorder—see? they fit in my hand—but the speakers are too big" (17). The reason that they attempt to colonize the planet at all hinges on the problem of temporally delayed reception. Their laser distress signal, moving only at the speed of light, might reward them with a rescue mission "in as little as a couple of centuries, a century, eighty years even. Even little Lori will be dead" (20)—a problem of spacing, then, common to all writing, which is ruptured, as Derrida writes, by the "spacing which constitutes the written sign: the spacing which separates it from other elements of the internal contextual chain . . . but also from all other forms of a present referent."[56]

At the same time that the problem of transmission bodes poorly for rescue, it lends a strange persistence to their lives and deaths, whose "light . . . may not reach you for a thousand million years" (8). Black-boxed, with no framing narration to explain how we are reading this story whose future-technology tape recorder becomes increasingly more difficult to find in our present, the story situates itself in the impossible present of television repeats. Even more than written narrative, television relies on serial reproducibility, recyclings of identical narrative arcs whose closure always leaves open the possibility of doing it all again. And like television, the illusion of narrative convention and the physiology of sound and vision give words to individual mouths rather than speakers from which they issue, in this case only and always the narrator, no matter whose indirect discourse she performs. Yet, the content of a television narrative sits uneasily next to the physics of its materiality. Each broadcast, in its repeatability, eludes direct address and perfect contextualization, spinning out, as the narrator says of her lost music, "into the ionosphere" (17).

"Who are you?" the narrator asks of her reader several times through her narration, playfully assigning alien biology, flippers, gills, and differently constructed voice boxes to her voice's receiver. "Writing orphaned,"[57] as Derrida describes all writing, finding its condition of possibility in "being severed from its referent or signified" (120) as well as from "the self-presence of a total context" (128), does not condemn to failure the investment in writing as a politically effective force. It just demands a more generous interval, a more complex field, and more room for the productivity of error and misprision. While Lori is made into the perfect machine for reproduction, the narrative insistently highlights the problem of transmission.

Such, perhaps, is the lesson of two memories the narrator relates to the voice recorder as she starves to death in her cave. Though she is haunted by the ghosts of her immediate past, her direct addresses to the reader primarily relate her experiences as a radical political activist. As a member of the Populars, a movement grounded in communist ethics, she is invited to lecture. Onstage preceding one of these events, she suddenly finds herself the target of the crowd's hostility: "Something I can only describe as a growing volume in the infra-bass as if the floor were preparing to rise and the walls come tumbling down, an ominous, slowly-rising roar" (116). The "cutting edge of change" (119) occurs here not as a surgical incision separating the longed-for future from its fully formed arrival but as movement producing sound and sound amplifying movement, the rumble of voices and bodies that portends violence less against her rather than against the edifice they all occupy. Her words do act, even before she can speak them, but with unpredictable and areferential results.

The narrator relates another story about her revolutionary past that turns on the question of dissemination. When still a Popular, she designed a graffito too unwieldy to become a slogan: "Money doesn't matter when / Control is somewhere else" (123). She thinks it forgotten until, years later, she finds it tagged on the wall of a New Zealand subway station, continents away. Each of these stories stages the indeterminacy of direct control over dissemination as opposed to delayed reception and the tendency of text to find its own addressee.

All this discussion of sound's capture and the unlikely paths of orphaned graffiti prefigure the ultimate irony of the book: she locks it. "By

writ and tort, by hullabaloo and brouhaha, I declare this tapedeck locked
to all voiceprints but mine, locked *re* playback, locked *re* print out, and
may God have mercy on your soul" (77).[58] We might suppose that the
fact of the text means that she did not commit suicide, that her grim
joke came true and she was rescued somewhere outside the frame of
the diegesis. Or we might conjecture that some alien civilization in the
far future found her tape deck, unsealed, and transcribed it, just as her
asides to her beflippered readers foretell. But I find these to be dubious
attempts to resuscitate the kind of exact reproduction that Lori embodies.
I'd rather think the whole thing a sham and the locked voice recorder a
little, winking punctum deflating any sense of narrative origin, continuity,
and truth. By so emphatically denying the reader the ability to identify
with the text, the locked tape deck blasts open the closed loop composed
of the embodied story and the rescued reader, leaving only remainders
without gravity floating away from each other in the ether to be dissemi-
nated across time — transtemporal, indeed.

Planet

Framed by the mystically transformative force of the rescue thematic's
performative locutions, *We Who Are About To . . .* looks less like a decon-
struction than like a wholesale massacre of all those metonymic children
and mothers who congregate around Russ's work and its critical reception.
The second half of the novel, however, which describes her long starvation
period, does provide a future. During this long starvation period, the planet
suddenly returns and, with it, an alternative to the sacralized future and
the sacrificial present. Without the symbolic overlay the group insisted
upon, and without anyone to convince of the possible harm awaiting
them, with indeed the harm already accomplished, the ecology emerges
as alien: neither threatening nor comforting, just alien. Only in the very
last pages of the novel, and coming as if a sign of her readiness for death,
does she see the planet as utterly indifferent to her. First, she experiences
the landscape as a symphony, specifically as Handel's *Messiah* bellowing
"Forever and ever!" but soon sees her own mistake:

> And they played and they sang and I wept, everything I ever knew, for Baroque
> music is keyed into Isaac Newton's kind of time; it's the energy of that new

explosion of philosophic time: perspective, mathematics, instant velocity, the great clock, the great wheel, the Great Godly Grid. . . .

Over here the Phoenix Reaction and God as Engineer. Over here entropy, suffering, death. And then the real Einstein, too complicated for me although I know what I am supposed to like, Stravinsky and after; it makes my head ache, referring to things in all dimensions and sometimes backwards. And then it turns primitive, this is a bloody great dynamo and this a laboring flute. (164)

In this final meditation, the struggle over which narrative will structure the colonists' lives on the planet appears as two versions of the "Great Godly Grid" of Newtonian physics and purposeful teleology forever and ever under the reign of reason. Beneath the comforting regularity of the "great clock," however, lurks the apprehension of mechanical failure and encroaching decay. As a story about the future, the law of entropy offers the timeless conservation of energy only by projecting an increasingly lifeless and uninhabitable world. As I have been arguing, conserving future life by constraining its form is an entropic strategy requiring deathly immobility. By moving away from replicative Newtonian time to the "real Einstein," the narrator gives up controllable predictability, and its attendant anxieties, for the complexity of a future that moves in its own course, offering some plenitude and some harm but always resisting our projections and predictions, always an epistemological void that no fence can contain nor narrative subdue. It is here that we can discern a future without future harm, for this is an understanding of the future robust enough to recognize the complex historical, ecological, and textual dynamics swerving all human intention.

I have been arguing that the erasure of consent in the commitment to generational survival underscores the deeply gendered dimensions of the (allegedly prepolitical, prediscursive) value of life. Key to this formation is the conviction that the future has been mapped fully enough that intercession into it will produce desired effects. Rescue requires everything to hold its shape, to remain as it is, long enough to be rescued. The point isn't that the world is acausal but that causality is richer and stranger than rescue and survival narratives imagine. Ideologies of reproduction, in other words, are one of the modes by which we attempt to manage biological, chemical, and ontological affectivities. In the next chapter, I turn to the genre of the postapocalypse through Cormac McCarthy's 2006 novel *The Road*. It is in the postapocalypse, I contend, that the revelation of complex, nonhuman causalities are most fully disclosed in the ruined planet and most phobically enclosed behind the generational promise of the child.

3

Planet

The myth of the cave, for example, or as an example, is a
good place to start.
LUCE IRIGARAY, *Speculum of the Other Woman*

The Road[1] begins twice. The first beginning relates a familiar postapocalyptic scene. It is early morning and we are in the woods. A man awakens, checks on a sleeping child, and looks around himself at the featureless, ruined world. In a sort of descriptive chiasmus, the second beginning repeats the details we've already seen, but with slight alterations. Where the first beginning is gray and fireless, the second is black and firelit; where the first is silent and empty, the second is silent and full; in the first, there is nothing to discover; in the second, each step reveals another unexpected detail. The first describes an actual place, the novel's setting, whereas the second recounts a dream-place. In the plot, the Man leads his son, the Boy, on a journey across a postapocalyptic United States, whereas in the dream, the Man follows the Boy. The prominence of this dream at the opening of the novel, the canted repetition of details from the setting, and the presence of firebrands, which serve as the central metaphor for civility throughout the novel, indicate that the dream expresses something importantly inexpressible within the diegesis proper. For this reason, it bears close scrutiny.

In the dream, the child leads the man into an earthen cave, which the narrator compares to "the inward parts of some granitic beast" (3). Hand in hand "like pilgrims in a fable swallowed up and lost" (3), the two explore what their light allows them to see. They discover a "black and ancient" (3) lake and, on the shore of the lake, a beast. The beast is blind, and its eyes appear as "dead white" as "the eggs of spiders" (3–4). The figures in the dream slot together like a set of nesting dolls. Metaphorically, the

85

cave is a "granitic beast." The cave-beast swallows them up, and in its belly they discover another beast. The beast inside the cave-beast is itself comparable to a nest of beasts—the squirming spider larvae of its dead eyes. Though this beast crouches to drink at the lake like a bear or a dog, it has no hair. It is "pale and naked and translucent" (4), its bones, bowels, heart, and brain visible through its skin. Exposed, atavistic, quadrupedal, mutated, but clearly human, this beast inside the beast retreats from the light they carry and leaves them alone.

This second beginning summarizes in condensed form McCarthy's novel's mutation of the postapocalyptic. Unlike the postapocalypse whose rupturing event stages a new beginning for society, McCarthy's novel keeps looking for a narrative line, a true beginning capable of compelling a telos, and keeps finding itself in the middle, in an interminable apocalyptic nowhere. The dream of the cave inscribes the desire to find a new origin point but also the apprehension that they may already belong to it. As Irigaray puts it in the passage I have taken as the epigraph to this chapter, the cave is a good place to start. She continues, "Read it this time as a metaphor of the inner space, of the den, the womb or *hystera,* sometimes of the Earth."[2] As a figure for the womb, the cave stands in for the origin and makes their wanderings into an exploration, a story whose ending will recode the territory they move across as conquered, human space. It is no accident that the origin, implicitly female, also serves as an image of the Earth whose bounty nourishes only after it is pacified through cultivation. In the novel's setting, too, the sterility of the land serves as a metonymy for the absent disaster. The dream doesn't include the beast's sex, but the weave of its figures, its arrangement of positions and gazes, makes clear what Irigaray would call its *scenography.* She writes,

> If there is no more "earth" to press down/repress, to work, to represent, but also and always to desire (for one's own), no opaque matter which in theory does not know herself, then what pedestal remains for the ex-sistence of the "subject"? If the earth turned and more especially turned upon herself, the erection of the subject might thereby be disconcerted and risk losing its elevation and penetration. For what would there be to rise up from and exercise his power over? And in? (133)

All the beasts in the dream of the cave are female: the naked beast at the lake whose mutated body promises weird progeny; the womb- and earthlike cave that swallows them up; and, most importantly—what all of these figures figure—the postapocalyptic Earth through which they travel in their waking lives. If this dream of the origin frightens, the source of that fright comes from the continued survival of life outside of reproduction. Cast into the light by the Boy's brand, the beast and the Earth she figures illumine the impropriety of the properly reproductive couple, their need for a spurned third term to guarantee progeniture, and the sacred trick that conjures that term away again.

From its beginning, then, McCarthy's novel thematizes male relations against an uncannily inwardly turned Earth. In this way, it partakes in the longer apocalyptic tradition stemming from the Revelations of St. John. In "Representing Apocalypse: Sexual Politics and the Violence of Revelation," Mary Wilson Carpenter argues that the violence of Revelation is *male* violence and that it is violence *between men* and *to* women."[3] Citing the burning and cannibalization of the Great Whore of Babylon, the denunciation of the female prophet Jezebel, and the expulsion of the woman clothed in the sun after she bears the male heir, Carpenter contends that the logic of the apocalyptic narrative positions the feminine as the abject ground of redemption. She concludes that Revelation functions to restore the triumph of sons over mothers and warns that even the most self-conscious attempts to unsettle the apocalyptic schema might fail to derail this project: "Gender hierarchy," she writes, "appears essential to 'apocalypse,' whatever it may be" (124).

Carpenter's description of the figurative labor of women in the apocalypse does describe the mother in *The Road*. Well before the novel opens, she commits suicide rather than face what she sees as their inevitable rape, murder, and cannibalization. When the Man asks her to think of them as survivors, she retorts that they are not survivors but rather "the walking dead in a horror film" (55). Their competing figurations point to the generic nature of their argument. They can't agree on which type of story they have been thrust into and thus the ending that their two narrative choices would predict: death in hers, redemption and renewal in his. Her explanation to her husband is couched in explicitly apocalyptic terms:

> You say you cant [survive alone]? Then dont do it. That's all. Because I am done with my own whorish heart and I have been for a long time. You talk about taking a stand but there is no stand to take. My heart was ripped out of me the

night he was born so dont ask for sorrow now. There is none. . . . As for me my
only hope is for eternal nothingness and I hope for it with all my heart. (56–57)

Framed by the apocalyptic tradition as the savior's mother, her only op-
tion is to occupy the other position, as whore: "You can think of me as a
faithless slut if you like. I've taken a new lover. He can give me what you
cannot" (57). The jockeying between them for the authority to name their
circumstances and her sneering capitulation to his narrative framing ("you
can think of me" [57]) implies that the presence of the apocalyptic tradition in the text comes from the Man. However, in this the novel seems
to collude. Her death, after all, means that the novel proceeds without
any female characters until the return of a proper mother-figure in the
conclusion, after the Man's death. That the narrative must dispense with
the birth-mother points toward the process by which apocalyptic narratives locate a single, stigmatized woman to stand in for all women, then
abstract and reify the feminine from out of her death, and finally embody
a newly purified feminine in a new mother-figure.

The novel's two beginnings, however, paint a more complicated picture of its relationship to the apocalyptic tradition. Together, these dual
beginnings suggest less a triumphal restoration of the paternal line and
purification of the abject feminine than a bifurcation that binds together
the novel's twin figures of futurity: the mutational beast and the sacred
child. That this bifurcation creates a fold that binds rather than a split that
divides can also be seen in the doubling of the narrative function. As in
many of McCarthy's novels, the dialogue is not set off from the narrative
by any grammatical marks. Except where the lines break for dialogue, the
narrative voice seamlessly merges into and out of the consciousness of
the Man. These two voices dramatically differ in their depiction of the
postapocalyptic world. This distinction within indistinction puts into crisis
the same opposition it compels. Though it is tempting to read the Man
against the narrator and the Boy against the beast, those neat oppositions
reveal themselves instead as a doubling and a haunting.

Much like the coinciding of the son's birth with the apocalyptic Event.
As if the mother had born twins, the novel's single depiction of the Event
and its only allusion to the Boy's birth happen in the same paragraph:

The clocks stopped at 1:17. A long shear of light and then a series of low concussions. . . . He dropped to one knee and raised the lever to stop the tub and then turned on both taps as far as they would go. She was standing in the doorway in her nightwear, clutching the jamb, cradling her belly in one hand. What is it? she said. What is happening?

I dont know.

Why are you taking a bath?

I'm not. (53)

The novel allows the Man, not the woman, to fully apprehend the dual birth to which he will play nurse and guide: the redemptive male child and the newly alien Earth. In one reading, then, only the Man gets full access to the meaning of the Event, while the woman merely acts and reacts within it. In this reading, we might say that the proximity on the page and in the timing of the Event and the birth indicate the novel's endorsement of his role of savior. The Event, then, might be thought to have segregated good from evil, concentrating the former in the Boy and the latter in the cannibal hordes who dominate the United States (or, as Naomi Morgenstern renders it, "Patriarchy loves the apocalypse!"[4]). But the same scene could also signal the critique of that idea in the co-constitution, literally the twinning, of violent purgation and redemptive purification. The folding together of the Event with the Boy's birth twines together the cave and the womb, making pregnancy into the only narrative figuration of a sterility-inducing catastrophe. The evidence for the former is identical to the evidence for the latter. Rather than opposed possibilities, these two interpretations double each other and rebound on each other as each other's constitutive conditions.

Middle Apocalypse

At every level in *The Road,* there is the fold that binds and doubles: the concussion–contraction of the apocalyptic Event; the internal externality of the narrative voice; the cave-womb; and the haunting absent presence of the preapocalyptic world in the newly alien Earth. It is against the intuition of the identity of these doubles, far more than in the struggle to survive, that the Man and Boy journey. They trek across the eastern United States less to find their own refuge than to recode the space as a part of a journey with a unified meaning. To this end, the Man salvages and uses the everyday technologies of domination, not least among them the eponymous road and the map with which they navigate. These are technologies that represent space as if it were an unchanging unity rather than sharing a generative fold with its double, time.

A whole poetics attends these devices. For instance, toward the end of their journey, the Man unfolds the map he's been carrying and shows the Boy:

> He sat looking at the map. The man watched him. He thought he knew what that was about. He'd pored over maps as a child, keeping one finger on the town where he lived. Just as he would look up his family in the phone directory. Themselves among others, everything in its place. Justified in the world. (182)

Tracing distances vis-à-vis a locating finger is the quotidian preapocalyptic material–discursive technology of domination. The Man trusts in the road to obey the twentieth century's compression of time into space and to act as a technology of transfer. In that equation, time on the road becomes space on a map whose divisions promise differences. As an artifact, the road provides a supplementary body for the epistemological order implied by the even ranks of phone numbers listed in the directory, just as, indeed, the Boy provides the supplemental–sacrificial body for a temporal order gone cross-eyed. Like the road, the Boy promises a horizon of difference that's really a restoration of ordered progression. Despite his incarnation of proper order, the Boy, like the translucent beast, has always lived exposed and without community. In different ways, but for them both, the *polis,* the political community that binds time as space, has given way to a profound homelessness:

> He walked out in the gray light and stood and he saw for a brief moment the absolute truth of the world. The cold relentless circling of the intestate earth. Darkness implacable. The blind dogs of the sun in their running. The crushing black vacuum of the universe. And somewhere two hunted animals trembling like ground-foxes in their cover. (130)

The novel offers as an alternative reading to the redemption the Man sees in his son, what the narrator calls "the ponderous counterspectacle of things ceasing to be . . . hydroptic and coldly secular" (274). Such a reading counterposes an entropic end—the world's death—to the redemptive end the Man imagines for his son. But the preceding passage introduces a third term: the possibility that they have been abandoned in the middle, as they ever in truth were. Martin Heidegger calls this homelessness "the symptom of oblivion of Being. Because of it the truth of Being remains unthought."[5] The preceding passage reverses Heidegger's terms and announces homelessness as the revelation of Being. This revelation of the ahomeliness of the world is what Eugene Thacker calls "the world-without-us," which allows us to think "the world-in-itself."[6] Timothy Morton goes even further by arguing against the notion of world entirely: "world," he writes, "is a function of a very long-lasting and complex set of social forms that we could roughly call the logistics of agriculture."[7] If the cave's roof is the sky and they are stuck on the ground without the elevation necessary to view their situation objectively and plan for the future, then the chronology of their travels will not describe a cartography of escape. In the crisis of the redemptive–entropic model, the revelation of being comes not from the ending of the world or from the nadir of their loss, whose depths mirror the height of the coming zenith, but from the world's unending middle. As an artifactual body like the map, the Boy promises escape; as progeny, however, he recalls the beast. If the beast and the Boy are bound to each other, rather than posed against each other, it is in the crisis of the middle that their kinship shines forth. By the same token, the crisis of the middle, always present, compels their polarization.

We might therefore extend Carpenter's conclusion to argue that the beloved son not only stands in the place of and covers over the violence enacted in his name but also that the son as beloved child poses as the primary problem the proper transmission of patrimonial inheritance as futurity. McCarthy's novel not only features as its primary protagonist a father whose fierce commitment to his son's survival in the face of civilizational, agricultural, and familial decay drives the plot, it also bears the name of his son on its dedication page.[8] This dedication binds the postapocalyptic world of the novel to the world of its composition and makes the book itself an object of patrilineal transmission. The apparently unremarkable use of a foreclosed future as the setting for the story indicates that some threat troubles the drama of patrilineal transmission in both contexts.

The problem of proper reproduction, then, is located not only in the soil but also at the center of the novel and in the figure of the child. If apocalypse narratives have historically maintained the link between women, nature, and origin, on one hand, and men, civility, and progress, on the other, then we might construe the son-who-is-child-of-the-father as a mediating term between them. Still bearing the vestiges of the womb, the male child-figure bridges the father's civility to the mother's originary force and, in so doing, sacralizes the future as such. Thus the radical foreclosure of human futurity implied by the postapocalyptic setting may be undone by the future contained within and purified by the sacred child. In this sense, purgation and purification act as the inaugural gestures in the drama of patriarchal transmission whose proper name is love:

> He'd stop and lean on the cart and the boy would go on and then stop and look back and he would raise his weeping eyes and see him standing there in the road looking back at him from some unimaginable future, glowing in that waste like a tabernacle. (273)

The dream of the cave, however, intimates a third unimaginable future alongside the Boy's glow and Earth's waste. As metaphor for the postapocalyptic Earth, the cave should be barren. Instead, they find it already inhabited. The life the torchlight illumines hints of more such alien lives. Framed as a part of the text's unconscious, the dream insinuates that the threat does not come from the collapse of the future but from its uncanny duration beyond the end. Thus the double valence of the cave: it may serve as a fantasied origin point, but this dream is a nightmare of enclosure and of forms-of-life that prosper without cultivation. If they are enclosed in many mouths, swallowed up and lost in their search for an exit, it is because there is no exit. The Earth has lost the grid work that subtended narrative progression. Though the conceit of the novel hinges on the idea that the apocalyptic Event has rendered the soil no longer suitable for cultivation, the dream suggests that some life continues to thrive.

Oikos and *Chora*

Reviews of the novel tend to begin with a recitation of the death of nature. Bob Hoover, writing in the *Pittsburgh Gazette,* says the setting is a "world nuclear winter, killed by fire and constant ash." William Kennedy begins his *New York Times Book Review* article by listing the signs of nature's death: "Fire and firestorms have consumed forests and cities, and from the fall of ashes and soot everything is gray, the river water black." Writing in the same paper two years later, Charles McGrath similarly begins by reciting the novel's grim setting: "The sky is gray, the rivers are black, and color is just a memory."⁹ It is true that the Event made it impossible to grow and preserve food, leading to the frantic search for increasingly rare canned, powdered, pickled, or salted foodstuffs (a point to which I will return at some length), but it is not the case that the collapse of the agrarian infrastructure is synonymous with the death of nature. Comparing the narrator's description of the world after the Event with a memory from a time before the Event and both with the dream of the cave intimates that the loss is not of nature per se but of a particular relationship to the natural.

As in the dream, the narrator speaks the description, slipping into the Man's thoughts as the Man is falling to sleep, emerging into a middle voice whose source seems to be the novel itself and then returning at the last moment to a first-person voice unconnected to the third-person narration that begins the passage. In the moments preceding this strange reflection, the Man and the Boy have once again made camp. The Boy, who rarely speaks, asks the Man what would happen if he died. The Man answers that he "would want to die too" (11). The Boy asks if that means that they will be together after death, an idea that the Man affirms. Nothing intercedes between the Boy's final "okay" and this:

> He lay listening to the water drip in the woods. Bedrock, this. The cold and the silence. The ashes of the late world carried on the bleak and temporal winds to and fro in the void. Carried forth and scattered and carried forth again. Everything uncoupled from its shoring. Unsupported in the ashen air. Sustained by a breath, trembling and brief. If only my heart were stone. (11)

At the very end of the novel, after the Man's death, a man and woman adopt the Boy. Using the same figure as the narrator employs here, the woman tells the Boy that he can talk to his father even though his father is dead because "the breath of God was his breath yet though it pass from man to man through all of time" (286). Reunited with a mother, sheltered in her arms, inhaling and exhaling the breath of God shared by all men—justified again in a world made distinct from all the others by man's sovereign right of existence, bearing up under the fluxions of a crisis that will pass because men will breathe through all of time—this is not the world whose ontology the narrator describes in the dream and in the preceding passage. Like the cave, that world is dark, wet, enclosed in bedrock, cold and silent. The image of bedrock conveys the stripping away of topsoil, in this case of the human world built up from the earth, to reveal the foundations. These foundations, however, are themselves ungrounded.[10] In this unveiling, the loss of the human world reveals the foundation as void. Without the ballast of human production, nothing remains shored up, everything moves. The foundation is the wind and its originary capacity to carry, what the novel calls "something nameless in the night, lode or matrix" (15). Beyond the unveiling, at the foundation, the novel asserts two opposite visions of ontology: on one hand, that we are breath, and on the other, that we are lost in the cave.

This fissure is not the product of the apocalypse. Compare the prior block passage with this memory from before the Event of a trip the protagonist took as a young man with his uncle:

> The shore was lined with birch trees that stood bone pale against the dark of the evergreens beyond. The edge of the lake a riprap of twisted stumps, gray and weathered, the windfall trees of a hurricane years past. The trees themselves had long been sawed for firewood and carried away. His uncle turned the boat and shipped the oars and they drifted over the sandy shallows until the transom grated in the sand. A dead perch lolling belly up in the clear water. Yellow leaves. (13)

This passage describes the world before the Event, and yet it is strikingly consonant with the colorlessness of the postapocalypse: the trees, like the trees they pass on the road, are compared to bone; the stumps are twisted; the fish are dead in the water. Yet the Man points to this memory as an emblem of what was lost. For him, "this was the perfect day of his child-hood. This the day to shape the days upon" (13). Like the Man's journey with the Boy, this is a story of the generational inheritance of knowledge gleaned from watching and imitating. As in his present, the Man is engaged in manipulating natural resources, in this case towing a stump to shore so they could chop it for firewood. I can point to little in this passage that testifies to the fullness of life it is supposed to represent, except for the promise of the "window-lights coming on along the shore" (13) and the woman who is sure to be in the house when they return. Perhaps, though, that is enough to cover over the fissure: the trail between the outside and the inside, their separation from each other and their contiguity to each other, and the accessibility of both to men.

In their travels on the road, the Man and the Boy often cross the threshold into private houses in search of food, but the Event has flattened their differences and made them uncanny and exposed. In their alienation from an *oikos*,[11] a domestic[ated] interior, the Man and the Boy unveil its uncanny other: the *chora*. Whereas the house encloses space so that men may move through it, the *chora* takes up the duplicitous position as the constitutive outside. But the *chora* and *oikos* are not separate ideas, except in the rending that accompanies the apocalypse. Just as the postapocalyptic Earth loses the grid work that not only allowed us to locate ourselves in space but also allowed us to locate our surrounds as made in our image and becomes instead the earthen cave of the novel's opening dream, so the difference between the *oikos* and the *chora* depends on the human relation to it rather than any immanent quality. Earth, like the *chora,* is what it has always been.

A second dream testifies to the novel's apprehension of this identity of the *chora* and the *oikos*. In one of the very few images in the novel of a lushly growing Earth, the Man dreams that "his pale bride came to him out of a green and leafy canopy. Her nipples pipeclayed and her rib bones painted white. She wore a dress of gauze and her dark hair was carried up in combs of ivory, combs of shell" (18). In the metaphoric economy of this dream, the fecundity of Earth, those "green and leafy" (18) canopies, and the cultivation of a women's beauty in the service of her husband's appreciation, those pipe-clayed nipples, are identical; farming is fucking;

the death of one requires the death of the other. But something cavelike, *chora*-like, lurks in this depiction of the pacified Earth as "pale bride" (18). The shell in her hair recalls the lake in the cave; her gauzily transparent dress the transparent skin of the beast; her white rib bones its rounded and sepulchral interior. Like the separation of the *oikos* and the *chora,* the difference between the beast at the lake and the bride in the forest is a function of the dreamer.

The notion of the *chora* comes from Plato's *Timaeus,* in which the titular speaker narrates the production of the cosmos by the Craftsman-God.[12] As John Sallis notes, despite Timaeus's explicit desire to recount the origins in a properly ordered succession, so that his discussion matches the construction of the universe, he instead succumbs to the "disorder, the errancy,"[13] of human discourse, first by narrating the creation of the body of the universe before narrating what preceded it in creation, the soul, and then, most significantly, by breaking off his narrative completely and turning back to remember the *chora,* or what Timaeus calls "the errant cause, necessity" (47). Here are the opening lines:

> Now our foregoing discourse, save for a few matters, has set forth the works wrought by the craftsmanship of Reason; but we must now set beside them the things that come about of Necessity. For the generation of this universe was a mixed result of the combination of Necessity and Reason. Reason over-ruled Necessity by persuading her to guide the greatest part of things that become toward what is best; in that way and on that principle this universe was fashioned. . . . If, then, we are really to tell how it came into being on this principle, we must bring in also the Errant Cause—in what manner its nature is to cause motion. (47)

In the first section of the discourse, Timaeus makes the foundational cut between "that which is always real and has no becoming and that which is always becoming and is never real" (16). All creation fits the second criterion; its model and maker-mover, the first; what could be that does not fall under the jurisdiction of these two categories? A whole new beginning must be made for Necessity, the errant cause of motion,[14] and the two divide into three:

> If, nonetheless, one calls it a third kind, then the discourse will already have begun to get entangled to a degree that cannot but broach difficulty and

expose the discourse to danger. It will already have begun to do something other than just say the third: for one will have to say also that it is a kind of kind beyond kind, a kind of kind outside of kind.[15]

This third thing, allegedly outside of intelligible kinds, which threatens to ruin the whole ordered system of likenesses, creators and models, movers and moved things, must be convinced to lend its power of motion to Reason, to allow itself to be bound to "things that become toward what is best."[16] This astonishing admission allows that there is a force in the world, though convinced to labor to produce the good, that is not of the same order as the rest and has no stake in its continuation. Bound, we might call necessity the *oikos*; released from its promise, *chora*. Indeed, it is directly after he recounts the binding of necessity that Timaeus first calls it a receptacle:

> For our earlier discourse the two were sufficient: one postulated as model, intelligible and always unchangingly real; second, a copy of this model, which becomes and is visible. A third we did not then distinguish, thinking that the two would suffice; but now, it seems, the argument compels us to attempt to bring to light and describe a form difficult and obscure. What nature must we, then, conceive it to possess and what part does it play? This, more than anything else: that it is the Receptacle—as it were, the nurse—of all Becoming. (48)

What emerges from this receptacle, this "matrix for everything" (48)? What always comes out of wombs: children. I might now restate the argument that I have been working toward throughout this chapter: the sacred child, the fruit of the binding of necessity as errant cause, comes to restore a lost proper order, to obscure the beginning before the beginning, the kind that isn't a kind, and to turn Earth back from matter to matrix. Like Timaeus's discourse, the postapocalypse, in attempting to restore order, produces the generative fold. For Timaeus's attempt to restrict the meaning of the *chora* to the womb violates the logic of his argument.[17] In her reading of Plato's cosmogony, Judith Butler explains that the *chora*, given Timaeus's definition, cannot really be a receptacle either, and certainly not a womb, because these would be metaphors and the *chora*

> is not a metaphor based on likeness to a human form, but a disfiguration that emerges at the boundaries of the human both as its very condition and as

the insistent threat of its deformation; it cannot take a form, a morphe, and in that sense, cannot be a body.[18]

In *Bodies That Matter,* from which this passage is drawn, Butler argues for what she calls "the irruptive chora" (41)[19] whose motion is no longer bound to the motives of the mover but irrupts to distort and deform all distinctions. In the next section, I contend that the apocalyptic disruption that has produced the *irruptive chora* issued from the domestication of Earth.

Tables

In a series of scenes I've come to think of as the Mars theme, the Boy asks the Man about extraterrestrial life:

Do you think there might be crows somewhere?
I dont know.
But what do you think?
I think it's unlikely.
Could they fly to Mars or someplace?
No. They couldnt.
Because it's too far?
Yes.
Even if they wanted to.
Even if they wanted to. . . .
Do we know where Mars is?
Sort of.
If we had a spaceship could we go there?
Well. If you had a really good spaceship and you had people to help you I suppose you could go.
Would there be food and stuff when you got there?
No. There's nothing there.
Oh. (157–58)

I've been arguing so far that McCarthy's apocalypse destabilizes the gendered relations of power between matter and form and gives rise to the sacred male child as its antidote. But the novel doesn't reject matter. Instead, it evinces a complicated relationship to the material world. In this passage, for instance, the Boy tests his intuition that there will be no exit for them when their journey ends at the Atlantic Ocean. They need a Mars, a place where there would be "food and stuff" (158). At the same time, his questions expose how much of the benignity of the planet is the result of technologies of control—like the map and the phone directory and the technologies they represented—that "justified [them] in the world" (182). What they need isn't nature itself, which they have in terrifying abundance, but what Hannah Arendt calls a durable, human world:

> Things and men form the environment for each of man's activities, which would be pointless without such location; yet this environment, the world into which we are born, would not exist without the human activity which produced it, as in the case of a fabricated thing; which takes care of it, as in the case of cultivated land; or which establishes it through organization, as in the case of the body politic.[20]

For Arendt, who channels her reading of *The Human Condition* through her scholarship on the ancient world, the private home is where men are "driven by their wants and needs" (30) and for this reason is the space of unfreedom. Like the nature it relies on, the household produces "the least durable of tangible things . . . [whose] consumption barely survives the act of their production" (96). Food is grown to be eaten and, if it isn't eaten, decays and becomes earth again. Undesirable in itself, the private realm maintains the polis. The free movement of men between the private sphere of necessity and the polis, where all are of equal standing and none tends to each other's needs and wants, makes up the human world:

> This world, however, is not identical with the earth or with nature, as the limited space for the movement of men and the general condition of organic life. It is related, rather, to the human artifact, the fabrication of human hands, as well as to affairs which go on among those who inhabit the man-made world together. To live together in the world means essentially that a world of things is between those who have it in common, as a table is located between those who sit around it; the world, like every in-between, relates and separates men at the same time. (52)

The fabrication of things not only preserves them from "the natural ruin of time" (55) that drives nature's metabolism but creates a world, a human world, from out of the rapacity of the natural. The distinguishing mark of the world as distinct from nature is that it "transcend[s] the life-span of mortal men" (55) and can be handed down from one generation to the next as patrimony. This world of fabricated things, and the world it creates for men, is exactly what McCarthy's postapocalyptic ontology lacks: the connection of the past with the future in a line that produces tables, children, and narratives.

The Man sees his son as the restoration of this line of connection that would reinstate lineage and ordered sequence; for this reason, he eschews new creation, using only the things that remain. Another group, however, has begun to fabricate, and in particular, to fabricate weapons and children:

> An army in tennis shoes, tramping. Carrying three-foot lengths of pipe with leather wrappings. Lanyards at the wrist. Some of the pipes were threaded through with lengths of chain fitted at their ends with every manner of bludgeon.... The phalanx following carried spears or lances tasseled with ribbons, the long blades hammered out of trucksprings in some crude forge upcountry.... Behind them came wagons drawn by slaves in harness and piled with goods of war and after that the women, perhaps a dozen in number, some of them pregnant, and lastly a supplementary consort of catamites. (91–92)

This is no desperate pitch at survival but a well-established and well-functioning political economy based on fixed capital, direct ownership of the means of production and military expansion. In this case, the product is meat and the process is agricultural. For the cannibals, farming is also fucking. Though there are many cannibal groups employing many production processes, including scavenging of the dead and culling fresh meat by amputation, all the groups use women's continued fecundity as a replacement for the husbandry they would have practiced on their farm animals if they had not become extinct.[21]

The Man and the Boy rarely encounter cannibals. More frequently, they are alone and vigilant. Yet these few encounters stand in for everything that motivates them on their journey. Their distinction from the cannibals is the source of their civility even when they must kill the cannibals to survive. In the wake of one such murder, the Boy asks if they are still the good guys. The Man answers, "My job is to take care of you. I was appointed to do that by God. I will kill anyone who touches you" (77). The terms of this distinction are absolute: the Man does God's work by killing cannibals, who show themselves to be unworthy of life by pursuing cannibalism. Poised against the sacralization of the Boy, the use of pregnancy as food production appears particularly debased. Yet the same rigid distinction the Man pursues—the ability to discriminate between those worthy to live and those who will be sacrificed—also informs the cannibals' practice. And both receive their sustenance from the child.

Like the Man's wife, the women's job is to produce the future, either literally as nourishment or metaphysically as redemption. Where the Man hopes to restore the grid work of the world through his son's divinity, the cannibals have begun to rebuild a human world, a world of fabricated things, through the exploitation of women's reproductive capacity. Both strategies attempt to rebind the *chora* to the *oikos,* and both do so through what Arendt calls *biopolitics* or the management of life-itself.[22] For Arendt, biopolitical governance disrupts the balance between the private realm of need and the polis where men are separated and related.[23] This disruption she names the social, which has come to usurp both the home and the polis in modernity. Whereas the classical polis rigorously delegated the labor of life to the household, modern society puts the life process at the center of governmental and economic production. For Arendt, then, the modern world has already become postapocalyptic in the specific sense that its overvaluation of life has already overwhelmed the separation characteristic of the human world. Rather than reestablishing the boundaries between the polis and the *oikos,* the Event continues the basic form of contemporary biopolitics. In the figures of the sacred child and the sacrificed child, we can see the dominance and centrality of the biopoliticized *oikos* where Arendt contends the polis once stood:

> They walked into the little clearing, the boy clutching his hand. They'd taken everything with them except whatever black thing was skewered over the coals. He was standing there checking the perimeter when the boy turned and buried his face against him.... What the boy has seen was a charred human infant headless and gutted and blackening on the spit. (198)

The sacred child faces the sacrificed child across the fire, whose guise as domestic cooking hearth never quite disguises its power to burn, just as meat betrays its origins in death. Their redemptive morality comes from their gustatory abstinence, but their recognition that meat requires death does not translate into a refusal to sacrifice. The sacredness of the child is his sacrifice in the service of reestablishing the separation between the production of life and the freedom of men.

In their instrumentalization of reproduction, the cannibals engage in one form of the biopolitical elicitation and management of life; however, they do so by re-creating the rigid distinction between the polis and the *oikos,* the free and the enslaved. As a form of sovereignty within biopolitical governance, the cannibals separate life-itself, in the form of meat, from the livingness of a person and elicit the former to care for the latter. The Man reverses this. His overvaluation of the living spirit of man causes him to sacrifice the present to his idea of the future. Neither group will accept the absolute exteriority of life, its beastlike fecundity, its systemic complexity and its tendency to move beyond the regulation of any ostensible center.

Such as, for example, the Event. Though never concretized beyond the "shear of light and . . . series of low concussions" (53), the shape of what remains testifies to the power of the irruptive *chora* and its coincidence with biopolitical governance. Whether nuclear, natural, or divine in origin, the Event's reorganization of the properties of matter continues, rather than breaks with, the industrial production processes whose absence defines life in the postapocalypse. Arendt argues that industrial production, the form of technicity correspondent to biopolitical governance, has "let loose an unnatural growth, so to speak, of the natural."[24] What interests me here is Arendt's recognition that industrial production processes are a form of nature's productivity made uncanny by their very profligacy. Rather than an imposition on, or corruption of, nature by culture, this unnatural growth comes from the hyperabundance of nature. Thus the same industrial products that maintain the social also render the polis indistinct from the *oikos* by generalizing the natural: "It is against this growth, not merely against society but against a constantly growing social realm, that the private and the intimate, on one hand, and the political (in the narrower sense of the word), on the other, have proved incapable of defending themselves" (47). At her most prophetic, Arendt warns of a total waste economy in which the unnatural growth of nature's metabolism would result in

> things [that] must be almost as quickly devoured and discarded as they have appeared in the world, if the process itself is not to come to a sudden catastrophic end. But if the ideal were already in existence and we were truly nothing but members of a consumers' society, we would no longer live in a world at all but simply be driven by a process in whose ever-recurring cycles

things appear and disappear, manifest themselves and vanish, never to last long enough to surround the life process. (134)

Under conditions of late capital (for what else would we call this waste economy?), the problem with stuff isn't its impermanence but its monstrously outsized permanence.[25] Things no longer perform the role of mediator of human life but instead threaten to overwhelm civilization with an onslaught of used-up product. The absorption of the public by the social and its biopolitical economies of production inaugurates a new, inhuman duration that uses the world-making capacity of stuff to entrench humanity in a newly menacing nature: on one hand, the steroidal strength of industrial production in globalization, on the other, the endless life-span of the plastic disposable. Whereas generationality promises continued action within human permanence, the inhuman duration is indifferent to man.

Industrial production processes and waste economies may seem like the antithesis of the problems introduced by the postapocalypse, whose lack of industry conditions the need for cannibalism. The novel, however, often takes time away from the plot to note instances of the sudden indistinction between the newly menacing postapocalyptic nature and the legacies of human production processes when unbound from their stabilizing grid work. In this scene, for example, the lake the Boy points out on the horizon reveals itself on further inspection to be the legacy of man's fabrication, specifically of a dam:

> What is that, Papa?
> It's a dam.
> What's it for?
> It made the lake. Before they built the dam that was just a river down there. The dam used the water that ran through it to turn the big fans called turbines that would generate electricity.
> To make lights. . . .
> Will the dam be there for a long time?
> I think so. It's made out of concrete. It will probably be there for hundreds of years. Thousands, even. (19–20)

The monumentality of dam construction, so evocative of modernist industrialism and its confident conquest of nature, so often erected on human suffering, bridges Arendt's two durations. Without the promise of patrimony and a human world, the dam is revealed as what it always had been, an instance of matter's mutability rather than the basis for those winking houselights the Man saw from his uncle's boat.

Is this to say that the end of the world is equivalent to the end of capitalism? On the contrary, nature's sudden implacability leaves the remnants of industrial processes as the only source of survival given the Boy's and the Man's gustatory abstinence. The novel even goes so far as to incorporate at its center a miniature of the lost human world. In an extended scene of restored domesticity that literalizes Jameson's notion that "it is easier to imagine the end of the world than the end of capitalism"[26] and repeats in even fuller fashion the small moment of redemption enabled by the Man's discovery of an unopened Coke,[27] the Man and the Boy stumble upon a fallout shelter:

> Crate upon crate of canned goods. Tomatoes, peaches, beans, apricots. Canned hams. Corned beef. Hundreds of gallons of water in ten gallon plastic jerry jugs. Paper towels, toiletpaper, paper plates. Plastic trashbags stuffed with blankets. . . .
> Is it okay for us to take it?
> Yes. It is. They would want us to. Just like we would want them to. . . .
> There were knives and plastic utensils and silverware and kitchen tools in a plastic bag. A can opener. . . .
> He took two paperware bowls from a stack of them wrapped in plastic and set them on the table. (138–41)

In one sense, this scene constructs a heroics of capitalism. In its recitation of the goods that will assure a few more days or weeks of survival, the passage seems to urge its readers to appreciate the material wealth capitalism provides. In another sense, though, the juxtaposition of material abundance with starvation uncomfortably mimics the inequalities of contemporary capital and the tendency of mass-production processes to create both deprivation and overproduction. For Arendt, the poverty of mass culture comes from the rapid and prolific production of petroleum-based consumer goods, the steroidal strength and the endless life-span of the plastic disposable. She writes,

> The weirdness of this situation (in which things last far longer than they are used) resembles a spiritualistic séance where a number of people gathered

around a table might suddenly, though some magic trick, see the table vanish from their midst.[28]

I'd like to offer the vanished table as a symbol of the postapocalypse. Yet, I don't mourn its passing. The table formed the space of patriarchy. In its guise as grid or ledger, the table delineates inside from outside, proper from improper, actor from acted upon, *zoē* from *bios*. As calendar or chronology, it relates men to the past they represent and the future they pioneer. As grid or zone, it marks off spaces of privileged privacy from the spaces of abjection that sustain them. In the postapocalypse of late capitalism, the insistence on these distinctions is directly proportional to the menace of a nature no longer amenable to them and no longer willing to be passively acted upon. The "picnic table"[29] at which the cannibals and the Man and the Boy sup may be a diminished version of the table of patriarchy, but it represents nonetheless an attempt to refurbish the *chora* as the *oikos,* to decorate the house of man so that it no longer resembles the cave. Yet waste economies rely on and hyperstimulate the mutability of matter. Little wonder, then, that the same mass-production processes that undermine the human world would elicit this postapocalyptic setting. The unnatural growth of natural processes, as Arendt puts it, relies on the near-uncontrollability of nature, its tendency to move. At stake in McCarthy's postapocalypse is less the authority of sons against the fallen feminine than the apprehension that nature under conditions of capital might return as the irruptive *chora* to threaten patrilineal transmission.

The distinctions enabled by the table are first of all distinctions in space. Walking through a ransacked library, the Man "picked up one of the books and thumbed through the heavy bloated pages. He'd not have thought the value of the smallest thing predicated on a world to come. It surprised him. That the space which these things occupied was itself an expectation" (187). The metaphysics of the table applies just as well to the gate between the domestic interior and the exposed exterior or to the fence that marks off the plot of land that will become resource from the plot that remains nature, as it does to the ordered rows of books on the shelves and shelves in the room. These sorts of material–discursive technologies separate one space from another, but they also order time as if it were space. Like the cells of a calendar, time in its movement becomes ordered rows and ranks of days and weeks. This, too, the Event undoes. Without the grid work that maintained the distinction between Earth and the human world, days become middle durations without end, enduring exposure deprived of causal progression.

Not only the books as bound objects ordered in rows but narratives too act as material–discursive technologies. The Man bemoans the new sort of day, unimpeded by "lists of things to be done. The day providential to itself. The hour. There is no later. This is later" (54). Unmoored from spatial distinction, time shifts away from the satisfying arc of narrative and with it from the narrative conventions of community.[30] In "Endings, Continued," Frank Kermode argues that narratives create patterns, and the end of the narrative seals those patterns, thus opening them to interpretation as a unity. Deprived of an ending, the story strands all those "ticks that [would] become tocks, seasons that [would] replace mere seconds, antitypes [that would] fulfill remote types"[31] in a finished work. As examples of the legibility produced by knowing how something ends, all of these refer to time. Endings, it seems, make time predictable. Surveying the whole pattern, the tick becomes legible as precedent to the tock. Without this total pattern, the tick would stand without import or prophetic message, a singularity whose presence repudiates the hermeneutic project because it means only itself, without predicates.

It is therefore all the more compelling that the novel refuses to end. Much as it began twice, so it ends twice. The first ending we have already had occasion to explore: the Boy finds a new mother in the wake of his father's death. Her reassuring vision of ontology as a great chain of breath passed from God to man and from father to son down through time promises restored succession and renewed temporal order, exposure hypostatized as continuity with the divine. Here is the second ending:

> Once there were brook trout in the streams in the mountains. You could see them standing in the amber current where the white edges of their fins wimpled softly in the flow. They smelled of moss in your hand. Polished and muscular and torsional. On their backs were vermiculate patterns that were maps of the world in its becoming. Maps and mazes. Of a thing which could not be put back. Not be made right again. In the deep glens where they lived all things were older than man and they hummed of mystery. (287)

Note how the voice shifts here. No longer wrathful or awed by an alien Earth, perhaps not even the same narrator, this voice encompasses and surrounds the Event. "Once," it says, as if beginning a series or a storybook. "Once there were brook trout," and if brook trout, then birds, and if birds, then perhaps Mars too carried the imprint of a map legible to man, to the Man, a map whose mystery names a location, an egress from the maze or a point from which to survey the whole wonderful, mysterious, conquerable pattern.[32] Yet the attempt to create a cartography of the end generates a temporal crisis. Becomings are unmappable. Only what has already become meets the requirements for representation. "Maps of the world in its becoming" (287) can only be written by a cartographer who has slipped outside of time. But for the timeless cartographer there would be no such thing as becoming, only plans and patterns and maps. Thus, while the apocalypse provides the formal closure necessary for the cartographic perspective, the postapocalyptic aftermath in which the cartographer is located opens the apocalypse to further—unmappable—becomings in time.

Whatever Being

Such is the import of a long but structurally unnecessary scene whose skewed repetitions of the conventions of the postapocalypse, and especially of the figure of the road, complicate a too-close alliance between the novel's import and the Man's choice of narrative frames. Interestingly, the novel's own encoding of the spatiotemporal apocalyptic problem comes in the form of a critique of community. In this scene the Man and the Boy meet a man named Ely, whose name and blindness suggest that he is a prophet. After satisfying themselves that he is not going to harm them, they ask him to share their dinner and question him about his life on the road. A scene of this nature, and it is the only scene of noncannibalistic communal consumption in the novel, should inaugurate what Jameson calls the apocalypse's "secret Utopian vocation" to "assembl[e] a new community of readers and believers around itself."[33] Instead, it plays with the terms on which we recognize community. Like the dream of the cave and its doubling of the barren wastes of the world with the intimation of subterranean fecundity, so the Man and the Boy's encounter with an apparently senile old man suggests a form of community that remains after the disaster.

Critics of the novel have used this scene to argue for the importance of the Boy's compassion, his worthiness of protection and valorization.[34] And, indeed, the Man and the Boy stop to eat with Ely only because of the Boy's insistent appeals, first to give him a can of mixed fruit in syrup and then to invite him to have supper with them. The Man begrudgingly allows it, but Ely takes more convincing. The Man asks, "When did you eat last?" and after a little back-and-forth Ely answers ambiguously, "I ate just now" (166–67). His evasions are defensive; they anticipate malice. But their quality of missed reference and obscured meaning begins to take on new resonances. At first, Ely's answers seem designed to make him appear harmless:

> Do you want to eat with us?
> I dont know
> You dont know?
> Eat what?
> Maybe some beef stew. With crackers. And coffee.
> What do I have to do?
> Tell us where the world went.
> What?
> You dont have to do anything. Can you walk okay?
> I can walk.
> He looked down at the boy. Are you a little boy? he said.
> What does he look like? his father said.
> I dont know. I cant see good. (166)

The spare prose in this section reveals little of gesture or tone; yet, it seems clear that the Man asks his question—"Tell us where the world went" (166), perhaps the only real question he could pose—because he believes Ely incapable of understanding it, but also because he should have understood it if he were in possession of his faculties, just as the Man takes it for granted that Ely tells him of his blindness in answer to his question about the Boy. As the conversation continues, however, the problem of reference comes increasingly to supplant the question of Ely's sanity. Once again, the Man poses a question about survival that presumes a shared set of references tied to their shared postapocalyptic setting:

How long have you been on the road?
    I was always on the road. You cant stay in one place.
    How do you live?
    I just keep going. I knew this was coming.
    You knew it was coming?
    Yeah. This or something like it. I always believed in it.
    Did you try to get ready for it?
    No. What would you do?
    I don't know.
    People were always getting ready for tomorrow. I didnt believe in that. Tomorrow wasnt getting ready for them. It didnt even know they were there. (168)

For the Man, the road is a synecdoche. His question makes clear that he believes in the limited duration of anyone's stay on the road. Limited on one side by the Event and on the other by the to-be-determined telic ending, the Man believes that the road will literally run out and so no one should be forever on it. Ely's apparent lack of comprehension, especially concerning the Man's query, allows him to slyly refute these assumptions. Although it might well be an admission of a literal pre-Event homelessness, Ely's assertion that he was "always on the road" also blurs the line of demarcation the Man labors to establish between the "world" (166) the Event took away and the road they travel in the wake of its disappearance. For the Man, tomorrow is a place on a map and a step on a carefully planned journey whose end point is the world's restoration. Ely replaces the Man's figurative use of the idea of the road with a figure of his own: a personified tomorrow. Much like Ely himself, tomorrow is just a stranger on the road, a figuration that slyly repeats the Man's spatial understanding of the future. Moreover, his personification of tomorrow casts into doubt the Man's assumption that Ely's foreknowledge that "this was coming" (168) references the same "this" the Man means. For Ely, in other words, every day contains its own "this-ness," its own unplanned-for event. While the Man believes that he offers hospitality to Ely, his hospitality comes at the price of committing to a shared narrative line. Instead, Ely represents what Derrida calls the stranger "who is already found within":

> more intimate with one than one is oneself, the absolute proximity of a stranger whose power is singular *and* anonymous, an unnameable and neutral

power,[35] that is, undecidable, neither active nor passive, an an-identity that, *without doing anything,* invisibly occupies places belonging finally neither to us nor to it.[36]

Ely does not refuse to recognize the difference between then and now; he refuses to recognize the difference of that difference or their ownership over their circumstances. Instead, in his most explicit overturning of the terms the Man brings to the conversation, he tells the Man that they are not survivors in the sense he means: "If something had happened and we were survivors and we met on the road then we'd have something to talk about. But we're not. So we don't" (172). Of course, the hypothetical situation the old man negates is exactly the narrative context, and his invocation of it here, even in negation, demonstrates that he understands it. What he refuses is the name; he refuses to accede to the specification of language. As Derrida writes,

> now, all *this, this* about which we have failed to say anything whatsoever that is logically determinable, *this* that comes with so much difficulty to language, *this* that seems not to mean anything, *this* that puts to rout our meaning-to-say, making us speak regularly from the place where we want to say nothing, where we know clearly what we do not want to say but do not know what we would like to say, as if *this* were no longer either of the order of knowledge or will or will-to-say, well, *this* comes back, *this* returns, *this* insists in urgency, and *this* gives one to think, but *this,* which is each time irresistible enough, singular enough to engender as much anguish as do the future and death, *this* stems less from a "repetition automatism" (of the automatons that have been turning before us for such a long time) than it gives us to think all *this, altogether other, every other,* from which the repetition compulsion arises: that every other is altogether other.[37]

The distinguishing *post-* of contemporary postapocalypses marks the crossing of these two figures, the place where the bent figure of time that won't stop coming despite the concussive effect of catastrophe meets the figure in whose form is announced the revelation of redemption: blind, shuffling Ely meeting the Boy. Rather than meeting the odd convolutions of time in the apocalypse, the novel seeks to rectify them, to set them straight. But Ely refuses the narrative community such straightness implies. Like the Boy and the beast, Ely is a product of the Event, a figure of the wayward, the disjunctive, and the queer. As prophet of McCarthy's apocalypse, Ely proffers the end of ends, not the end of the world but the end of the future that houses the possibility of the end and thus the end of an apocalyptic telos. While literally postapocalyptic, Ely's assertion that he "was always on the road" characterizes life as an interminable middle. They are not survivors, because such a name would imply that they could define themselves against a determinate past and toward an ultimate conclusion. "You just dont want to say it in front of the boy" (172), he scoffs. What the Man doesn't want to say in front of the Boy is that they may not have a story at all. "Do you think your fathers are watching?" rages the narrator, "That they weigh you in their ledgerbook? Against what? There is no book and your fathers are dead in the ground" (106). As the novel's representative, Ely rebukes the Man for even asking for a predicate or a nomination, a shared story that would bind them together in a quest. Without such a story to tell, the novel can't meet our expectation that Ely will become a member of their little group. There can be no group. Ely's insistent refusal of communal sentiment tasks them instead with imagining a new form of political community indifferent to definitional predication beyond what Giorgio Agamben in *The Coming Community* calls "being the *thus*" or being as "whatever being."[38] Toward the end of his elaboration of this concept, Agamben asks,

> What could be the politics of whatever singularity, that is, of a being whose community is mediated not by any condition of belonging (being red, being Italian, being Communist) nor by the simple absence of conditions (a negative community, such as that recently proposed in France by Maurice Blanchot), but by belonging itself? (85)

His answer is suggestive for this context. He begins by asserting the utility of predication for the state. Predication should not be taken as a cosmetic adornment overlaying being but as a form of subjection whose political utility comes out of the close association of a qualified being with a representative state. Being American, for example, effaces the difference between "being" and "American," locates the source of being or vitality in the designated identity, and associates both with a national spirit never quite captured by the necessarily changing physical territory, national history, and governing bodies. "This is what," he writes, "in our culture, the hypocritical dogma of the sacredness of human life and the vacuous declarations of human rights are meant to hide" (86). That is, the predication that makes life sacred to the state also makes people willing to sacrifice their being in the name of predication, beginning with the community of believers whose presence endows the sacred with its role and its significance.

As we have already seen, the predication the Man desires—the justification that comes from a list of names in a phone book—slides easily into the redemption promised by the single, sacred life around which a community of believers might gather. As singularities whose belonging cannot be questioned because it is not justified through predication, Ely the prophet and the beast at the lake express the narrator's nightmare recognition of Earth's lack of predication, which keeps "trundling past the sun and return[ing] again as trackless and as unremarked as the path of any nameless sisterworld in the ancient dark beyond" (181). The telephone book and the calendar, the sacred child and the redemptive apocalyptic story, are all technologies of predication designed to obscure the irreparably contingent whatever being of Earth.

Perhaps this then is why Derrida calls the moment of sight the most dangerous of the apocalyptic movement. He calls the moment of seeing "more serious . . . sometimes more culpable and more dangerous than what follows."[39] In illuminating the interior of the cave, the Man and the Boy see Earth without the covering of the human world, that is, without predication. Thus the apophacy of revelation; it has no story and precisely nothing to reveal. The danger of such a revelation comes from what Derrida calls the "apocalyptic *pli* [fold, envelope, letter, habit, message]" (157), the invaginating manifold, which, as in the cave, presents the *post*-apocalypse as its double, the womb. If the postapocalypse seems to have moved no further up the list in the endless waiting room of unredeemed time called history, it is because the *pli* folds the announcement of the apocalypse's imminent arrival directly onto the "upheavals, the thunderbolts and earthquakes, the fire, the blood, the mountain of fire and the sea of blood, the afflictions, the smoke, the sulphur, the burning" (157), that restart the predication game of hierarchical authority and telic triumph. As Derrida suggests, as a moment beyond the order of moments but destined to return in what cannot be measured as a moment, the apocalyptic sight of the exterior "can only be anticipated in the form of an absolute danger. It is that which breaks absolutely with constituted normality and can only be proclaimed, *presented,* as a sort of monstrosity."[40] As I have endeavored to suggest, to think the future or the absolute exterior may indeed require releasing the predication that separates monstrosity and normalcy, the present and the future, the sacred and secular, the eternal and temporal, into what Pheng Cheah calls "the structural openness of finite being."[41] Cheah calls on Derrida's elaboration of *différance* to "deform the opposition between the transcendental and the immanent" (131) to give an account of "the peculiar dynamism of the given, which is prior to the distinctions between activity and passivity, form and matter" (134), or the forms-of-life that prosper without reproduction or cultivation:

> An interval must separate the present from what it is not for the present to be itself, but this interval that constitutes it as present must, by the same token, divide the present in and of itself, *thereby also dividing, along with the present, everything that is thought on the basis of the present, that is, in our metaphysical language.*[42]

This divide, this fold, this interval, invaginates the present in itself and produces the future from out of its splitting. There is no awaiting future; the interval of time in its passing is all we ever get of futurity. And it is quite a lot. When this split, however, finds its way into a metaphysical language premised on the unity of truth and personified in the single, shining face of the sacred, sacrificed child, the generativity of the cave becomes a scandal.

Chora and Matrix

In *Hospitality of the Matrix,* Irina Aristarkhova observes that abstracting the *chora* from the maternal in readings like Butler's (and Derrida's and Levinas's) has the funny effect of nonetheless solidifying the analogical correspondences between the male figures. While the maternal becomes an ontological predicate, Aristarkhova writes, "there is an uncritical transition, conceived as an (obligatory?) anthropomorphism, between Craftsman, philosopher, father, and son."[43] She reads this ontologization and decorporealization of the *chora* as the ground on which philosophical and biomedical models of hospitality misrecognize the maternal matrix and its generativity, resulting in the easy correspondence between doctors, technicians, scientists, philosophers, mathematicians, and various forms of matrixes (cell matrix, incubator) from which women themselves are excluded. Women may be absent, she argues, but the imaginative and material work of the matrix is not. She cites Emanuela Bianchi's claim that "the feminine generativity of the receptacle/*chōra* is inalienably tied to the reproductive, maternal function,"[44] each calling on the other even if one is obscured.

In this chapter, I have been arguing that the planet is imagined as a kind of domestic interior for men. In this metaphysic, the threat of ecological apocalypse discloses the apprehension of the *chora*—Earth's own agency—even as it labors to shutter it again behind generationality. But, as I have endeavored to demonstrate, the generativity of the matrix cannot be wholly denied because of its centrality to industrial production. The next two chapters flow from this point, that the apocalypse threatens to rescind the gift of nature's labors—a threat negotiated through the figure of human reproduction. The rest of the book will be concerned with the status of fertility under conditions of somatic capitalism.

4

Birth

Every technology is a reproductive technology.
DONNA HARAWAY, "The Promise of Monsters"

In the first of three promotional posters advertising the film adaptation of Cormac McCarthy's novel *The Road,* the Man and the Boy walk side by side down the middle lane of a highway, the child gripping the Man's hand but falling slightly behind his pace. The Man stares vigilantly past the camera, revealing his full face: deeply shadowed where it pits and crags, pale white in its smooth planes. Most of the Boy's face is obscured by an oversized hat, but what shows beneath glows with the full light of the picture.

The second poster defines the movement of the set. The Man and the Boy are on the same highway, but whereas the first poster shows them walking toward the camera, in the second they walk away from it. They are farther down the road, while the camera has remained rooted in place. Though all the viewer sees is their figures in retreat, the Man's arm, slung this time behind the Boy's back, tells us that the Boy has now advanced in front of the Man.

In the final poster, the road is empty, and the tall, leafless trees take the place of the human figures, transforming the road into a clearing in the woods.

This grouping illuminates the figure of the child as it operates as a fold[1] in contemporary discourse. Luminous in occlusion, the Boy draws our eye as he draws back from full presence, lingering behind in the first frame, pushed ahead in the second, protected but also coyly reserved, as if to suggest pursuit. Like the movements of the signifier to which Lee Edelman compares him, the child-figure remains tantalizingly out of reach, deferring full revelation to the next frame "in [a] narrative dilation that endlessly begets the future by always deferring it."[2] Drawing and repelling our gaze, the child thrusts us toward the position of the Man, who looms up before us, his lunar face fully available, fully adequate to house our gaze. The Boy's transposition across the Man's body, on the contrary, marks him as the place of the inaccessible. Arriving too late or too soon, the child never fully reaches the hands that hold him, and yet, luminous and supplicant, he presents an image of suffering that demands redress.[3] As Edelman writes, the image of suffering is "always the threatened suffering of an image: an image onto which the face of the human has coercively been projected such that we, by virtue of losing it, must also lose the face by which we think we know ourselves" (108). Thus the hat that hides the child's eyes chastens us to reach out and preserve the life that glows in him at the same time that the erasure of his eyes suggests what might be revealed underneath the hat's drape. The suffering face of the child always threatens to dissolve back into the woods to which it leant its spectral humanity.

Thus far, we have pursued this child as representation and as figure, as character and as signifier, as ideological icon and as discursive technology. The questions I have addressed to the child-figure concern the meanings it circulates. I asked what we should make of the face of the child, of the pathos that demands and seduces by threatening its own dissolution, and what it makes of us. I looked at novels that feature child characters, therefore, to see what meanings the child makes available, such as the valorization of the human future. And I looked at the rhetorical use of the child-figure to see the distribution of those meanings across apparently unrelated discourses. I have looked at what forces animate the child-figure and the capture and control of force through the child-figure.

But why should the child continue to circulate at all? What sentiment attaches to the child under conditions of neoliberalism and its regimes of flexible accumulation? Once upon a time, perhaps, the figure of the child served as a link between the domestic interior and the national domestic, thus centralizing sexuality and reproduction as the basis for economic vitality and designating the vigor of the household as the mechanism by which the nation rises and falls. As Theodore Roosevelt put it in his

1905 speech to the National Congress of Mothers, "the welfare of the state depends absolutely upon whether or not the average family, the average man and woman and their children, represent the kind of citizenship fit for the foundation of a great nation."[4] In her *Wayward Reproductions,* Alys Eve Weinbaum calls this obligation not only to bear children but to bear proper children "the race/reproduction bind."[5] Rightly raised and rightly raced, these children contribute to the "stock" of the nation, a term that coordinates market economics, racialist ideology, and animal husbandry.[6] Biologized, the nation's future wealth is in its present reproductive choices, which are fostered and supervised by a whole roster of experts. It is to this state-based biopolitics that Michel Foucault's description in *History of Sexuality 1* best applies, for the production of Roosevelt's "average family" comes from the state's investment in and extension of its disciplinary procedures. Not for nothing is the twentieth century both the century of biopolitical governance and the century of the child.[7]

This era is rapidly fading. As Eve Kosofsky Sedgwick trenchantly observed, "since the beginning of the [Reagan-era] tax revolt, the government of the United States . . . has been positively rushing to divest itself of answerability for care to its charges, with no other institution proposing to fill the gap."[8] While certain forms of pastoral care and disciplinary control continue, they do so as vestigial strata—often with punitive intent—within an overarching ideological framework that privileges deregulation, privatization, and risk amplification. In this context, stock ceases to designate the tenderly marshaled wealth of the nation in its variety of forms and instead becomes the financialized object of speculative market manipulation and its unevenly distributed *necropolitical* consequences. Stock, in this sense, relies on surplus: surplus value, surplus vitality, surplus populations.[9]

Yet, as the fervent pro-natalism of the past several years has shown, reproductive futurism has lost none of its efficacy under neoliberalism. If anything, the child has become more available and more pervasive even as economic and legislative policies undermine the very social vitality the child supposedly indexes. Why should this be the case? One possible explanation for the persistence of reproductive futurism is that the child provides a justificatory rhetoric of future growth, a kind of reproductive economics that matches the vehement vitalism of anti-abortion activism.

In these terms, we might look to the homology between reproductive and economic futurism as inspiriting the money relation and lending the child's innocence and utopian promise to the debt form, fulfilling what sociologist Melinda Cooper calls "the prophetic, promissory moment of capitalist restructuring, the kind of utopia that is celebrated in neoliberal theories of growth."[10]

For as convincing as this argument is, however, it neglects the literal and material conjunction of the child and capital, or what I will call *somatic capitalism*—the intervention into and monetization of life-itself.[11] Rather than focusing on the domestic household, somatic capitalism operates above and below the level of the individual subject to amplify or diminish specific bodily capacities. It siphons vitality rather than exerting discipline, swerves and harnesses existing tendencies rather than regulating their emergence. It differentially distributes exposures and zones of safety, but with the implicit acknowledgment that no system is ever really closed enough to be safe. Its accelerant is capital, and it rides on the profits to be reaped from catastrophe. It is an expression of the move from state biopolitics with its rhetoric of concern to neoliberal speculation. Its focus is on species as repositories of recombinant capacities. Thus its paradigmatic artifacts can be found in all that biological plasticity makes possible: stem cells and transgenic animals, genetically tailored medicines, and bioweapons.[12] The converse of this activation of organic plasticity is the catalysis of systemic complexity in the autonomous agency of natural forces, brought home by biospheric change, genetic mutation, and epidemic disease. That reproductive futurism continues unabated into the twenty-first century, in other words, has less to do with ideologies of unfettered growth and more to do with *uncontrolled biological growth*.

In this and the next chapter, I consider the effect of somatic capitalism on the child-figure. The extraction of nonhuman liveliness from the child, I argue, has spurred a host of efforts to graft the culture of life over the culturing of life. By the same token, however, the child-figure that emerges from this labor is a queer child, in Kathryn Bond Stockton's sense of that term, or what we might call the *queerly human* child.[13] Stockton argues that the construction of the modern child as the fragile interval of innocence before the inevitable fall into adulthood, far from generating a smoothly teleological progression into normative heterosexuality, instead enables the proliferation of lateral potentialities. By shifting the terrain to think about the child's relationship to the reproduction of the species-qua-species, I am arguing that these queer potentialities inhere biologically as well: we are not the smoothly self-similar species we wish to imagine. The child is strange, in other words, and stranger still when given the work of obfuscating the strangers we have already become. The grafting of life is thus a reproductive futurist response to the burgeoning of life that nonetheless provides a glimpse of the apprehensions of mutation that, I contend, structure and fuel that response. And to the extent that this phobic mode of response denies the very effects that somatic capitalism seeks to induce, its consequences should be of vital concern for everyone—human and nonhuman alike.

This chapter takes up this problematic by exploring the space of encounter between reproductive futurism and reproductive futures or the profusion of liveliness rendered visible by the harnessing of life-itself in modern production processes under conditions of somatic capitalism. We are accustomed to thinking about economic-growth futurism as resulting in the actual despoliation of the present. In those terms, the fetishization of the child is a bitterly ironic fiction that occludes the harm done to future generations. The examples I have given, however, point in another direction. Taken together, these forms of liveliness suggest other-than-human profusions that threaten to dissolve the bond that seals the child to the future.[14] I argue that reproductive futurism in the neoliberal present is a response to the threat of nonhuman profusion that harnesses the associations of the child with the future to reconsolidate liveliness back into human, at the same time that material practices in the life sciences make this sovereign fantasy harder and harder to maintain.

To get at the historical transition between a biopolitical mode of reproductive futurism and its emplotment in somatic capitalism, I turn to several novels by Margaret Atwood. The first part of this chapter tracks the continuities-in-difference between Atwood's 1986 dystopia *The Handmaid's Tale* and her 2003 postapocalypse *Oryx and Crake*. Although the two novels have very obvious differences, both, I argue, use reproduction to give face to a latent anxiety about nonhuman vitality. For *Handmaid's Tale,* human infertility is both the warrant for state-enforced reproductive futurism and the volte-face of human mutation brought on by industrial waste accumulation. For *Oryx and Crake* and its full-throttle somatic capitalism, reproductive futurism takes the form of direct control over the germ line through species-wide genocide and our replacement with humanoid transgenics. Though both instances leverage reproductive futurism against reproductive futures, they simultaneously make apprehensible the specter of liveliness within the circuit of wealth (and waste) production. Thus the historical transition that I am narrating through these novels is more accurately posed as a historical torsion or torquing. What was marginal, inchoate, and without clear determination in *Handmaid's Tale* is central to the logic of *Oryx and Crake.* By looking across these novels, we can see particularly starkly how the shifting relations to nonhuman vitality affect the political stakes of women's reproductive autonomy.

The chapter's second half turns to the two books that follow after *Oryx and Crake* and that complete the MaddAddam trilogy. In these books, Atwood imagines a utopian future for the survivors of *Oryx and Crake*'s apocalypse. What appears to be a critical mapping of somatic capitalism in the first novel transforms through the trilogy's unfolding into a reconstitution of reproductive futurism. In this way, *Year of the Flood* and *MaddAddam* recast the first novel's apocalypse as the necessary precursor for the series's utopian conclusion. This is, to say the least, a twist ending. In the chapter's second half, I work through the meaning of this resurgent reproductive futurism, looking more attentively at the plot of the novels than has thus far been my practice. The cost of such attention, however, is rewarded with another surprise. In thinking about the circumstances that drive Atwood back to a formula she so thoroughly trounced in her own earlier novels, I find something unexpected: a set of ontological predicates that appear to apply the brakes to *Oryx and Crake*'s somatic capitalism and its apparently uncontainable vitality. These limits—and here is the chapter's final twist—are not only key to Atwood's reproductive futurism but help to explain the return to an ethics of care in feminist thought.

Of course, Atwood's trilogy is also and inescapably about mass murder. Its utopianism carries the stench of rot. The two never resolve, leaving the reader with no clear ethical mandate beyond the wolfish premise that all survival comes coupled to harm. And despite everything that this book has already argued, it is still deeply alarming that the joint that joins care to harm takes the face of the child.

Cultures of Life

Nowhere has the antimony between biotechnical life and the life celebrated by anti-abortion activists been more fraught than in the realm of reproduction itself. We have already had occasion to note that reproduction is a privileged instrument of social order. Weinbaum argues that "competing understandings of reproduction . . . became central to the organization of knowledge"[15] from the late eighteenth century onward. Alongside Foucault's famous contention that "the whole thematic of species" serves "to obtain results at the level of discipline,"[16] Weinbaum's formulation helps to delineate the reverse correlate: that the disciplining of populations through the regulatory apparatus of sex, gender, and race also serves to shore up the only apparently natural relations of reproduction, relations whose plasticities were made newly visible in the period in which Atwood was composing *The Handmaid's Tale*. Valerie Hartouni, for example, records the July 1986 headline news of the surgical removal of a fetus from the womb of a comatose woman, Marie Odette Henderson, noting that in such cases, the fetus appears rhetorically unmoored, "an independent life form floating about in the world . . . loose, lonely, abandoned, in need of being saved."[17] Donna Haraway and many other feminists writing in the 1980s and 1990s made a symmetrical point with reference to the continuing discursive effects of intrauterine fetal visualizations.[18] These visioning technologies render the fetus fully representable: "not just the signifier of life but . . . the-thing-in-itself."[19]

While this visual and discursive instantiation of the solitary fetus is incontrovertibly attuned to a pro-life politics dedicated to effacing the woman whose body the fetus quite literally is, there is also something anxious lurking behind this adamant isolation. In its monotonous repetitions, the life-itself made sensual in the image of the fetus betrays the lurking presence of another kind of life-itself engendered by reproductive technologies. From the test tube birth of Louise Brown in 1978 to our current "embryo-strewn world of the 21st century,"[20] assisted reproductive technologies have begun to unravel the bond between sex, pregnancy, and childbirth and to intimate that life may be neither fully controllable nor fully controlled. As a manipulable object of medical knowledge and intervention, reproduction is shown to be just one of many biological functions. In the process, assisted reproduction has blurred the distinction, as Susan Squier delineates, between the unique event of human birth and the kinds of breeding practices long associated with animal life. Indeed, it is under the pressure of in vitro fertilization technologies and their extraction of bodily capacities from the housing of the individual subject, and in the mix-and-match practices of human and animal surrogacy, that the equation underwriting the fantasy of heteroreproduction—that $1 + 1$ will always $= 1$—dramatically transforms. The reaction-formation Lauren Berlant names "fetal motherhood,"[21] then, responds to this transformation by collapsing the reproductive woman into the juridical and discursive primacy of the fetus, retooling the apparatus of fertility as adjunct to the single, sacred child.

The Handmaid's Tale has garnered much critical commentary. As a dystopia, it is often considered in light of that genre, especially through Atwood's formal choice to write it as a first-person oral record discovered by a later society for which it serves as a historical archive. As a feminist dystopia, it is read as an "if-this-goes-on" warning that asks, as Atwood herself puts it, "how thin is the ice on which supposedly 'liberated' modern Western woman stands?"[22] And as a work of feminist science fiction, it engages in the critical distance from the sorts of received notions of the natural and the transhistorical that Darko Suvin calls "cognitive estrangement" and that motivates both Carl Freedman and Earl Jackson Jr. to assimilate science fiction with critical theory tout court.[23] Both science fiction and critical theory strive to formulate "a worldview in which the subject is not the cause but the effect of the system that sustains it."[24] Indeed, Atwood's novel gives us three different narrative presents—the dystopic future, the remembered past that most closely resembles the period of the book's composition, and the far future in which the other two texts function as testimony. In juxtaposing these moments, the reader comes to see the differences in their assumptions and thus the "creation of the gendered subject within language and culture."[25]

Despite this broad array of approaches to *Handmaid's Tale,* however, surprisingly few seriously engage the profound shifts in reproductive technologies that were occurring contemporaneously with its composition. In this, Heather Latimer's account is both perspicacious and telling. Latimer first describes the novel as "tap[ping] into the time period's politics" by extrapolating from the 1980s backlash against reproductive rights to imagine "a world where maternity is so tightly linked to state oppression that any move against the state, from unlawful sexual interaction to contraception is considered a radical one and punishable by death."[26] Latimer's insight is to see in this extrapolation a satiric rejection of the terms in which the abortion question has been framed, one whose positing of life against choice is always capable of turning inside out.[27] This satire only works, however, if the primary political context encoded through the novel—violent opposition to abortion rights—is understood as a technology of gender oppression, without further inquiry into the reasons for such resurgent misogyny.

Yet *Handmaid's Tale* is a novel *about* reproductive technologies. In an earlier essay, Anne Balsamo casts the novel as a critical mapping of the new technologies of reproduction and their effect of breaking reproduction "into discrete stages: egg production, fertilization, implantation, feeding, and birthing."[28] Her particular focus on the criminalization of maternal drug use, however, reads reproductive technologies instrumentally as "the means for exercising power relations on the flesh of the female body" (233). In picking up on Balsamo's analysis, Squier emphasizes the divisibility engendered by new reproductive technologies and their confusion of inside–outside, part–whole, and human–animal distinctions.[29] While crucial, their focus on how these newly unstable body boundaries are managed by the state diminishes the vibrancy of the vibrant matter that is their subject. In getting a handle on the circulations of knowledge and power through the biomedical body, it is easy to overlook the extra-discursive consequentiality of these procedures in their ongoing ecological intra-actions. That reproduction needs to be managed, in other words, is indicative of its unruly escape from that management. As biologist Lynn Margulis and essayist Dorion Sagan argue, reproduction far outstrips sexual reproduction, which is really just a province in its great domain.

Reproduction, they remind us, refers to the "process of making living copies" that also enables mutational transcription errors, while the genetic transfer that typifies sexual reproduction can likewise be achieved through such variegated means as "cosmic irradiation, acquisition of viruses or symbionts, or exposure to ambient chemicals."[30]

Unbabies

In *The Handmaid's Tale*,[31] the moral imperative of reproductive futurism comes at the end of a cattle prod. In its dystopian present, America has become the young Republic of Gilead, a theocratic military dictatorship whose response to the crisis of fertility is to strip women of their employment and their property and sort them according to their social roles: the wives of highly ranked men retained their positions, as did religiously and morally acceptable married women of lower rank. Proper unmarried lower-caste women were divided into laboring Marthas—cooks and housekeepers for upper-caste households—and the Aunts who train the Handmaids. It's around the Handmaids and their fertility that the social structure turns. They are its constitutive exclusion, the abjected groundwork around which the machinery of state labors. As Offred the narrator sourly remarks in connection to the state's brand on her ankle, "I am a national resource" (65). Offred's name, like that of all Handmaids, derives from the family she serves and changes as she moves from house to house—three high-ranked infertile families, three shots at producing the child that will redeem her and spare her from the label of Unwoman and a life in the colonies clearing toxic waste.[32] Assigning names to the classes of women is just one example of the disciplinary mechanism by which the women of Gilead are made to disappear behind their social roles.[33] They are not allowed to read; their money has been replaced by government script correlating with a small number of shops; and their uniforms, the same color and cut for every woman in her role, are issued to them.

"Think of yourselves as seeds," says Aunt Lydia at the Red Center during Offred's training. "The future is in your hands" (47). It is not her hands, however, that bear the future:

> I used to think of my body as an instrument, of pleasure, or a means of transportation, or an implement for the accomplishment of my will. I could use it

to run, push buttons of one sort or another, make things happen. There were limits, but my body was lithe, single, solid, one with me.

Now the flesh arranges itself differently. I'm a cloud, congealed, around a central object, the shape of a pear, which is hard and more real than I am and glows red within its translucent wrapping. (73–74)

Handmaids are "ambulatory chalices," "two-legged wombs" (136). Offred's disappearance behind her womb, and the social relations that make it more real than she, exemplifies Berlant's notion of fetal motherhood or the production of the heteroreproductive household through the enormous privilege transferred to the child as the index of the vitality of the nation. Given this, it is apparent why so many readers of the novel have treated the specter of infertility as a ruse. After all, for all the weight placed on childbirth and the dire consequences for Handmaids who do not succeed in becoming pregnant and birthing healthy children, the mechanisms by which such impregnation is supposed to happen are absurd. In light of the once-monthly Ceremony of Copulation triangulated through the body of the infertile wife with its restriction on female orgasm and the legal sanctions against claiming that any man is infertile, the discipline taught to the Handmaids begins to look like exactly that: a disciplining technology. No abstaining from liquor or coffee, no amount of Kegel exercises, will make up for the exclusion of male-caused infertility if the point is indeed to produce more children.[34]

Clearly, then, infertility serves to naturalize patriarchy. Not for nothing does the book underscore that "gender treachery" (43) is as much a capital crime as religious deviance and a history of providing abortions. Since Handmaids escape punishment for these crimes only by virtue of their fertility, their failure to produce life is tantamount to their death. As Latimer writes, Atwood offers "a picture of what the world would look like if a woman's only reproductive 'choice' is pregnancy or death."[35] In a different sense, however, infertility is indeed a ruse. For the novel also includes a third possibility that splits open the opposition of pregnancy and death and that links Handmaids and Unwomen through their shared encounter with reproductive futures: that is, the Unbabies and the mutagens responsible for their deformities. "The chances are one in four," Offred tells us.

The air got too full, once, of chemicals, rays, radiation, the water swarmed with toxic molecules, all of that takes years to clean up, and meanwhile they creep into your body, camp out in your fatty cells. Who knows, your very flesh may be polluted, dirty as an oily beach, sure death to shore birds and unborn babies. (112)

The rhetoric of spatial permeability—the constitutive openness in the meeting of radiation and skin, the keen hospitality of fatty cells to chemicals—intersects with the temporal permeability of the "once," signaling the bleed of other moments into the apparent solidity and permanence of the present. Although never foregrounded in the novel, the conjunction of toxic pollution, infertility, and mutation suggests that Gilead's militarized reproductive futurism responds as much to the uncontainable liveliness of biological and ecological forces—including those extradiegetic reproductive technologies whose absence the novel so conspicuously underscores—as to the threatening breakup of heteropatriarchy in precoup America.

In this sense, the differences between a state biopolitics of sexuality and population and a neoliberal biopolitics of subindividual capacities and algorithmic databases appear as differing strategies for negotiating and organizing what Hannah Arendt identifies as the key characteristic of modernity and which I explored in the previous chapter: the unnatural growth of the natural. Unlike Foucault's designation of life as the new entrant into the political, Arendt's biopolitics is less concerned with the new form of subjectivity it engenders than with the effect on the planet of the demand for ever greater efficiency in the creation of an ever expanding repertoire of goods and services. This increase in production is accompanied by two contradictory demands: that extracted resources retain their animacy so that their vitality can be operationalized *and also* that they are not so active that they transform too quickly from value to waste. Industrial production relies on precisely timing the duration of a good's durability and therefore on the management of the metabolic process of production, consumption, and decay. The ideal result of such control is a world in which things "manifest themselves and vanish," but the reality is a "waste economy"[36] in which the vibrancy required of the production process is never rendered fully sterile no matter how many layers of lead separate out the spent uranium, to take a paramount example, from the surrounding bedrock.

"The force of life is fertility," Arendt writes. And yet the example of nuclear waste makes clear that biological reproduction is hardly the only source of liveliness. For this reason, queer theorist Mel Chen prefers the term *animacy* for the rich fields that inhere in the interstices of molar binaries like "life and death, positivity and negativity, impulse and substance."[37] In this context, reproductive futurism promises to consolidate the explosion of other-than-human liveliness under the figure of the child at the same time that it suggests an accelerating horizon of unrecuperable vitality. Through the figure of the shredder child, the mutant child, *The Handmaid's Tale* shows us the reproductive future behind the sacred child of reproductive futurism. Indeed, the only child born in the space of the novel—in a collective ritual of sympathetic identification so powerful it causes phantom pains and false milk in the bodies of the women who attend—is an Unbaby. While this may seem less like liveliness than death and despair (a conjunction that resonates with the mandate "breed or die"), a lyric description of an egg, which directly precedes both Offred's explanation of Unbabies and the birth scene that brings another Unbaby into the world, gives us another combination of deathliness and liveliness. I quote from it in full:

> The shell of the egg is smooth but also grained; small pebbles of calcium are defined by the sunlight, like craters on the moon. It's a barren landscape, yet perfect; it's the sort of desert the saints went into, so their minds would not be distracted by profusion. I think that this is what God must look like: an egg. The life of the moon may not be on the surface, but inside.
>
> The egg is glowing now, as if it had an energy of its own. (110)

The egg hiding under a cozy the shape of a woman's skirt, the egg Offred imagines incubating between her breasts, the egg that reminds her of the moon but is also the shape of God, is inescapably the fertilized egg of Handmaidenly ambitions. As she notes, "This is how I am expected to react. If I have an egg, what more can I want?" (111). And yet this egg, with its arid, barren landscape repelling all profusion, glows with its own energy—an extrareproductive vitality whose liveliness like the "swarms of toxic molecules" alerts us to the profusion that surrounds us. As Offred reflects, "the desire to live attaches to the strangest objects" (111). In fact, her gaze insistently picks out these signs of liveliness, from the "worms, evidence of the fertility of the soil, caught by the sun, half dead; flexible and pink, like lips" (17) that she spies in the back garden to her hermaphroditic vision of the tulips "redder than ever, opening, no longer wine cups but chalices, thrusting themselves up" (45). For Offred, this profuse display of natural fecundity offers an alternative mode of conceptualizing futurity—"all flesh is grass," as she acutely observes.

In *Oryx and Crake,* it is exactly this life that is the target of techniques of control trained on the production of agricultural, biological, and ecological liveliness.

Somatic Capitalism

As a young boy in the world before the apocalypse, Jimmy lived at OrganInc, a multinational biopharmaceutical firm and suburban compound. In one of Jimmy's earliest memories, he and his father attend a bonfire at the compound. They are burning dead animals. Jimmy, who is five at the time, worries that the disinfectant poison they have to walk through will hurt the ducks painted on his boots, but his father assures him that the ducks aren't real. Jimmy's confusion is understandable. He is also anxious about the sheep and cows on the pile. "The animals are dead," his father tells him. "They were like steaks and sausages, only they still had their skins on."[38] His father is joking, but Atwood's language is precise. These are not really animals at all; they are containers for capital. *Sus multiorganifer*—a transgenic animal species composed out of domestic pig DNA and called "pigoons" in the colloquial—grows human organs for transplant. A rapid-growth gene splice allows each animal to be reaped over and over again. It's "much cheaper than getting yourself cloned for spare parts," Jimmy's father quips, "or keeping a for-harvest child or two stashed away in some illegal baby orchard" (23).[39]

In a *PMLA* article released a year after the publication of *Oryx and Crake,* Atwood objected to the link readers and critics had been making to *The Handmaid's Tale.* While both novels are set in a dystopian near-future America, they differ markedly in the features they extrapolate. These differences appear most emphatically in their two visions of the place of the market in the organization of society. Whereas *Handmaid's Tale* appears to have only two modes of commodity production—agricultural and military—*Oryx and Crake* is wholly given over to commodity innovation: electronics, entertainment, beauty products, fertility clinics, snack foods, vitamin production, coffee, and biomedical devices dominate the markets. As might be expected, where *Handmaid's Tale* divides the population into a small number of acceptable social roles based on race, class, and gender, the future America of *Oryx and Crake* has only a single great division, that between the rigorously sanitized compounds and the anarchic, immiserated Pleeblands. Like *Handmaid's Tale, Oryx and Crake* enforces the boundary between Compound and Pleebland with barbed wire, but whereas the body exerting regulation in the world of *Handmaid's Tale* is the state and its abiding interest in the welfare of its citizens, the communities inside the fence in *Oryx and Crake* are owned by multinational corporations and policed by the private CorpSeCorps security service.

In summary, then, the differences in social and economic organization between *The Handmaid's Tale* and *Oryx and Crake* reflect the cultural shift from a regulatory state, militarized in *The Handmaid's Tale,* to a neoliberal control society that has shucked off the carapace of nation entirely. The boundary concerns that fueled the plot of *Handmaid's Tale* (disciplining fertility by controlling women's movements) morph in this new context. For *Oryx and Crake,* the most serious boundary breaches have to do with controlling the flow of proprietary information, patented life-forms, and engineered diseases.[40] OrganInc, with its clever conflation of organic marketing with the "Inc." of incorporation, highlights the property relationship at the heart of somatic capitalism[41] and thematizes the deepening and broadening of the capture and monetization of life.

OrganInc and its competitor businesses are unabashed in their ambition to convert all of nature to patentable standing reserve for human consumption. Jimmy's early experience at the bonfire tutors him in the relations that attend somatic capitalism or what the novel elsewhere describes as AgriCouture: to exhort life, to summon its vitality and torture it to efficiency through careful control over its somatic capacities. But exhortation and control sit uneasily together. OrganInc and the other corporate compounds have no doubt that they can convert all of nature to patentable products. They are far less certain that they can perfect the containment systems that make such patenting possible. And, sotto voce, they are even less clear about what they might do if they succeed. Such is the lesson of the burning animals. The bonfire is an attempt to contain an engineered disease. In a conversation Jimmy relates, a friend of his father blames the animals' destruction on a rival company that, it is thought, intentionally infected the animals. "Drive the prices up," he opines. "Make a killing on their own stuff" (18). His metaphoric use of killing reminds us that what we are witnessing is a scene of slaughter conducted to preserve profit and so to "make a killing" is by no means restricted to the hypothetical other company. In the final analysis, though, it's neither OrganInc's purifying fire nor the deliberate dissemination of a hostile disease that matters but the failure of containment. "I thought our people had us tight as a drum," Jimmy's father complains.

They do not. Indeed, the most pressing difference between the two novels is generic. *Handmaid's Tale* is a near-future dystopia. *Oryx and Crake*'s near-future dystopia (the world of Jimmy's childhood) is the near-past of a postapocalyptic present.[42] The dystopia-that-was comes to the reader by way of Jimmy, who recounts his memories of his life in the compounds before his best friend Crake intentionally spread the deadly and easily transmissible virus he cooked up in the labs of his employer and that killed off most of the world's human population.

As we learn, this was not entirely his own idea. It had also long been the secret strategy employed by the compounds for assuring profits. Before Crake engineers his disaster, he makes a discovery that he relates to Jimmy by way of a hypothetical scenario. What happens if you're a drug producer like HelthWyzer and you've cured all the known diseases? You produce them instead:

> Listen, this is brilliant. They put the hostile bioforms into their vitamin pills. . . . They embed a virus inside a carrier bacterium, E. coli splice, doesn't get digested, bursts in the pylorus, and bingo! Random insertion. . . . But once you've got a hostile bioform started in the pleed population, the way people slosh around out there it more or less runs itself. (211)

It is this discovery for which Crake's father was killed, pushed off a highway overpass outside of the compound's walls, and it is the discovery of his discovery that led Crake to his genocide and to the reproductive solution that follows it. For alongside his development of the extermination pill, Crake is also developing a transgenic humanoid species he calls his children.

It's a funny thing about that genocide. In "Arguing against Ice Cream," her review of environmentalist Bill McKibben's polemic *Enough: Staying Human in an Engineered Age,* Atwood seems to concur with McKibben's assessment that although human genetic engineering might be fun, it's a form of fun we should deny ourselves.[43] A similar sensibility informs her retelling of the Scrooge narrative in *Payback: Debt and the Shadow Side of Wealth,* in which she poses the ghosts of Earth Day past, present, and future.[44] Like her account of genomics, Atwood discusses environmental exploitation as an appealing indulgence with a nasty down side. All this contributes to a reading of *Oryx and Crake* as advocating on behalf of an Earth rendered Tiny Tim–ish in its innocent woundedness and expectation of future harm: on one side, the exciting choices available in designer babies ("The line forms to the right, and it'll be a long one"[45]); on the other, the ill effects on our species and our environment of "pigging out" (130) on biotechnology.

However, the opposition between environmentalism and science is not supported by the novel. Crake's given name is Glenn. He takes Crake as a pseudonym from a species of extinct bird and uses it as his handle on Extinctathon, a protected social media space for environmentalists interested in civil disobedience. Crake the scientist, Crake the architect of genocide, is one of them. "As a species we're in deep trouble," he tells Jimmy.

> They're afraid to release the stats because people might just give up, but take it from me, we're running out of space-time. Demand for resources has exceeded supply for decades in marginal geo-political areas, hence the famines and the droughts; but very soon demand is going to exceed supply for everyone.[46]

For Crake, genocide is just a quicker version of what will happen anyway as *Homo sapiens sapiens* becomes one of many species in the great die-off, with one notable exception. His helping it along wipes the slate clean enough to give his Children a chance to thrive and to breed.

The Children of Crake are officially prototypes for designer genomics clinics promising custom-designed beauty, immunity from microbes, and UV-resistant skin. But, as Jimmy comments, they have a number of implausible traits as well. They are herbivorous, hard-wired against hierarchy and racism, and unlikely to have a carnivore's attachment to land and conquest. Most important of all, their estrous cycles have been altered so that they can have sex only when they are fertile. Here, too, he is only thinking of the planet's future. For Crake, reproduction as a fantasy of the future is what's most damaging about *Homo sapiens sapiens*:

> Men can imagine their own deaths, they can see them coming, and the mere thought of impending death acts like an aphrodisiac. A dog or rabbit doesn't behave like that. Take birds—in a lean season they cut down on eggs, or they won't mate at all. They put their energy into staying alive. (120)

Crake styles himself immune to the relation between sex and the imagination of death. But this too is wrong. Crake is the apotheosis of the link he draws between sex and death: his Paradice project is designed to be the last and most successful human eugenics program, leveraging the enormous curatorial power of genomics in the service of reproductive futurism on a mass scale. It is precisely Crake's certainty in his own prognostication, his conviction that his imagination of death is empirical rather than emotional, that allows him to believe in the morality of his genocide. What appears as an opposition between a self-indulgent commodity culture and a threatened ecological inheritance is in fact a dialectical movement between reproductive futures and the reactionary reinstallation of reproductive futurism. For the formula works in both directions. Crake duplicates the logic of somatic capitalism, but in the name of environmental futures. Like the corporate compounds he destroys, Crake dreams of encircling proliferation and putting it to work.

Thus, whereas *Handmaid's Tale* attempts to disguise the emergent conditions of reproductive futures in the armature of reproductive futurism, *Oryx and Crake* renders reproductive futurism biological. Caught between the dual demands for control and for a reserve of vibrant potentiality, somatic capitalism breeds the conditions for its own catastrophe, as Crake—shining son of the compounds and the architect of the apocalypse—makes so emphatically clear. But Crake's vision is also subject to the surplus vitality triggered by somatic capitalism. After all, the virus cares not at all why it was created or whose research animals it infects; the pigoons, rakunks, and wolvogs bred in the exuberant early days of created species quickly run feral. And though feral pigoons may be the paradigmatic emblem of somatic capitalism, it is the apocalypse itself that takes up the position of the shredder child as the system's own constitutive exclusion. Containment fails. And so the promise of control in reproductive futurism cannot but attend the somatic capitalist production of reproductive futures just as the dream of reproductive futurism needs the fecundity of reproductive futures.

This chapter began by asking why the child continues to loom so large even against the waning of the liberal, protectionist state. In response, I have argued that although somatic capitalism differs from eugenic biopolitics in its modes of address (moving from population and demography to algorithmic incitement and capacity extraction), this shift merely deepens and intensifies the paramount biopolitical project of the twentieth century: the elicitation and management of surplus vitality. In the corporate compounds of *Oryx and Crake*'s America, we see how biopolitics in its somatic capitalist phase extends the long-standing logic of surplus extraction to forms-of-life that previously escaped instrumentalization, commodification, and financialization. All of this has prepared us to see Crake as the object of Atwood's critique, misguided precisely to the extent that he speaks the doubled-sided logic of somatic capitalism. It is all the more shocking, then, that the remaining two books fulfill Crake's vision and, in so doing, turn emphatically *back* to reproductive futurism.

ChickieNobs

The world of *Oryx and Crake* is one in which all life is subsumed into the imperatives of somatic capitalism. It is in this world that Glenn was raised, excelled, and was richly rewarded. And it is in this world that Glenn becomes Crake. As Crake, he takes a very particular lesson from this world, one we are invited to ponder. If genetic engineering may be pressed into service to produce capital, might it not be made to serve other purposes as well?

While a student at Watson-Crick, Crake requests that Jimmy spend a few days with him. During their tour of the campus, Crake makes a point of stopping in on the NeoAgricultures division, where they visit strange new forms-of-life, including a prototype ChickieNob, "a large bulblike object that seemed to be covered with stippled whitish yellow skin" (202). It is "sort of like a chicken hookworm" a student tells them (203), but with each individual animal producing only one cut of meat (breasts, drumsticks, wings, etc.) to amplify each individual animal's efficiency. With all of their original chicken capacities retooled, these animals produce chicken breasts in two weeks. "Picture the sea-anemone body plan," Crake counsels. But Jimmy wants to know what it's thinking (202). Jimmy has no problem with the industrial agricultural processes that make some animals available for slaughter and rendering. But the transformative genetic engineering performed by the NeoAgricultures group makes the processing of living beings for surplus wealth production too obvious for Jimmy. In response, Jimmy thinks that all chickens should have the dignity of their own purposes, including in something as extrasubjective as body plan. For Jimmy, species specificity functions as a limit case of interiority even for those organisms otherwise easily objectified and expropriated. Crake, on the contrary, is not at all concerned about interiority, subjective depth, or organic wholeness. He sees forms-of-life as "meat machines" (209), skin-bound bags of capacities only contingently held together and which may therefore be extracted and recombined with those derived from other creatures—like chicken tissue on a sea anemone body plan.

In his own offhand way, Crake is a philosopher. "You know when people get their hair dyed or their teeth done?" Crake asks Jimmy rhetorically, in response to Jimmy's attempt to distinguish the "real" life-forms from the newly created ones. "After it happens, that's what they look like in real time. The process is no longer important" (200). "If you can tell they were fake," Crake tells Jimmy about breast enhancements, "it was a bad job" (200). Despite his capitulation to the language of the authentic and the fake, Crake's claim here is far broader than customer satisfaction. His point is not that *Jimmy* won't be able to tell the difference but that *nature* won't. A job well done is a job done to the satisfaction of everyone involved. The breast must accept the material used to enhance it; the chicken must be subtly solicited so that it is willing to hold hands with the sea anemone. The promise of a commercial application may give Crake the excuse to do what he does, but otherwise he has little interest in market logics. He is driven instead by what he can *make*. He doesn't wonder which comes first, the chicken or the ChickieNob, nature or culture. He works with whatever has the most traction, and he recognizes that the traction it has comes from the constraints it imposes. Jimmy may see the NeoAgriculture projects as callously instrumentalizing animal life, but Crake cares just as much for the dignity of life as Jimmy does. He just cares about it differently.

Thus while Jimmy worries that "some line has been crossed"[47] in separating living capacity from evolutionary morphology, Crake concerns himself with the limits immanent to those capacities. In transgenics, as in chemistry, some things work together and some things just don't. What really matters about any organism is the set of constraints it offers, the stops it puts on runaway vitality and that allow form to take shape. In Crake's worldview, the stasis needed to maintain current species boundaries is itself a strenuously produced staving off of mutation. "To stay human is to break a limitation," his fridge magnet quips (301). Jimmy's moral constraints are themselves a part of that apparatus for maintaining form. "Nature is to zoos as God is to churches," he tells Jimmy on their way out of the Biodefense unit, the last stop on their tour. "Those walls and bars are there for a reason," he continues, "not to keep us out, but to keep them in" (206). From what aspects of God does a church protect us? A God without a church is by extension a God without a scripture, without a set of laws inscribed and passed down, without a chosen people. By analogy, nature without walls is like a God without a covenant, powerful, unpredictable, and beholden to no one. But Crake is no animal liberationist. His aim is not to return nature to its original state but to strip away the protections that keep it static. As he says in response to Jimmy's incredulous "I thought you didn't believe in God," "I don't believe in Nature either . . . or not with a capital N" (206). Jimmy hopes for some reassertion of moral and ethical law, but Crake isn't lawless. He follows different laws, the laws set down by the immanent antipathies and affiliations of subindividual capacities. And those he deeply reveres.

Crake's disbelief in nature "with a capital N" might remind us of arguments in queer and feminist theory against a nature used as a bludgeon against antinormative forms of thriving. If we are indeed encouraged to see Crake as a philosopher of nature, and I think we are, then we might characterize his philosophical position as a version of feminist new materialism. Like Karen Barad, Crake's central question concerns rethinking culture "as something nature does."[48] In answering to this challenge, he dispenses with conceptions of identity that posit essential self-similarity, originary unity, or individual independence. Like her, he thinks of the world in terms of agential cuts or the ontological primacy of entangled relations that "radically rework relations of joining and disjoining" (46). He just happens to enact his agential cuts through the genetic splice and the chemistry of death. We might be inclined, here, to remember Barad's commitment to our entangled "relations of obligation" (47) in processes of spacetimemattering. Or perhaps we would object that Crake's sense of the inbuilt constraints offered by any Earthly being pulls against the mobility of mattering, its lack of fixity. These objections, however, apply with equal rigor to feminist new materialism's ethics of care, an ethics that requires that we "nurture living" by getting better at "facing killing" and indeed at "dying instead of killing," to paraphrase Donna Haraway's *When Species Meet*. After all, Crake, who murders humankind, who arranges to have himself killed by his best friend's hand, does so in the name of life. More specifically, he does so to circumvent the ontological predicates that he has come to see as baked into the world and that bracket the mobility of matter. The first, which we have already explored at some length, concerns reproduction. The second, new to us, has to do with eating.

In these final sections, I consider why the trilogy seems to have so emphatically returned to reproductive futurism and what the unexpected conjunction of eating and birthing tells us about that return. For the need to feed is also a familiar problem in feminist thinking about posthuman ethics in the shadow of industrial meat production and in the lee of the sixth great extinction. In *MaddAddam*, as in feminist inquiry, the specter of extinction does surprising things to a politics of multispecies flourishing. In what follows, I turn first to a key moment of culinary boundary making in *MaddAddam* before considering how feminist theorists have taken up the question of the edible. Finally, with both of those knocking around together, I endeavor a brief reading of the novel's troubling final chapter.

Blood and Roses

While Crake's reverence of the laws of biological affinity results in the appearance of an infinitely malleable world, at the root of Crake's worldview is a sense of the limited number of forms in which sociality might take shape. In many ways, Crake crafts his worldview and justifies his actions on the basis of his understanding of these basic laws of the world. Those laws come from a computer game. As children, Jimmy and Crake play Blood and Roses. This game trades the beautiful creations of human history for acts of horror and murder. Each player starts with a small store of cards from either side, Blood or Roses. Every hand begins with a roll of the dice. If a Blood item turns up, the Roses player has the chance to stop it from happening by trading human achievements back to the bank. If the roll of the dice turns up a Roses item, the Blood player could acquire it by turning over an atrocity (78–79).

The game contains a structural irony, however. If the Blood side wins, the cost of salvaging human achievements is an empty, wasted world. If the Roses side wins, wars, disasters, riots, and tyrannies evaporate alongside art, science, and culture. On one hand, death; on the other, boredom. The two soon abandon Blood and Roses for Extinctathon, but the logic of the trading game recurs throughout the novel. In their time together at Watson-Crick, Crake muses that the legacy of human misery originates in "a series of biological mismatches" (166) that leads to imperfect monogamy and thus to sexual jealousy, territoriality, and warfare. Jimmy defends jealousy and its sublimation as the basis for art and, when pushed, retorts that art "is all that's left over" (167) when civilizations perish. Jimmy offers art as consolation for the biological mismatch on which Crake blames human misery. Crake sees art as predicated on an inefficient model of sex selection. Inefficient courtship generates art but also war; efficient courtship eliminates war at the cost of art. And on both sides, the fulcrum that turns biology into culture is sex.

In fact, it is safe to say that Crake is obsessed with sex—not with having sex, as Jimmy is, but with working on it. The appeal of purchasing sexual ecstasy in pill form is, of course, the way that Crake engineers the apocalypse, but it is equally at the heart of his other act of engineering: the Crakers. While the reader is distracted by Jimmy's romantic escapades and sexual neuroses, Crake is quietly building a theory of culture that takes sex as its keystone. As is manifest in their huge, blue, swaying penises, the Crakers are least human in their reproductive anatomy. In fact, though, even the Craker penis is a sideshow from the most important alteration Crake makes, which is not to male anatomy but to female biology. Human women have menstrual cycles, which uncouple sexual pleasure from reproductive consequence far more foundationally than the birth control pill. Craker women, conversely, have estrous cycles—they are sexually available only during fertile periods—and during those fertile periods, they can only select among male suitors; they can't withhold consent.

These alterations are made in response to the same arguments that Crake makes to Jimmy at Watson-Crick, and they employ the same trading structure as Blood and Roses. The Crakers are a solution to a design problem: "War, which is to say misplaced sexual energy. . . . Contagious diseases, especially sexually transmitted ones. Overpopulation, leading . . . to environmental degradation and poor nutrition" (293).[49] What Crake does is to systematically eliminate each one of these three areas, not through culture but precisely by way of nature. He becomes a student of human behavior and its origins in biochemistry, the reproductive cycle, metabolism, and brain development, and he designs a version that better fits the ends of social transformation. Mobilizing atrocity against itself, Crake's apocalyptic two-step plays the ultimate Blood card to clear the game board and wipe out both art and atrocity by eradicating their shared source: the aberration of menstruation.

Ultimately, then, Crake is not a capitalist. He is not a humanist. He is not an environmentalist. And he is no determinist. He is a radical utopian whose medium is genetic (rather than social) engineering. His ambition is to change the social order. Because he sees the social order as an epiphenomenon of hard-wiring, he reengineers the wiring. "You've got to work with what's on the table," he says (292), a Frankensteinian allusion that makes current capacities the basis for new forms while also acknowledging the limitations that stymie even the maddest of mad scientists.

Hospitality is thus the first principle of Crake's nature philosophy. And yet, as Jimmy argues, it is impossible to ignore the force involved in exhorting hospitality, which always involves some infringement, some sacrifice. Atwood, too, has theorized the violence implicit in the desire of each living thing to continue in its own way. In her critical work, Atwood defines her own writing as *ustopian,* a word she coined to conjoin the dystopian and utopian perspectives she argues are at work in any community.[50] As she puts it, "better never means better for everyone."[51] This sense that someone always pays for another's happiness chimes with her autobiographical writing about animal stories, which she writes profoundly shaped her worldview. In these stories, she writes, "the main thing was to avoid dying, and only by a mixture of cunning, experience and narrow escapes could the animal . . . manage that."[52] Or to put the point as she renders it in one of her novels, "all stories are about wolves."[53]

At the heart of Atwood's ustopian perspective is the predator–prey relationship and the problem of eating. Even the vegan Crakers with their kudzu diet borrowed from the two-stomach system of ruminants can't help but infringe on the grasses they eat. The ChickieNobs are merely an extreme version of the more general Atwoodian platitude: utopia is always dystopia for someone. Some thing's survival is always some other thing's loss. No one of us can escape the need to feed. Nor is this necessarily, for Atwood at least, reason to mourn. In the acknowledgments page of the final book in the series, *MaddAddam,* Atwood gives thanks to her husband "with whom [she] wanders through the afternoon woods of life, foraging for nutritious bioforms, battling hostile ones wherever they appear, and eating them when possible" (394). The autumnal hush of the woods and the careful gathering of seeds, nuts, and plants transform in the final clause. In the Red Riding Hood meeting of wolf and girl, while one of them will certainly get eaten, it might be Atwood herself who is the wolf.

Life

As the title announces, *MaddAddam* is a creation story, the tale of the coming into being of what the Craker Blackbeard calls "this safe and beautiful world"[54] and the birth of the first generation of hybrid Craker–human children. The penultimate section of the novel ("Moontime") names the four newborn children and announces the pregnancy of a sixth woman as well as relating the construction of the first pieces of repre- sentational art, the plans for expanding the compound's one house, the health of the garden and the bee colonies, and the variety of acceptable meat sources discovered in the area. All of which starts to sound like a dead baby joke: what's the difference between an infant and a nutritious bioform? Or maybe, to torque a line from Lewis Carroll, how is a baby like a body? And if the Hatter's famous raven and writing desk riddle confounds for its evident lack of relation, the body–baby problem does so for its uncanny identity. In fact, everywhere in the novel, reproduc- tion comes twinned to consumption, as the unabashed celebration of life meets up with boundary-drawing and death-tethered practices of eating. Indeed, *MaddAddam* insists on their contiguity.

MaddAddam tells two stories—that of what is and that of what has been. In the present of the narrative, it is a few months after the murder of most of the world's human population. The plague that Crake orches- trated to clear the way for the Crakers has left only three groups, all of whom know each other: a few members of an ecologically minded utopian community called the God's Gardeners (focalized through Toby), the handful of scientists Crake coerced into working on the Craker project by threatening to expose their work with the direct action ecoterrorist group MaddAddam, and two survivors of the brutal Painball punishment arena. And, of course, the Children of Crake, who have spent the first two books of the trilogy making myths out of the improbable tales told to them by Snowman-the-Jimmy, singing songs in praise of Crake, and engaging in group copulation on the edge of the sea. Prior to this book, the present was the space of bare survival, isolation, and despair. (*Oryx and Crake* opens with Jimmy eating his last mango.) It is in *MaddAddam* that the groups find each other and, in finding each other, begin to rebuild a community.

MaddAddam is the story of that rebuilding and of the two battles that bring it into being. For the first time that the groups encounter each other is through the Painballers and their hostage, Amanda. And the first time they recognize themselves as a group with a shared com- munity ethos is when they gather to vote yea or nay on the execution of those same Painballers. That four hundred pages and several lost lives intervene between the two battles marks the difference between the Toby who would not shoot and the Toby who would—or rather, between the correct alignment between her capacity for violence and her recognition of friend and foe. The founding of the nascent Craker–human complex doesn't really begin until they have established themselves through these acts of boundary making.

If this is the plot, then the pigoons are the catalyst.

As I have already suggested, the trilogy might be best described as an apocalypse in its classical valence as revelation and witnessing, even as a new testament. The second two novels are especially thick with biblical allusions. The God's Gardeners use the term Waterless Flood to refer to Crake's plague; Jimmy's attempt to provide himself with a regular meal leads to the association of fish with Jimmy's oracular storytelling; together the deified Oryx and Crake and the very Earthly Jimmy form a new trinity; the God's Gardeners' secret hideout is in the Scales and Tails Gentleman's Club; even the rhythms of Craker speech evoke the cadences of the Old Testament. None of these are as overt as the covenant with the pigs. As is well known, pork products are restricted in both Islamic and Jewish dietary codes. The pigs that parade to the gates of the human–Craker compound, however, are not really pigs at all, but pigoons, one of the many transgenics from the time before the Flood. Unlike the AgriCoutured ChickieNobs that so disturbed Jimmy in *Oryx and Crake,* the pigoons weren't created as food but as living incubators of human organs for medical transplant. It was rumored that some even grew human neocortex tissue for brain injury patients. It is these pigoons' feral cousins who approach the human–Craker compound. They come to the gates bearing on a litter between them the flower-strewn corpse of a dead piglet.

In this encounter, the humans learn just how intelligent the pigoons really are, and at the same time, they learn of another aspect of the Craker design. It turns out that the Crakers' high-pitched singing, which has annoyed Jimmy and the other humans throughout the trilogy, is not really singing at all. It's the way they talk to animals. Through their Craker translators, the humans find out that the pigoons want to form an alliance. In the absence of other meat sources, the humans have been killing and eating pigoon, and so have the Painballers. The pigoons therefore seek to strike a bargain. They will battle the Painballers together with the humans, and in exchange the humans will agree to make pork products taboo and the pigoons will promise not to raid the humans' gardens. Through the implicit threat posed by their intelligence and organization, the pigoons' demand lifts them out of the category of merely instrumental life, the category of most animals whose deaths may not be mourned, and into the realm of rights and intrinsic worth. Into the human, that is, whose humanist ordering must shift to compensate this new alliance of non-human life and political agency.

Despite the seriousness of this point, it is also curiously campy. Are we really expected to swallow a new testament that puts the prohibition on pork on the ample shoulders of a few mournful pigoons? The idea is so ham-handed that were it not surrounded by other swine scenes, it would be tempting to see it as a comment about the scandalously low origins of origin myths rather than a blueprint to our posthuman futures. But it is apparently quite sincere. The alliance with the pigoons comes to the reader already infused with spiritual significance and reproductive resonances. In an earlier chapter, titled "Farrow," Toby embarks on a vision quest to ask her dead Gardener mentor Pilar what she should do about Amanda's pregnancy, which may have resulted from rape and, in any case, might kill her if anything were to go awry. As a healer, Toby knows that she could induce an abortion, but the chemistry is delicate and, if mixed incorrectly, fatal. And so she cooks up the hallucinogens, journeys to the elderberry bush where she planted Pilar's remains, and asks Pilar's spirit for a signal. She soon gets it:

> Toby turns her head. Crossing the path, within a stone-throw, there's one of the giant pigs, a sow, with farrow: five little piglets, all in a row. . . . Such enormous power. (223)

Already at this point Toby's vision swells with significance. The sow and her farrow rewrite the vision of Amanda, a leash around her neck, half-dragged through the ruined landscape by her Painball rapists as a resource to be used up and left to die, or at the compound after her rescue, so wounded by her experience that she sits and stares at nothing for weeks.

Instead of these, the vision presents Toby with redemptive motherhood. Even her phrasing recalls the idealized motherhood of children's finger games like Five Little Pigs. And the Crakers concur. "Why is [Amanda] sad, Oh Toby?" they ask. "We are always happy when our bone cave is full" (216). Toby's "mystical quasi-religious experience" (228) sacralizes what had previously been a question of this woman, these circumstances, and turns it into a categorical imperative about which there can really be no dissent. *We* are always happy, after all.

"Life, life, life, life, life," Toby repeats to herself as the sow begins to turn away. "Full to bursting, this minute. Second. Millisecond. Millennium. Eon" (223). "She was here," Blackbeard relates, and while Toby wonders what he means, the novel leaves little room for doubt. The mother pig is the signal that Pilar has sent, her young akin to the fetus that Amanda carries. Life, the virtue nature speaks, even (maybe especially) when that nature started in the AgriCouture labs of the corporate compounds. And so it is that Toby, having dreamed "piglet dreams" (261), refuses the ham and kudzu fritters on offer for breakfast the next morning. Well before the pigoons promise to ally with them, then, Toby's vision has already redrawn the boundary between animal and human life, that is, between a cherished child and a nourishing bioform.

As is so often the case with Atwood, however, that's not quite all. After the deal is struck, the pigoons begin to file away from the compound, leaving behind them the funeral bier and the dead piglet. "It is a gift," Blackbeard explains. "It is dead already. They have already done their sadness. . . . They say you may eat it or not eat it, as you choose. They would eat it themselves" (271). This "no-holds-barred recycling," Toby reflects, is life too, the kind that values survival over dreams of piglets flying with "white gauzy dragonfly wings" or "prancing like some old animated film" (261). In the gift of the piglet's corpse, we see the literal convergence of child and food, the contingency and reciprocity of their moral categorizations. "Everything digests, and is digested" (221), Toby reflects. It is survival, in other words, that turns delicacy into taboo and could easily turn it back again. Indeed, the whole scenography of the pigoon meetings makes sense only in light of the trilogy's otherwise obsessive interest in tactics for staying alive in a world truly reducible to predator–prey relationships.

Far from a lamentation, however, this assumption of harm is the premise from which *MaddAddam* offers its course in survivalism. Look sharp, act big, trust rarely, and don't get caught. There is bound to be a wolf in every story, and some time or another, that wolf is going to be you. What's a little genocide, after all, to stand between certain annihilation and a return of agrarian utopianism? Life, the virtue genocide speaks.

Accounting

In a number of recent small pieces, Donna Haraway has directed her readers back to Ursula K. Le Guin's much-anthologized 1989 essay "The Carrier Bag Theory of Fiction,"[55] which opens by telling a little evolutionary narrative linking the development and purpose of the literary, in the form of the heroic quest narrative, to the processes of finding and preparing food. The problem is one of time and also of attention. In the Paleolithic and Neolithic periods, our hominid ancestors were largely grazers, sticking to weeds, nuts, seeds, and a few small woodland-type creatures. This didn't take very much time, and so to pass the hours, they went on large-game hunts, which turned out to be a fabulous way not only to waste time but also to provide entertainment in endless rounds of killing-the-mammoth stories. These stories had little to do (says Le Guin) with the actual conditions of life in hunter–gatherer communities, but they had a far more satisfying arc than the concentrated focus on the very small and very many involved in husking wild oats. And so our human legacy is stories in which heroism looks like one group of territorial mammals "bashing, sticking, thrusting, killing" (151) other territorial mammals. In contrast to this story of death, Le Guin proposes the "carrier bag theory of fiction"—a "life-story," that is, a story about collecting things that are "useful, edible or beautiful" (153) and putting them together, higgledy-piggledy, into a bag so that you can survive and share that survival and sustain the survival of that which sustains you. And so the story itself is a kind of bag, and it nests inside of other bags, this world a "vast sack, this belly of the universe, this womb of things to be and tomb of things that were" (154), to quote Le Guin.

In the carrier bag, Haraway finds an apt model for what she calls "staying with the trouble" or the ethics of care. For Haraway, the recognition of entanglement within multispecies relations of symbiosis and symbiogenesis, of legacies of past damage and potentialities for future flourishing, calls on us to act responsibly in full recognition of our and other species' abilities to respond. Indeed, for Haraway (and for Karen Barad, from whom she derives the term), respons-ability is not an act of sovereign human will but an inevitable consequence of our enmeshment in an open-ended process of worlding. The call, then, is to respond in ways that promote flourishing for all of the companion species jostling together in the carrier bag that is the world and to be accountable to those that do not flourish. Both tasks require close attention to the tendencies and orientations of agents enmeshed together—the circuiting of material agencies through the biological, ecological, chemical, political, social, and cultural apparatuses of our world—and also a refusal to forget the paths by which we maintain our bit of that world. In an astonishing chapter on suffering, Haraway uses the trope of the face to insist that we act politely toward each other even when in entangled relations with "significantly unfree partners"[56] whose suffering we are causing. "The needed morality," she writes,

> is culturing a radical ability to remember and feel what is going on and performing the epistemological, emotional, and technical work to respond practically in the face of the permanent complexity not resolved by taxonomic hierarchies and with no humanist philosophical or religious guarantees. (75)

Or, as she glosses a few pages later, "Try as we might to distance ourselves, there is no way of living that is not also a way of someone, not just something, else dying differently" (80). Caring, in other words, must account for killing, because causing to suffer and die is inevitably built into the structure of entanglement. All good stories, even the carrier bag of stories, contain a wolf.

"Getting better at facing killing" (81), for Haraway, means counting ourselves into the calculus in an accounting that is explicitly actuarial. Properly counted and extrapolated, such minute tracery enables a care-taking that is also a world-making, what Haraway calls "terraforming" and presents in the form of a calculus whose variable terms include stuff, sociality, capacity, and materiality:

> $\Omega \int \text{Terra}[X]n = \int \int \int \ldots \int \int \text{Terra}(X_1, X_2, X_3, X_4, \ldots, X_n, t) dX_1 dX_2 dX_3 dX_4 \ldots dX_n dt) = \text{Terrapolis a } X_1 = \text{stuff/physis}, X_2 = \text{capacity}, X_3 = \text{sociality}, X_4 = \text{materiality}, X_n = ??a$ (alpha) = not zoe, but EcoEvoDevo's multispecies

epigenesist Ω (omega) = not bios, but recuperating terra's pluriverse t = world-ing time, not container time, entangled times of past/present/yet-.-to-.-come[57]

Haraway insists that this calculation is in fact incalculable, a becoming-with that can never be rendered fully known ahead of time. Yet the calculation remains, a combinatorial whose promise of pastoral care of the future might be understood as the only properly ethical response to mass impoverishment and immiseration of the world. Such a calculation might well look like the formula for BlyssPluss pills, and especially so if the problem is taken to be rooted not in the story but instead in the (genetic) sequence. And if it is indeed, as Crake asserts, as much a matter of bioengineering as it is of social change, then where does that leave the imperative to reproduce that code? For Haraway's multiplex ethical calculus seems to come down to two basic (and familiar) constraints: killing and birthing.

In the final chapter of *When Species Meet* (titled "Parting Bites"), Haraway relates the story of the northern hairy-nosed wombat, a species facing imminent extinction. "Being female in such a world," she writes, "never comes without paying the price of value."[58] What value? "This would not be the first time that forced reproduction was employed as an evolutionary and ecological rescue technology" (291). Just as we must get better at facing killing, Haraway argues, we must likewise get used to the idea that being female is inevitably tied to reproductive value so crucial to the flourishing of the species that it outweighs any individual compunction in the calculus of survival.

In a worldview in which killing and birthing represent the limit cases of freedom, if they are what we see when we face the material constraints of this our world, then perhaps reproductive futurism is a kindly ruse. Better to embrace than to fight what is anyway inevitable. The very end of *MaddAddam* gives us a sense of what this entails. It tells the story of Toby's death and of the disappearance of her lover, Zeb, who went in search of the source of a thin column of smoke visible on the horizon and never returned. This contact is not repeated, and the novel closes on the announcement of a seventh pregnancy. Certainly Zeb might have been waylaid by anything: an accident, an animal attack, even a case of wanderlust. But the novel leaves open the possibility that they are not the only group of survivors and, in the violence that attended this intimation, the potential that their new neighbors might have a very different culture indeed. And so it begins again: from survival to community and from there to protection, territory, boundaries, institutions of governance. It is possible, now, to offer a different reading of Atwood's wolves, not as the inevitability of evil stamped into the fabric of the world but rather as the obverse face of reproductive futurism. Like the wolf in grandmother's clothing, the rhetoric of care in the commitment to responsible terra formation disguises the lurking presence of boundary-drawing, death-tethered extirpation—of choosing, in other words, what to eat and what to raise.

Labor

Of course, it can't end there.

I want to return very briefly to the AgriCouture labs at Watson-Crick University and specifically to Crake and Jimmy's conversation about the real and the fake, the evolved and the engineered. That conversation began with Jimmy's curiosity about a species of butterfly—bright pink with wings the size of pancakes (200)—that they encountered on their tour. "These butterflies fly," Crake says, dismissing Jimmy's question. "They mate, they lay eggs, caterpillars come out" (200). The proof that they have been made well, in other words, is that they behave as any other butterfly would. This answer, however, also contains a subtle admission. For a new species to take form, every actant in its construction must be satisfied, which in turn means that each must have its agency respected— thus the religious overtones of Crake's philosophizing. For Crake to test his hypothesis, he needs a mechanism by which his engineering will not be lost with the individuals themselves. He needs them to culture, in both senses: to reproduce like cells in a petri dish and to develop the culture that he has conjectured that they will develop. He needs them to have babies. Reproductive labor is not just about the flourishing of the species; it is about the willingness of nature to turn over the gift of its labors. But what if it were to refuse? The next chapter takes up the sterile woman as the figure for life's withdrawal.

5

Labor

Capital comes dripping from head to foot, from every
pore, with blood and dirt.

KARL MARX, *Capital*

In her 2008 monograph *Life as Surplus,* sociologist Melinda Cooper characterizes neoliberalism by its "ambition to overcome the ecological and economic limits to growth,"[1] a characteristic it shares with biotechnology and biopolitical governance. The speculative vitalism that emerges from these three great regimes makes growth without end the default economic logic of the postindustrial period. Celebrations of this expansionary vision, however, are markedly in contrast to one of the most prominent motifs in popular genre representations: that of *outbreak,* a motif in which growth all too easily turns into overgrowth. In this, Atwood's plague narrative is hardly alone. From Ridley Scott's 1979 film *Alien*[2] to the AMC series *The Walking Dead* (2010–), contemporary genre fictions have taught American audiences of the menace posed by overanimated nonhuman life. Zombies who rip through walls, aliens that pass unnoticed in human form, viruses on the run from quarantine zones: the anxiety to which these fictions give voice is less about human extinction per se than about the exposure of a restive and agential nonhuman surround against which human security systems provide only temporary safety. That we might be subject to another species's depredations, in other words, or that we might merely be in the way of forces that outstrip our regulatory systems, indeed that regulatory systems themselves contribute to the amplification of those forces — these are some of the anxieties that drive the welter of medical thrillers, postapocalyptic fictions, zombie narratives, survivalist manuals, space invasion films, climate change literatures, and other visions of contemporary catastrophe.

The representational apparatus of genre fiction is thus an ambivalent expedient in the "public pedagogy"[3] of the Anthropocene—ambivalent insofar as these fictions acclimate us to the idea that we are not alone in the universe at the same time that they coordinate human salvation through the very surveillance and containment strategies that failed to provide safety in the first place. This ambivalence has another dimension. For containment never means extirpation, just as the fear of overgrowth merely extends out of equally prevalent neoliberal celebrations of growth. That growth *requires* containment at all teaches us a crucial lesson about the difference between neoliberal ideologies and their unfolding as biopolitics. For the limitless potential for expansion extolled in the rhetoric of neoliberalism in fact hinges on the modulation and control of living systems to interpellate life "between labor and capital."[4]

Future-oriented, speculative, and preemptive, neoliberal biopolitics (or, as I prefer, somatic capitalism) is a strategy of adjustment that relies on life living itself before it can produce the specific variables that will optimize its movements.[5] It cannot make life, it can only make more or less of it, push it in one direction over another, contain it in reservoirs to siphon its constrained vitality or allow it to dissipate into other systems to diminish its potency. For the same reason, somatic capitalism cannot simply eliminate life, which is its proper subject and the source of its wealth, even if "the dream of contagion control is eradication."[6] In this sense, these visions of the mass that overwhelms, the horde that overruns, and the swarm that brooks no boundaries give us back in exaggerated form the very potency that underwrites the biopolitical as such and that threatens its continuation. Containment thus shadows growth as its necessary corollary.

This recognition, then, opens onto another. If too much growth turns potential profit into life-choking peril, it is equally the case that no system of elicitation—biopolitical or biotechnical—can generate the original wellspring of vitality that underwrites living systems. That wellspring is not identical with any particular organic or nonorganic system and therefore is beyond the ken of biopolitical management. The extraction of value from life processes begins from and is absolutely premised upon natural increase, both autopoietic and reproductive, without which nothing else moves. Fecundity is thus central to but outside of the economic machinery of late capitalism. Even cajoling life from life, as in the case of the stem cell, harnesses the cell's own willingness to reproduce itself. But what if it were to stop? As the constitutive outside, this gift of nature's labors (construed in both of its senses) opens onto another and less explored vista: *life's withdrawal.* Because life provides the motive force for technical infrastructures, infrastructures that shape forms-of-life but cannot elicit life-itself, the whole edifice of somatic capitalism finds itself vulnerable from within.[7]

This vulnerability to the wayward agency of life is the problem posed by the contemporary upwelling of sterility apocalypses, an old genre given new relevance by the apprehension that life-itself falls outside of the apparatuses that contain and rely on it. Coincident with the production of the nonhuman world as terrifying in its lush and ravenous abundance, sterility apocalypses tell another story of life's (in)tractability. Some of these narratives (such as *Children of Men,* to which I will be turning in the next section) frame species extinction through mass infertility.[8] In others, infertility is coupled with species-level threat from a different source, such as alien invasion *(Extant, Prometheus),* divine retribution *(Noah),* environmental causation *(Code 46, Lost),* or synthetic biological design *(Battlestar Galactica, Windup Girl).* Across this wide swath of texts, women's reproductive capacity is the beachhead. Women sit in the place of life-itself, coordinating its translation from élan vital to species-being, and so women's fertility is invested with all of the mysticism of that which eludes control. As Sarah Franklin writes in her book *Dolly Mixtures: The Remaking of Genealogy,* "the heightened sense of technological potency associated with modern, industrial design, scientific advancement, precision engineering and so-called smart weapons is seemingly mocked by forces beyond its control, or even comprehension."[9] Ultimately, fertility is beyond technical know-how. In the parlance of the genre, it takes a miracle.

It is this miracle, obsessively reiterated, that sterility apocalypses offer. For the crucial dimension of the genre is less the *loss* of fertility than its *restoration.* Infertility is the conceit, but restoration is the point. The withdrawal of life's withdrawal, in these narratives, is inexplicable, unwarranted, without cause or cure; the single fertile woman appears out of nowhere, her pregnant body promising the return of a calculable future guided by human sovereignty over Earth's abundance. In her pregnant form, all threats are erased, and the covenant between God and man—to be fruitful and multiply—finds its new Eve.[10] The child that results from her pregnancy is thus not only the living guarantee of a continued human future but a condensed metonymy for all of those living systems whose acquiescence in what Eugene Thacker calls "biomaterial labor" allows for the continued production of surplus value.[11]

In this chapter, I argue that these fictions must be read in the context of overabundant life, on one hand, and life's withdrawal, on the other. Together these limit states set the conditions by which it becomes possible to imagine a wholly economized life or what I am calling the new enclosures of reproduction. Enclosure refers in aggregate to the many acts of the British Parliament from the eighteenth century onward that shifted agricultural land from "common and customary use rights"[12] and the social relations that went with them to a profit-driven model of high-yield private ownership. Enclosure thus functioned to consolidate some of the primitive accumulation that would fuel the development of capitalism and enforce the separation between producer and means of production. Enclosure and primitive accumulation likewise define the contemporary moment, in which natural resources like water are the subject of more or less successful, geographically variegated privatization campaigns.

In the form of biotechnological enclosures—focused on life to produce profit regardless of the cost to the living substance that provides the means of production—somatic capitalism finds itself facing two equally pressing problems: it must not only control distribution in the form of management but also get as close as possible to replicating life-itself and enclosing it through patent law. By delivering the redemptive dynamism of fertility alongside the redemptive stability of infertility that puts a check on overgrowth, sterility apocalypses promise that the antinomy between these two tendencies might be held in suspension long enough to regain mastery over nature in the specific form of the production of surplus value. In what follows, I consider the conventions of sterility apocalypses as a displacement onto the human of the enclosure of the commons in general and in particular of the reproductive potentiality of agriculture.

The Human Project

Near the beginning of Alfonso Cuarón's 2006 sterility apocalypse *Children of Men,* there is a welcome moment of levity. Jasper, the aging hippie, former political cartoonist, and father-figure, tells a long, rambling joke to the film's protagonist, Theo. Both Jasper and Theo are white men, both are citizens of the United Kingdom, and (as this scene unfolds) both inhabit a fragile zone of privilege hedged around with insecurity. The year is 2027, and the joke is about the Human Project, a radical underground research collective dedicated to solving the infertility crisis that has gripped the world for eighteen years. The joke goes like this:

> The Human Project gives this great big dinner for all the scientists and sages in the world. They are tossing around theories about the ultimate mystery: Why are woman infertile? Why can't we make babies anymore? Some say it's genetic experiments, gamma rays, pollution, same old, same old. Anyway, in the corner this Englishman is sitting. He hasn't said a word. He's just tucking into his dinner. So they decide to ask him. They say, Well, why do you think we can't make babies anymore? And he looks up at them, chewing on this great big wing, and he says "I haven't the faintest idea," he says, "But this stork is quite tasty isn't it?"[13]

Quite a tasty stork. Jasper's joke relates something important about the premise of the film and sets up for the viewer its ethical orientation. The joke depends for its humor on the conflation of the diegetic past and the viewer's present. It is in our present that the world's scientists gather to make sense of an increasingly unpredictable natural world while the leaders of the Global North enjoy Earth's final fruits. More precisely, the joke implies a causal link between the present of its composition and the future it describes. It is because some powerful men in the viewer's present wouldn't give enough credence to the scientists and sages to stop their enjoyable consumption of the world of the film's present—"This is a tune from back in 2003 when we refused to see the future," as a disc jockey in the film puts it—that our future is now barren.

On the bus Theo takes to see Jasper, who lives in the suburbs outside of London, ceiling-mounted digital monitors play short reels narrating the events of the twenty-first century as they are monumentalized for the

British public. On the screen, the names of the world's cities scroll past accompanied by images of panicked mobs, masked men, mass protests, bomb explosions, diseased animals, burning buildings, riot police, chemical spills, and wailing women. As if the catastrophic twentieth century with its genocides and nuclear blasts was condensed into two decades of unmitigated horror, the images blur past so quickly that they stop making individual sense. "The world has collapsed," the video concludes. "Only Britain soldiers on." Through the window we get a feeling for what this means. Cages of refugees (called 'fugees) line the train station platforms guarded by riot police, while the disenfranchised throw rocks at the train windows. Posters reminding women that it is a crime to evade the mandatory state-run fertility tests share space with witty graffiti that advise the last person alive to shut off the lights. In the pleasure gardens of the wealthy, the world's treasures pour in. Like the Englishman at the great big dinner, Britain's soldiering on is also a tucking in to the abundance that calamity provides. But while the stork may make quite a tasty meal, devouring the future also has consequences. The lesson the film intends here is clear even if the Englishman (and by extension the British state, and by further extension the Global North) refuses to know it: eventually, all birds come home to roost.

Clearly, then, the question is not really, Why can't we make babies anymore? for in its depiction of temporal gastronomy, the joke already provides an answer: we ate all the storks. Just prior to this scene, the film relates a little bit more of the history of the collapse in the form of a collage of news headlines: "90% Infertility," one reads. "Two Years Since Last Baby Born," reports another. "No Baby Hope," states a third. While the content reflects the film's primary conceit, the story told by these headlines in their collectivity is familiar from a decade of climate change journalism's careful presentation of empirically verifiable data: rates of glacial melt, methane release, and atmospheric CO_2 levels. Indeed, *The Possibility of Hope,* the documentary included as a bonus feature with the DVD to further explore the themes of the film, makes the connection between climate change and infertility explicit. In the documentary, the film's setting in post-9/11 state-of-emergency biopolitics (and particularly in indefinite detention camps) becomes the extrapolated reality not of the security state nor of infertility but instead of the ecological disasters brought about by global capitalism, disasters that will exacerbate the process of dispossession already under way, generate social chaos in the form of climate refugees, and increase corporate reliance on police and military violence to preserve what Naomi Klein calls "the global green zone."[14] The great mystery indicated by Jasper's joke, then, isn't really, Why are women infertile? but instead, How might humans be made fertile again? or even, How might nature be brought back into the fold of human management? In casting Earth as a barren woman, *Children of Men* aligns climate change with disruptions in proper gender relations and makes women's reproductive labor key to the salvation of humans.

Conjugated to labor, this child subtly shifts the figuration away from the redemption of human futurity so fully bodied forth by McCarthy's Boy. As we saw in the last chapter, however, the hoped-for future promised by the child is in fact a longing for the past and a dread of the planetarity caged within but never fully held by the tension towers and highway systems of human engineering. In this sense, *The Road* grounds its notion of human futurity firmly in the colonial civilizing project, which is far more than tendentiously related to the lost protections of whiteness that have thrust the Man into the exposure of the open. Like *The Road*'s aggrieved messianism, *MaddAddam*'s utopian hybridity and its literalizing of caste as color code racialization in terms of speciation.[15] By contrast, sterility apocalypses invert this coding, proffering the future of the species through the miraculously restored fertility of women who are both racially marked and in positions of extreme vulnerability to racialized state violence: pregnant refugees, detainees, double agents, and illegal aliens.[16] These figurations, I argue, are tied to the problem of surplus value, which (despite infertility) does not really concern the long-term future of the species but instead centers on short-term relations of production in general and on the question of labor more specifically.

The stork joke, then, cautions us to reconsider the analogic relations between infertility and the future of the planet. For the question of dinner is not easily discarded as so much analogic wrapping. Quite literally, global climate change is a problem of and for the production, distribution, and consumption of Earth's biotic and geochemical resources. In the image of the stork on the plate, the joke highlights the economic consequences of the Anthropocene, which shifts conditions away from the stable predictability necessary for the maintenance of food production, and particularly for the multiple and interlocking systems that go into the catered meat-based dinner. What is in need of salvation, then, isn't the human species but precisely the stork: the system that routinely delivers the single, sacred bundle of vitality. But neither is this to make reproduction the operative metaphor for agriculture. Reproduction, production, distribution, are contiguous processes. At most, reproduction is a metonym, a privileged instance, one among many other modes needed to maintain industrial relations. Reproduction doesn't just fill in for agricultural labor; reproductive labors are agricultural labors. And both are tightly woven into the histories of racialized and colonial violence. The central problem addressed by sterility apocalypses thus concerns who can be induced to do labor on another's behalf. And so it is that the fantasied solution offered by mass sterility, on one side, and miraculously restored fertility, on the other, disinters the racist and racialist systems at stake in species anxiety.

Surplus Flesh

This might seem like a counterintuitive assertion. After all, these fictions of redeemed fertility offer futures to and through their most vulnerable characters while condemning the powerful to extinction.[17] The reproductive potency of women of color—long a racist shibboleth underwriting the various "rising tide of color" panics—here takes on the positive valuation associated with Madonna myths and mitochondrial Eves. Despite this, I contend that we should see these fictions within the broader terrain of ecological and economic anxieties that informs the contemporary apocalypse more generally. As we have already had reason to note, the forms of laboring performed by these reproductive women spark the old questions of sacrifice and safety: who performs what labor, and for whom? In this case, we can render those question more precise: to whom is the spectacle of the fertile woman of color reassuring, and why?

In *Habaes Viscus,* Alexander Weheliye gives us a crucial clue.[18] He argues not only that racialization partitions the species into "the human, not-quite-human, and nonhuman" (43)—a familiar sort of claim—but also and more emphatically that this partitioning generates several forms of fleshy surplus. First and most emphatically, colonial and neocolonial racialization "yields a surplus version of the human: Man" (135). For Weheliye, "Man" denotes a category of person most able to use legal, economic, and social means to detach from embodied struggle (i.e., to be literally no-body). The surplus that engenders this detachment, however, doesn't originate with Man. No, that surplus that generates the regime of Man has been expropriated from those categories of persons recipro- cally responsible for bearing the flesh in pleasure, in pain, in labor, and in parturition, those most likely to be legal no-bodies (135).

Weheliye names this formation *habeas viscus* or "you shall have the flesh," in counterpoint to Giorgio Agamben's separation of forms-of-life into *zoē* (animal life, bare life) and *bios* (juridically protected populations). Where Agamben's distinction makes analytically available the supplemen- tarity of protected and exposed lives, Weheliye's revision insists that the partition of and supplementarity between *bios* and *zoē* yield a disavowed third term, a fleshy surplus that attends the "violent political domination" (2) required to support the world of Man (130). "The biological," he argues is "never anterior to racialization" (4). As a technology of racialization, the *zoē–bios* distinction opens the flesh to economic processes of extrac- tion, commodification, and enclosure while at the same time enabling the recipient of the resulting surplus to stay safely, cannily unknowing.[19]

The flesh that is made to be borne, however, is by no means inert. Its as-yet enduring willingness to gift itself comes through in what Weheliye, following Aristotle, calls a "natural sweetness" and, following Sun Ra, a "potential enfleshment" that may act as "transit visas to universes betwixt and between the jurisdictions of Man" (127). The flesh is a kind of gateway regulating the flow of energy from one stratum to another. It is the vestibule between biology and culture, between *bios* and *zoē*, but as such it has the potential to open "a vestibular gash in the armor of man" (44) and allow the outside in. A surplus flesh, a surplus of flesh, a surplus of suffering flesh, a fleshly surplus: in these alchemic equations, the excessive body, the laboring body, and the suffering body transsubstantialize as economic surplus and surplus populations but also as surplus vitality.[20] It is through the swinging door of the vestibular gash that surplus vitality transits from natural sweetness to biological (and bioeconomic) increase—or, in other words, into another body for the regimes of racialization.

Thus the salvation promised by the reproductive woman and her child, their gifts of vibrancy that can't be solicited but can be harnessed to turn the crank of industrial production, recalls the history of generational racial slavery and, in particular, the centrality of reproduction to plantation-based slave labor camps, particularly after the closure of the Atlantic slave trade, and thus to the making of American wealth.[21] For the child as a figure is inseparable from the reproductive processes to which she is temporally adjacent and whose sense of interlocking (and sometimes failing) non-"human" agencies she still bears, precisely as the promise of further births. As Dorothy Roberts trenchantly writes, "reproductive politics inevitably involves racial politics."[22] But where she rightly ties the economics of childbirth in generational enslavement to the many twentieth-century campaigns to control black women's fertility, these texts suggest a return to racialized reproductive labor as mystified "fleshly surplus." Thus I argue that not only is "the biological given . . . as such is immediately racialized"[23] (as Weheliye has it) but also that these racially marked reproductive labors perform a kind of ideological sleight of hand: they appear to iconize the reproductive woman of color and the community her fertility prophecies by proffering birth, labor, and the child against a backdrop of ecological devastation. But the promise she engenders through the gift of her fertility in fact reinstates a complacent nature capable of enclosure. In her fleshly surplus lurks a new form of wholly economized life.

The sweetness of the flesh finds its analog in reproduction and in sugar. As Weheliye writes, "the abundance of sugar was made possible via the conduit of racial slavery" (129). Kara Walker's recent installation *A Subtlety, or the Marvelous Sugar Baby* makes these historical continuities startlingly clear. Housed in the cavernous former Domino Sugar factory, the installation is dedicated to "the unpaid and overworked Artisans who have refined our Sweet tastes from the cane fields to the kitchens of the New World."[24] The focal point of the installation, however, isn't production (the tools for which have been cleared out of the factory space) but reproduction. Sugar Baby, who fills the main hall of the factory, comprises thirty tons of sugar on a foam molded base. She is modeled on the Great Sphinx of Giza, but where the Sphinx is crowned by a royal headdress, Sugar Baby has a kerchief tied around her head; where the Sphinx's leonine body ends in haunches and a tail, Sugar Baby frankly displays her vulva. Part Mammy figure, part fertility goddess, Sugar Baby's unpaid work isn't in sugar production but in the molasses children who work around her, carting woven baskets around the floor of the factory. But they can haul only because she pushes; their productive labor comes from her reproductive labor, as Marxist feminists have long reminded us.

Nor is her reproduction limited to those children. *A Subtlety* was commissioned as a place-specific installation to mark the demolition of the plant, which had been a landmark on the Brooklyn waterfront for 132 years. Before the neighborhood's rapid gentrification over the past two decades, the Domino plant had been one of many dockside factories that included refineries, shipyards, breweries, and a power station. The regional history of labor, which was also the sensuous surround for the people who lived in that place, is still imaginable in the sugar-high rush of the building's smell. But a warehouse also always exceeds its own location to tell other stories about production and distribution. In this case, the Domino plant sits in a network that connects the history of sugar production and the Caribbean slave trade to the colonial origins of industrialism. "Blood sugar,"[25] Walker calls it, in a pun that bridges obesity discourse to diamond mines. In Walker's vision, *Sugar Baby*'s vulva is at the center of these circuits, which bind her like the pillars of the factory. In this way, *Sugar Baby* insists that the unremunerated work of reproduction and social reproduction makes the machines run. *Sugar Baby* has the flesh, to recall Weheliye's neologism, and gives it.

There is a second way in which site specificity changes the meaning. The Domino building was scheduled to be demolished not long after *Sugar Baby*'s installation opened. Rather than try to preserve the sculptures, Walker built them to collapse. The show opened in May in a building with no air-conditioning. By July, many of the molasses boys had begun to melt in the heat. *Sugar Baby* herself was cascading away, her sides spilling sugar. In this final turn, the representational meanings the show gives to *Sugar Baby* and her children erode over time, the disfiguring conditions effacing the human story and foregrounding the show's material circumstance. In this accelerated ruin creation, Walker reminds us that the configuration of sugar, foam, heat, population density, even shifts in the land grade, form what Jane Bennett calls a "vital assemblage"[26] of actants whose unpredictability remakes the artwork as a temporal machine. I want to keep this image of Sugar Baby in the background as we turn back to *Children of Men* and to two other instances of animal life: one of dead sheep and one of living cows. I begin with the living.

Animal Capital

The most famous scene in *Children of Men* takes place in a barn. Kee, an Afro-Caribbean refugee, stands half-uncovered in the midst of cattle, one arm hiding her breasts, the other holding the dress she has lowered to reveal her pregnant belly. Around her, two cows low. Despite the stainless steel equipment hemming her in, the scene is unmistakably religious. Even if she were not the only pregnant woman in a world gone suddenly and inexplicably sterile, her stance and setting would still recall Marian iconography. Kee—a new character whose presence makes the film and its politics quite different from P. D. James's original novel—is a version of mitochondrial Eve, the single woman thought to be of African origin from whom all subsequent members of the species *Homo sapiens sapiens* emerged. But she is also the next Mary, whose pregnancy promises the start of a new messianic period; as the new Eve, she refigures that redeemed future as the return of the prelapsarian past; in both guises, she foreshortens her actual present—in which Britain detains refugees in vast, brutal camps while the political and economic elite plunder wealth from disinvested cities and suburbs—as the passage to a new Eden.

These cows are not the only livestock of interest in the film. Early on, we watch with Theo as he drives past smoldering pyres of dead sheep, their legs rigid in the sooty air. Though never explained—never even commented upon—these pyres are striking in their intimation that sterility is not all that is at stake in this apocalypse. Indeed, there is a real-world analog for these burnings: the millions of sheep exterminated in the United Kingdom during the 2001 outbreak of foot and mouth disease, a highly contagious but nonlethal disease whose pandemic spread was met with slaughter-on-suspicion policies. In *Dolly Mixtures,* Franklin explains that the cull of 3.8 million British sheep was not motivated by fears for the sheep's well-being or for the human populations that tended to them but instead for the national industry's standing as disease-free and thus for its reputation on the global market. It was "economically intolerable,"[27] Franklin notes, not epidemiologically necessary. Foot and mouth disease threatens the regularity of the natural world that allows for the production of profit. Literally backgrounded,[28] these dead sheep signify for the film the potential cost of too great a rupture in what Foucault calls "the disposition of things" through whose regularities a "domain of analysis" may be established.[29] The sheep pyre and the refugee cages are both attempts to restore the "laws of transformation and movement"[30] that allow for economic calculations. Against the background threat of uncontrolled proliferation, infertility appears as the antidote for, rather than the symbol of, climate change and its upending of rational management.

From the outset, then, *Children of Men* presents us with profitless, uncontrolled proliferation coupled to species-threatening sterility. And so it is no surprise that the film places the discovery of the end of sterility in a well-managed milking shed. Kee herself comments on the system of economic rationality that informs industrial farming techniques. As she attempts to convince Theo to help her find a way to the Human Project, she tells him about the facts of life in a milking barn. "You know they chop the poor cow's tits? They do—zzzt. Gone. Only leave four. To fit the machine. Why not make machines to fit the cow? Wacko, eh?" Positioned in the midst of the animals, Kee visually registers the transpositions between human fertility and control over agricultural production while her speech overwrites and is overwritten by the religious allusions in the composition. For Kee's pregnancy not only recalls the Virgin Mary's but also equally clearly cites the rape of enslaved women by plantation owners as a form of sexual domination and of increasing fixed capital.[31] In collapsing the dual meanings of labor—as childbirth and as economically productive activity—Kee's Madonna excavates the agricultural roots of reproductive sciences and points toward the many forms of contemporary bioscience descended from them: artificial reproduction, regenerative medicine, tissue engineering, nanotechnology, and the genetic modification of plants and animals. The fungible exchange of pregnant refugee and livestock reasserts the pastoral care of the population through the single pietà formed by mother and child.

Notably, however, this image never provokes race suicide discourse, inside or outside of the film. Kee's Madonna and Child suggests that while nativism is clearly at its most brutal, white racial "stock" is not the territory that state violence labors to protect, as has been historically true; instead, it labors to control the production of *habeas viscus*.[32] That Kee can signal the restoration of proper relations between *bios* and *zoē* has to do with the histories of enclosure her racialization invokes.[33] Reproduction is no longer preeminently a matter of disciplining population dynamics to assure the perpetuation of the proper national stock but instead works through differential access to the means of subsistence and differential vulnerability to accumulation by dispossession. In the rest of this chapter, I bring this analysis of Cuarón's film to bear on the SyFy series *Battlestar Galactica* (2004–9), whose themes included indefinite detention, genocide in the name of species survival, reproduction as a national asset, and the miraculous birth of the hybrid human–alien child Hera despite years of Cylon infertility. To explore the difference this difference makes in the long itinerary of *habeas viscus*, I turn first to earlier instantiations of race and reproduction and, in particular, to the figure of the barren woman.

Barren Women

The story of the barren woman is thickly woven into the culture of turn-of-the-twentieth-century America. The decades between the end of the Civil War and the beginning of the Cold War were a period of intense racial, ethnic, and class anxiety. By 1927, the year the U.S. Supreme Court decided *Buck v. Bell*, many states had already enacted forced sterility measures that were disproportionately applied to poor white women and women of color.[34] Such actions by the state found justification through recourse to the logic of biological essentialism, which argued that so-called degenerative characteristics such as feeblemindedness, nymphomania, and alcoholism were predictable symptoms of corrupt bloodlines that must be curtailed before they were reproduced in the next generation. At the same time, declining birthrates among Anglo-Saxon women in the United

States compared to those of immigrant women gave rise to race suicide panics. Combined with the colonialist fantasy that some populations are less advanced than others, whose primitivism was like a shard of the past lodged in the present, the question of reproductive capacity—of savage hyperfecundity and overcivilized enervation—reentrenched race, class, gender, and sex norms in a period of vast social transformations. For this reason, the call to medicalize, regulate, and eventually ban abortion was one tactic in the same overall strategy as enforced sterilization: tying race to reproduction regulated women's social mobility and maintained de facto and de jure race and class segregation at the same time that it gave access to power at the level of the population.[35]

Female sterility occupies an especially freighted and incoherent region within this broad epistemic grid work. The strange combinations of social Darwinism, eugenic sciences, and animal husbandry produced sterility as the mark of racial contamination. Miscegenation was often associated with cross-species hybridization and thus with "infertile hybrids and mongrels" sneaking under the line of "surveillance, discipline, domestic confinement, and control" of women's spaces and bodies.[36] Especially through the threat of racial passing, however, biracial women carried both the presumption of sterility *and also* a duplicitous promiscuity that might reveal itself as hyperfecundity. Adjacent to the pseudo-scientific theories of so-called racial admixture were physician's advice books like Nicholas Francis Cooke's 1877 polemic *Satan in Society,* which depicted female sterility as the consequence of unchecked masturbation: "The orgasm induced in the female organs by the conjugal act," writes Cooke, "is such that, if left incomplete [by masturbation], the congestion does not immediately relieve itself, and inflammations, ulcerations, and final sterility are the result."[37] His diagnosis mirrors the more general relationship established between moral conduct, natural health, and physical vitality by turn-of-the-century sexology. For example, part of the cure for infertility at the time was "infrequent coitus, pure air, quietude of mind, [and] temperance in food, drink, and sleep."[38] Sterility might be the sign of wayward reproductions across racial lines, in other words, or the result of solitary pleasures performed outside of the conjugal embrace. In either case, in the eugenic context of early-twentieth-century America, sterility was both the threat leveraged against sexual transgression and the point of insertion for medicojuridical oversight of women's lives and bodies. And in both cases, sterility was inextricably bound to racialist ideologies. Left out of the nation's stock, the sterile woman was the vindication and the nightmare of racial sciences.

At the same time that eugenic discourses were circuiting ideas about the health of the nation's future, infertility was playing a central role in the development of life sciences and agricultural sciences. In *Life as Surplus,* Cooper relates that the techniques that would become artificial reproductive technologies were originally pioneered in the post–World War II period for animal breeding, particularly for the cattle industry. In fact, though, the ties between livestock and fertility treatment go back to the mid-nineteenth century. U.S. historian Elaine Tyler May relates that in 1884, Dr. William Pancoast added the use of donor sperm to the already developed impregnator syringe to artificially inseminate a childless white woman.[39] Originally designed by J. Marion Sims, the infamous physician whose experiments on enslaved women led to the development of the speculum, the first successful vaginal surgery, and the modern constitution of gynecology,[40] the impregnator was one of multifarious techniques in the nineteenth century that shifted the imagination of the body away from the holistic humoral system and toward a mechanistic arrangement of semi-independent parts.[41] Yet, although attempts to make sperm more productive continued across the early twentieth century, it was not until the 1940s that breakthroughs in semen selection, collection, extension, and storage, as well as changes in shipping and distribution, made it possible to treat sperm as a widely marketable commodity. Tests for sperm motility and morphology and the addition of glycerol to cryopreserve sperm, both key techniques in artificial insemination of animals and the diagnosis and treatment of infertility in humans, emerged first from the dairy and chicken industries.[42] In these ways, sperm became "alienable, commercially evaluated reproductive tissue."[43] Concurrent with the industrialization of sperm, reproductive biologists were at work on embryo morphogenesis in animal ova. From the 1870s through the 1970s, experiments with rabbits laid the groundwork for what would become, in 1978, the first successful human in vitro fertilization (IVF)—a process that also involved the culture medium generated for research on hamster embryos.[44]

Although not all of these acts of transspecies reproduction were aimed at industrializing food through selective breeding, all were crucial to what Sarah Franklin describes as the postwar turn to the life sciences and the redefinition of life as a tool. "That biology has become a technology is not a metaphoric description," she writes.[45] As the contexts for marketization of biomaterials expand, the materials once considered commodities have become themselves new technologies for new kinds of biocommerce. In the production of induced pluripotent (iPS) cells, for example, "viruses are used to transport the required genes, and the genes, or factors, themselves become tools in the process of forcing a cell to reorganize itself."[46] The example of iPS cells allows us to chart what we might call the becoming-reproductive of the soma. With iPS, any cell might be forced back to its undifferentiated, pluripotent state to induce it to express the characteristics of the target cell. More than anything, then, assisted reproductive technologies "reincorporate the realm of social, sexual, and biological reproduction within the economic sphere"[47]—a logic of artifactualization that led to and was amplified by the landmark 1980 U.S. Supreme Court decision in *Diamond v. Chakrabarty*.[48]

The case, brought by biochemist Ananda Chakrabarty, concerned the sorts of work that qualified a natural resource to be recognized as a patentable invention. Prior to the *Diamond* ruling, the guiding common law tenet held that the labor of discovery was not enough to give the discoverer patent rights to the resource; rather, some process of extraction or modification had to be employed that would make the product significantly different from its natural state. For nearly a century before *Diamond,* patent law held that no process involving living organisms would be enough to meet the patent standard because the method of sexual reproduction was (1) natural rather than manmade and (2) imperfectly reproducible at the industrial scale.[49] In responding to the increasingly normalized framing of (reproductive) biology as a form of technology, a framing made available in no small part by the visibility of artificial reproductive technologies in the wake of the 1978 IVF success, the *Diamond* ruling also gave financial incentive to the burgeoning fields of biotechnological research.

It was a short ten years from the *Diamond* ruling to the first patented transgenic mammal: OncoMouse, genetically modified through techniques perfected in animal breeding to reliably produce human cancer cells as a living laboratory and model for cancer research. OncoMouse is an "ordinary commodity in the exchange circuits of transnational capital,"[50] in Donna Haraway's memorable terms. Its living vitality, its ability to manifest desirable traits at regularized and anticipatable timescales, are precisely what *Diamond v. Chakrabarty* allows to be enclosed as intellectual property in what I am calling the new enclosures of reproduction. For OncoMouse is not only a living tool, it is also living property, doubly rights-less as an animal and an invention. "Inventions do not have property rights in the self," Haraway writes, highlighting the spectral presence of the enslaved women whose suffering enabled J. Marion Sims to make his discoveries. "Alive and self moving or not, they cannot be legal persons."[51] Yet their value as salable technoscientific instruments derives from the reserve of constrained vitality they hold. In this sense, transgenic animals exemplify *habeas viscus*; their enclosure echoes the economics of enslavement at the same as it makes literal the biologization of caste in the new form of somatic capital.

No wonder Kee's pregnancy is revealed in a barn: her restored fertility stands in for all the creaturely life rendered as capital and for all the creaturely and geological vitality whose gift of labor might one day disappear. As Jasper tells Kee, "Your baby is the miracle the whole world has been waiting for." He means that the restoration of fertility her pregnancy portends will end the state of exception. And in a way, he is correct. His words find visual echo in the miraculous cease-fire scene. Kee has given birth in war zone conditions inside of the Bexhill refugee camp where she and Theo have gone to seek refuge from the Fishes (who have conspired to kidnap her child) and to gain access to the ocean (and thus the Human Project's ship) through a drainage ditch that starts inside of the compound. Their intentional self-internment is swiftly followed by a Fishes-inspired revolution (a screen to move Fishes fighters into the camp), which in turn triggers an all-out assault by the state militia and its war machines. This part of the film has an almost unbearably high body count as the people living in Bexhill find themselves in the crossfire of forces for whom no sacrifice of other people's lives is too great a price to pay for continued control over the enclosure of reproduction. It is into this melee that Kee delivers her child and through mortar rounds and gun battles that she and Theo find their way to the water. For a moment in the middle, however, as the threesome descend into the waiting gun barrels of a militia who are shooting on sight, the fire ceases. Kee reveals her child, the soldiers lower their weapons, and all kneel down to her.

The conjunction of the production of death and the worship of life begs us to ask what, in the face of such enormous loss of life, one more person could possibly mean. If we read this scene through a lens of reproductive futurism, an answer presents itself. The reproductive woman and her child must be protected for the restoration of the human future and the return of generationality their lives hold. Heather Latimer argues that the child–refugee dyad should be understood through contemporary fetal politics. "Fetal citizenship occupies a special position biopolitically," she writes, "one akin to how the refugee functions—just on the other side of the spectrum."[52] An inversion of the refugee whose life is retained by the state but not protected from its violence, the fetus receives the state's protection as violent appropriation. As Latimer writes, "there really is no 'life' prior to the state's deciding on the categories that render life into existence."[53] In this instance, however, it would be more accurate to say that there really is no life at all. The great wheels of the biopolitical state cannot turn by themselves, and so, in a real sense, all population is rendered surplus population. This is why the miracle of the child bends the soldiers' knees: the reproductive woman and her child promise a return to a looser and less threatening division of *bios* and *zoē,* one that, in reinstating the motive force of *habeas viscus,* returns the original storehouse of vitality that no amount of violence will by itself elicit.

The Farm

It is in the context of post-*Diamond* genomic control that I would like to read a central episode in the unfolding of *Battlestar Galactica*'s reproductive futurity. The series, a reboot of the short-lived 1970s show of the same name, engages a well-worn science fictional plot summed up in the first and second seasons' title sequence: "The Cylons were created by man. They evolved. They revolted. There are many copies. And they have a plan." This context reflects an important difference between the original

Battlestar Galactica and the Oughts version. In the contemporary series, the Cylons are built by humans; in the 1970s original, they are an invading alien technology. Like OncoMouse, Cylons were created to be self-moving laborers, living property, and like patented life-forms more generally, they inspire "desire and fear."[54] After years of uneasy détente following the original Cylon rebellion, the renegade Cylons have evolved a model nearly indistinguishable in form from their makers, giving the lie to their allegedly robotic or slavelike intelligence condensed in the derogatory name "toaster." The humanoid Cylons are designed to seduce the Caprican military elite in the lead-up to the genocide and colonization of the human planets.

There is a lot to be unpacked here, and I would like to do so by looking closely at a key episode. "The Farm" comes at the beginning of the second season, well after the humanoid Cylons have been detected by the Colonial fleet.[55] Kara Thrace—hard-drinking, cigar-chomping Viper pilot and begrudging mystical visionary—finds herself in a makeshift hospital recovery room on Cylon-occupied Caprica. Woozy from surgery, Kara awakens to the sympathetic face of Dr. Simon O'Neill, who tells her that she is in a Resistance hospital on the grounds of an old mental institution recovering from a hip wound. Kara's hospital room is rich with sunshine and so pointedly isolated that Kara questions Simon on the truthfulness of his story.[56] The episode returns again and again to this room, with its signs of medical authority juxtaposed with crumbling postwar infrastructure, tracking Kara's periods of lucidity between applications of pain medicine. It is during one of these returns that we see Simon administering a gynecological exam on Kara. In its questionable necessity, this exam recalls the history of eugenic sterilization procedures conducted in asylums like this one, a feeling exaggerated by Simon's unsolicited advice to Kara on the subject of breeding:

> Got to keep the reproductive system in great shape. It's your most valuable asset these days. I'm serious. Finding healthy childbearing women of your age is a top priority of the Resistance. And you'll be happy to know that you are a very precious commodity to us.

In this speech, Simon cajoles Kara to be like Kee and Sugar Baby and OncoMouse, that is, to become *habeas viscus*. But Kara pointedly rejects this description of her worth, retorting tartly, "I'm not a commodity. I am a Viper pilot." Her rejection, however, only triggers another round of persuasion from Simon:

> Do you see any Vipers around here? You do realize that you are one of the few women actually capable of having children. That is your most valuable skill right now. Take a moment to think about where you are and what's going on. The human race is on the verge of extinction. And to be quite frank with you, potential mothers are a lot more valuable than a whole squadron of Viper pilots.

This position is in fact in line with that of acting president Laura Roslin, whose feminism does not prevent her from banning abortion across the fleet in the face of dwindling population numbers, which she keeps tallied on a whiteboard behind her desk. The irony, however, is that Simon is a Cylon; his concern is not the fate of the human species, whose extinction he has been orchestrating, but rather developing reproductive technology for Cylons. He had been prepping Kara not for recovery but for resource extraction. In the next scene, Kara awakens from her drug-induced sleep to discover a new scar on her abdomen. She follows Simon, observes him talking to a familiar Cylon model, and, a few scenes later, stabs him to death with a shard of her room's broken mirror and stumbles into the corridor looking for an exit. What she finds instead is a farm. A half-dozen women recline on gurneys, legs splayed, in a circle around a central control terminal. Electrodes ring their faces and tubes rise from their abdomens to devices in the ceiling. In a verbal–visual transposition of Kee's speech in the barn, each woman has four tubes extending from her. They look uncannily like cows attached to milking machines.

In this scene, the dread suspicion that the monetization of life-forms may not be kept in check by the thin veneer of human exceptionalism is delivered in its most emphatic and historically freighted form. For the crosshatch of readings is thick here. One of the women Kara finds on the farm, and the only one with a speaking role, is a black woman named Sue-Shaun, who begs to be killed. This choice underscores the already intense associations with eugenic racism while the hoped-for product—hybrid human–Cylon children—highlights the miscegenation fears that subtend eugenics. But Simon the doctor is also the only Cylon played by an African American actor, and so the racial coordinates don't quite line up. Similarly, if it is easy to see the Cylons as genocidal racialists fueled by belief in their own innate superiority, they are equally readable as revolutionaries and freedom fighters. Moreover, the Cylons are themselves products with model numbers and branding names to match. Whatever merger of human reproductive organs and machine parts the Cylons orchestrate can only ever be a version of what was originally done to them. After all, the scene not only mirrors the milking machines of Kee's barn but also alludes to the factory floor of the Cylons' own creation as military technology with commercial applications. Its slippery incoherencies, then, result from the overcoding of eugenic concerns for racial "stock" with the commercial biology characteristic of somatic capitalism and the new enclosures of reproduction. In light of the foregoing discussion, Kara's whiteness stands out. That the series allows her to escape from the farm suggests something about the continuing racial alignment of somatic capitalism.

The baby farm fails, and its failure intimates that it is not enough that women of color labor to reproduce proper relations through reproduction. To align with the gift of nature's labor, that reproduction cannot be taken; it must be desired.[57] What stands out from this slippery set of allusions is the oddity that Cylons would want to be reproductive at all. They may not reproduce, but Cylons do procreate through a combination of synthetic biology and downloadable memories. In vast, hivelike Resurrection ships,[58] dead Cylons reemerge to new bodies in viscous birth tanks. Though the models are limited, Cylon numbers are potentially infinite and their lives eternal. Later in the episode, Sharon explains that what Kara witnessed was not at all unusual. Galvanized by their monotheistic religion's demand that they be fruitful, they have been conducting breeding experiments on human women in the thousands. And so it is fitting that as Kara is discovering the true purpose of the hospital, Sharon has already learned why those experiments have met with little success. By attempting to force birth, they have left out love. It is love that has made Sharon the first Cylon ever to conceive. Love, the mysterious, moves the mechanisms of biology where technological elicitation by itself fails. In the figure of a love that exceeds and catalyzes biotechnical life, *Battlestar Galactica*'s reproductive futurism functions as originary plenitude, the unsolicitable élan vital. Theo-ontologized,[59] love and love's child promise that nature's vibrancy might be tractable after all.

But how tractable? In scene after scene with hybrid human–Cylon child Hera, she is pictured by herself, in mother-and-child pietàs or in nativity arrangements. One by one, the series clears her of rivals for the title of mitochondrial Eve, who are either stillborn or shown to be purely human. Like Kee's daughter Dillon, Hera is racially marked: once by the actor Grace Park's Korean American background and again by her character's Cylon biology. In all these ways, she remains emphatically singular, and this singularity is heightened by comparison with her mother's people's multiplicity. The few times that the camera travels to the Resurrection ships, the impression of swarming life beyond the hivelike honeycomb reminds the viewer of the uncanny proliferation-in-sameness presented by Cylon clones. Moreover, although the metallic Cylons may terrify through their identically mechanized appearance, they are at least distinguishable from their human counterparts. The synthetic Cylons, as the first season of the show emphatically repeats, "look like us now." Visually indistinguishable, the only mark of their difference is sexual—their biomechanical vertebrae glow red during sex—and reproductive. I have been arguing that the reproductive woman's restored fertility promises a mystical mechanism for enclosing and making pliable the subtending vitality that is both central to somatic capitalism and eludes its full control. But Hera's singularity does more than ensure that nature will remain productive. It also sequesters the destabilizing proliferation of Cylon copies. For the obverse side of the fear of sterility is that of rampant and unproductive bounty. Like cancer cells, Cylons are all one thing, and in their enormous numbers and autonomous agenda, they threaten to turn everything into themselves.[60]

Yet the nightmare of Cylon abundance is an outgrowth of genetically induced sterility. In the years since the *Diamond* decision, not only have living organisms become intellectual property in biotechnology applications and commodity services in artificial reproductive technologies but plant reproduction has become a primary target of accumulation by dispossession through genetic modification.[61] GMO products are indistinguishable from ("look like") non-GMO plants, except that their seeds can be used only once. Like the Resurrection ships, vitality comes from elsewhere.

In this sense, the Cylon fantasy is holographic, revealing at one angle the voluntary rejection of withheld labor (i.e., the willingness to reproduce) and at another the involuntary withholding of that labor (the built-in fidelity to producing the selfsame). Or, in other words, the new enclosures of reproduction offer a loyal nature that can't help but be obedient to its patent holders. Hera's bispecies heritage grafts together without fully resolving the dual demands for vibrant potentiality, iconized here as romantic love, and total control. In the nonsolution Hera presents, we can see how deeply riven the contemporary moment is by the dramatic expansion of capitalist nature. Caught between increasingly precise genomic control and the sixth great extinction, the new mythos of sterility apocalypses must do double duty—reining in and eliciting, amplifying and tamping down—to solicit the return of the nature whose complacency made industrial agricultural production possible.

Right Relations

That this is a nonsolution is made clear by the series's finale, which ends with a literal return of the natural. While the majority of the episodes were set either in the confines of the ship's passageways or on the refugee planet of New Caprica, "Daybreak, Part 3"[62] narrates the final destination of the thirty-eight thousand human remnants and their few Cylon allies on an ostensibly unknown planet that is quickly revealed in the *Galactica*'s viewfinder as our familiar Earth. The ships hover over a perfectly recognizable northern Africa and, in the next frame, zoom down into a field of tall grasses. The whole sequence takes less than ten seconds, in part because the crafts' actual entrance into the atmosphere and touchdown on the planet's surface get elided by a fade between the cruising ships and the third-person camera's perspective. No friction interrupts their descent from the void of space to the field of grass, and nothing detracts from the Eden they find there. Gazelle graze in the high grasses; flamingoes stand in the shallow ponds; the sky is blue and sparsely clouded; the wind blows the heat away and the stands of trees provide a perfect canopy for their makeshift homes. The world they have found is perfect, as the episode tells us over and over again: "the perfection of creation," Galen calls it; "so much life," Laura Roslin whispers; "one might even say there was a divine hand at work," Gaius opines. Between man and nature, proper relations have been restored, and so they reject the engineering feats they could accomplish, the city they could lay out, and instead send their fleet to burn up in the sun.

I mean the phrase "between man and nature" quite precisely. For a series with no shortage of important female characters and a quest whose success hinges on the charisma of Kara Thrace, the determination of President Laura Roslin, and the political savvy of the Cylon women, there are strangely few women in the first scenes on Earth. In fact, there are none in the crucial first moments on their new home. In these moments, they learn that Earth has a native population and that that population shares enough of their DNA to be sexually compatible. In them, too, they decide that they will start over without technology. Their decision to "go native" (in both the technological and reproductive senses) reflects one strand of the history of colonialism, and the group that makes these decisions are themselves as colonial as it is possible to be: they are all men, they are all white, they are all adult, they are all in fatigues, and, with the single exception of Colonel Tigh, they are all human. When women are reintroduced, it is in order to leave more permanently. Roslin passes away from the breast cancer that she has battled throughout the series; Kara announces that "her journey is over" and literally disappears, thus demonstrating that her purpose had truly been mystical and visionary rather than tactical all along; the Cylon women walk offscreen with their spouses to pursue lives as farmers' wives.

In fact, the only woman given the chance to inhabit this new world by herself is Hera. She walks along between her parents, Karl and Sharon, swinging their hands lightly and smiling into the sunshine while they debate which of them will teach her survival skills:

KARL *(to Hera)*: Don't you listen to Mommy. Daddy is a great hunter.
SHARON *(to Hera)*: No, Mommy's gonna teach you how to hunt. Real hunting.
KARL: No, no, no, no, no. No.
SHARON *(to Hera)*: Yes, and I am going to teach you how to build a house and how to plant crops.
KARL *(to Hera)*: OK, maybe Mommy will teach you that, but I am going to teach you to hunt.

From a distance, her two sets of "grandparents" watch over the scene: the Tighs, who first invented humanoid Cylons, and Caprica Six and Gaius Baltar, who the series presents as her spiritual parents and guardians. And between them, the single moment of hybrid Hera running across the fields by herself: the survival of the colony, the salvation of three species, and the living embodiment of a restored nature and all the right relations that follow from it. Beginning, of course, with farming.

Unexpectedly, however, it is not Hera who closes the series but Baltar and Six. Six is one of the central architects of the Cylon attack on the Colonies. She was sent as a weapon to seduce Baltar into sharing with her the structure of the defense mainframe. Throughout, he has been haunted with a spectral version of Six only he can see, who chides him into performing further acts of sedition. In these final ten minutes, the series returns us to the secret scene of his guilt, the moment, long unrevealed, where he consents to give Six access to classified systems. "For love," as he says, ironically. And in response to her startled response, he amends, "Well, you know what I mean." Had he meant love in that moment, her relieved laugh suggests, the whole thing might have been avoided. Instead, it is only now that he recognizes love and at the same moment embraces his father's spurned profession as a farmer. The memory of that earlier moment, then, brackets their departure to find a field to till and their shared recognition that love was indeed what motivated them now that they have "fulfilled God's plan." "Over there between those two peaks," Gaius tells Six, "I saw some terrain that looked good for cultivation. . . . I know about farming, you know."

After the break, the series's brief epilogue picks back up with Hera by herself, still a child, but this time using a walking stick to make her way across a field. The camera fades out from her upturned face to race through fields and deserts, oceans and woods, until suddenly a city rises and with it the legend "150,000 years later." In this way, the series retro-actively reframes the show's historical location. What appeared through four seasons and a handful of specials, webisodes, and miniseries as a not-so-distant future of space travel and artificial intelligence instead returns to us in these last three minutes as our ancestral past. And literally ours; the final sequence implies that the hybrid child Hera is mitochondrial

Eve, whose traces were recently discovered. The setting of these last few minutes mirrors the opening on Caprica, which of course also mirrors our own glass-and-concrete present, but also more specifically the most recent memory of Caprica in the form of Gaius's treason. Coming as it does at the end, then, this ouroboros movement threads together the last days of Caprica and the Twelve Colonies with the future of the epilogue and compresses both into the present of the series's screening. By the end, in other words, we are again at the end; the Cylons' attack and the humans' counterattack may have purchased 150,000 years of right relations with nature, but a hundred thousand years later, and we are back at the edge of crisis.

"All of this has happened before," Gaius says, "but does it need to happen again?" Six wagers that this time might be the exception: "Let a complex system repeat itself for long enough," she argues, "and something surprising might occur." Ultimately, then, the series is not about cybernetics but about recombinant genetics; Cylons are not toasters, not robots, not metal machines, but capitalist nature, the enclosure of reproduction. Hera and all her progeny give us back the throw of the dice whose promise of surprise the new enclosures of reproduction strip away. As I have endeavored to show throughout this chapter, for it to be successful, somatic capitalism needs unanticipatable liveliness as well as a mechanism of capture and control.

CONCLUSION

Child

This book has argued that the child continues to circuit sentimental attention under neoliberal regimes of flexible accumulation more interested in extracting and monetizing subindividual capacities than in maintaining and protecting desirable populations. Broadly stated, I have argued that the child does double duty in what I have called somatic capitalism: on one hand, the child, in her innocence and plentitude, promises another generation of species-survival posed as physiological self-similarity even as she begs for protection against the many and varied harms of contemporary industrial practices. On the other hand, while the child appears to vouchsafe the future of the species, her connection to reproduction opens onto the interlocking biological and physical systems whose livelinesses compose us as much as we compose with them. That we too are subject to biotechnical control conversely reminds us of all that escapes from and exceeds that control: the specters of mutation, pollution, proliferation, and dehiscence. Thus the child grafts onto our burgeoning apprehension of nonhuman agency and binds it back, reconsolidating liveliness within the charmed circle of human futurity via sexual reproduction. At issue in both aspects of the child in somatic capitalism is the question of nature, nature's nature, so to speak—whether by nature we mean the manipulable stuff of industrial production practices or those vibrant agents that are our co-constituents in the real.

I have used the term *Anthropocene* throughout this work as an apt shorthand for all those relations thrown into new alignment by the "unnatural growth of the natural"[1] under conditions of industrial production. The argument that I have unfolded in the course of the book now affords us the vantage to wonder a little about the framing of the term. For all that the Anthropocene is a welcome heuristic, there is also something perplexing about it. This perplexity has coalesced for me in two questions. First, does the Anthropocene differ in substance from biopolitics? And if the answer is indeed, as I suspect, that it does not, then does it offer something otherwise obscured by the concept of the biopolitical? And here I think the answer is yes.

Of course, these are in some ways perverse or at least contentious sorts of questions since the Anthropocene and the biopolitical have such obviously different conceptual trajectories. As I have already had occasion to note, the Anthropocene was coined by Paul Crutzen and Eugene Stoermer to name the geological period that succeeds the Holocene. In his 2002 article "Geology of Mankind," Crutzen defines the Anthropocene as the first "human-dominated geological epoch" and dates its emergence to the late eighteenth century.[2] Biopolitics, by contrast, describes a mode of governance. It is a heuristic worked out by theorists as a way to discuss the entrance of life-as-such into the political arena. Despite these differences, situating the two next to each other reveals some compelling tangencies. Both concepts concern the relations between technologies of capture and the complex natural systems that are the subjects of that capture. We might say, then, that the Anthropocene is the earthly effect of biopolitics, its geological unconscious. Curiously, though, both concepts collapse the modulation of natural systems into their means of solicitation. In other words, both the Anthropocene and biopolitics begin from but also minimize the importance of nonhuman vitality to the functioning of technologies of capture. No electricity without the funny friction of the electron setting everything else in motion, to put the point once more again.

What the comparison of the Anthropocene and biopolitics thus so strikingly reveals is their shared attachment to the strength of human action. By focusing on the role of human action, the Anthropocene obscures a far more threatening reality: the collapse of the regulative. Here, I want to argue, is where the Anthropocene reveals something important about biopolitics. In the hyperstimulative environment of late capital, in which the acceleration of nature's metabolism has triggered unpredictable vibrancies ramifying across complex systems, what we see erupting is not the increased world-forming powers of the *anthropos* but the autonomy and wayward causalities of the planet. The Anthropocene is not the end of nature in total but the end of techniques of control premised on the manageability of natural processes and the end of nature as the repository of monetizable agency.

As a retrospective designation, the Anthropocene tells us what has been true at the very moment that it ceases to be true. For where we are now is not only at the terminus of those stabilities that enabled systems of management based on predicative control but also and concomitantly at the waning of respons-ability[3] premised on our ability to anticipate the consequences of our actions. Richard Grusin poses a congruent point when he writes that the Anthropocene is defined in recognition "that humans must now be understood as climatological or geological forces on the planet that operate just as nonhumans would, independent of human will, belief, or desires."[4] Thus the close relations between the Anthropocene and the apocalyptic. Call it, then, the anti-Anthropocene. The anthro-no-more-cene. The terracene, with terror fully voiced. Or call it nothing at all. For isn't the taxonomic just such a technology of stabilization whose own groundwork the closure of the Holocene radically unmoors? Perhaps, then, we should call it what it looks like to us here in the dirt—a relation of scavenge or an a-volitional restriction to the present tense.[5]

Biopolitical theory in fact already has a name for life outside of management. It is useful to recall here that for Agamben, *bios* (or the political life proper to the human) always results from the inclusive exclusion of *zoē* (or the biological being common to all living things).[6] *Zoē* is in this sense the originary bare life, held in the sovereign exception to support the production of the human over against his own animal being. And while Agamben proposes a transformed relation between *bios* and *zoē* as his ethicopolitical intervention, it is with the assumption that nothing can or will interrupt the smooth functioning of the anthropological machine given the continued efficiency of control mechanisms. The catastrophe for biopolitics inaugurated by the Anthropocene expresses itself first and foremost as the release of *zoē* from the anthropological machine that relies on it.

Assuming that Lee Edelman is right to say that the political as such cannot exist apart from the labor of the future,[7] what might emerge from the unreliability of causal efficacy in the Anthropocene? The issue, after all, is not that there is no future but rather that there is no sure way of orienting toward that future, either to save it or to survive it. This is likely a question without an answer; still, what seems clear is that scholars are not the only ones grappling with this transformation. Recent representations have also been wrestling with the false presentation of choice at stake in both the Anthropocene and biopolitics. I'd like to conclude by looking at a couple of case studies to ask how we might think a catastrophe that is first and foremost a catastrophe for biopolitics. (Of course, doing so makes its wager in the currency of speculation and should be considered accordingly.) By reading transversely across contemporary figurations, I conjecture that we can catch a glimpse of what I would like to offer as a wayward and insurgent *zoē* as resistant to stewardship and the politics of care as it is to the mass-production processes premised on a pliable natural world. In the first case study, I look at the future in young adult fiction, in the second, planterity or the world-without-us.[8] In each, the child is emphatically denied the restored relations with nature that we have observed are key to its functioning.

Figure/Ground Reversals

"Read what you want. But you should feel embarrassed when what you are reading was written for children." So ran the subtitle of Ruth Graham's *Slate* rant "Against YA."[9] Motivated by the number of young adult–based films that premiered during summer 2014, Graham takes crossover audiences to task for what she sees as the moral and intellectual torpor that must explain—but certainly results from—adult consumption of teen lit. Bracketing out "transparently trashy" supernatural, dystopian, and fantastic YA ("which no one defends as serious literature"), Graham turns her attention instead to realist fiction focused on plausible characters in sophisticated and nuanced emotional situations. Even these, however, miss the mark of adult literature for her. They may engage the reader in the character's emotional lives, but because young adult literature para-digmatically features young adult characters (and, typically, first-person narrators) in situations familiar to the ideal young adult reader, the reader is never challenged to rise to the tolerance for ambiguity, contradiction, and experimentation that mark fictions for and about adults. For Graham, this is why YA is pleasurable: it encourages escapism by being overly mimetic, so narrowly focused on the social lives of young people that it excludes adult judgments altogether. When adults read it, it is as if we all decided to stay in the "kiddie pool" rather than sinking into the deep waters of great literature.

In the way of the Internet, Graham's article inspired a small flurry of responses from places like *The New Republic, xoJane,* and the *Vulture* as well as three thousand reader comments.[10] Far and away the majority of these articles and the most popular comment responses abjured Graham's position. But they did so, interestingly, without shifting the terms of her description in any significant sense. For both Graham and her detractors, YA lacks subtlety, but it is this very lack that gives rise to what they all agree is its most common feature: its pleasure. Jen Doll, writing for the *Vulture,* describes herself as "sighing in pleasure because the heroine really does get the guy, the world has been saved, the parents finally understand."[11] In her autobiographical reader's narrative for *xoJane,* Sarah Seltzer castigates her younger self for her closet consumption of YA fiction. "What had I been thinking," she writes, "denying myself pleasure? Pure, unadulterated, unguilty pleasure? There may be no deciphering needed in these books, no head-scratching about meaning or metaphor, but sometimes, what a reader needs is just to feel."[12] The use of the word "unadulterated" here is curious and perhaps unintentionally telling. After all, the structure of reading generated by YA is rarely an actual one-to-one mimeticism such as in the case of S. E. Hinton, who wrote *The Outsiders* while still herself a teenager; far more typically, an adult author stands in the middle of and coordinates the encounter between constructed adolescent character and presumed adolescent reader. If YA mirrors the conditions of young people's emotional landscapes, as these authors suggest, then it is also the case that those landscapes are as much the *product of* YA literature as they are *reflected in* YA literature.

That, at least, has long been the authorizing conceit of writing for children, which developed before the field of YA and from which YA takes a number of its organizational strategies and common tropes. A product of the print revolution, early children's literature intended to instruct and so took the form of the moral lesson, the etiquette book, or the early reader, and while children's literature became significantly more literary through the Victorian Golden Age, it also never entirely lost its status as propaedeutic. Similarly, young adult literature came of age in the twentieth century alongside the great institutions of psychology—especially progressive reform, educational psychology, sexology, and psychoanalysis—and their variety of developmental models of subjectivity. Indeed, while the term *teenager* first appeared via popular journalism as a way of discussing postwar youth culture, the teen was in many ways prefigured by the American psychologist G. Stanley Hall's two-volume 1904 magnum opus *Adolescence, Its Relations to Physiology, Anthropology, Sociology, Sex, Crime, Religion and Education*[13] and its use of Ernst Haeckel's recapitulation theory to justify strict educational surveillance. Hall's adolescent tends toward criminality, is liable to get caught up in strong emotion, and must therefore be cultivated through civilizing impressions.[14]

Both children's literature and young adult literature grow out of and as disciplinary apparatuses trained on that fraught transit between the presumptive difference of those still in their minority and the socially necessary sameness that is inscribed into fully attained adulthood. Where for children's literature that transit is bound up with the problem of innocence and experience, YA novels are propelled by the movement from romance to realism, or the need to acclimate romantic young adult readers to the deflated expectations of realist adult lives. As Roberta Trites explores in *Disturbing the Universe,*[15] the problem is how to weave young adults into the fabric of the social when the institutions that represent that adult telos often feel inimical, constraining, malevolent, or just boring. So, she writes, the adolescent "must learn to negotiate the levels of power that exist in the myriad social institutions within which they function."[16] She contrasts these narratives of acclimation and accommodation to the romantic bildungsroman tradition and its greater emphasis on (masculine) self-actualization. Where bildungsromans use quest narratives to affirm the heroic individual, YA novels use social problems to mold adolescent subjectivity—that is, not only to install the qualities associated with properly achieved adulthood (diminished expectations, renunciation of idealism, recognition of mixed motives, etc.) but also to engender self-reflective subjectivity through the very movement from romantic to realist selfhood that is also and not for nothing the growth narrative at the heart of psychoanalysis.

Here we could list off a number of examples. In Madeleine L'Engle's *A Wrinkle in Time,* Meg discovers that her father can't help her defeat the evil brain; instead, she must help him. In Lionel Davidson's *Under Plum Lake,* Barry discovers a world where technology has defeated labor and the limitations of the body, but being in it nearly kills him, and so he must learn to live with its loss. In China Miéville's *Un Lun Dun,* Deeba the UNchosen One comes to recognize that she doesn't need an ancient prophecy to do what needs to be done to help her friends. Sherman Alexie's Junior (in *The Absolutely True Diary of a Part Time Indian*), in moving from an impoverished reservation school to a privileged white one, comes to recognize that his own personal and family tragedies are part of the same structural inequalities that make one school wealthy and the other poor and, in that light, sees his responsibility to his home as well as to his achievements.[17] Clearly this is a satisfactory heuristic for patterning YA fiction. But it is also a far cry from sighing in pleasure and reading after dark with a flashlight. Hadn't we been promised pleasures? Escapism? Unrealistically satisfying endings? What has happened in this gap between the reported experience of reading and the historical analysis of the discursive role of the genre?

I would like to propose a counterintuitive explanation. It comes in two parts, and I'll present them one at a time. The first part is easy and a little conventional, and that is that the pleasure of YA fiction is a part of what makes it work as a disciplinary mechanism. Here I am thinking back to Foucault and the perverse implantation.[18] As I discussed at length in the introduction, he argues that the modern *epistēmē* implants and intensifies the sexual secret and the corresponding agon of hiddenness and exposure as a technique of power that results in a depth model of subjectivity. YA novels' status as *guilty* pleasure, as trashy literature, without redeeming metaphoric complexity or recondite meanings, fulfills this role at a formal level. They are pleasurably quest-y, world building, character-quirky, formula repetitive despite that they tilt toward responsibilization in the form of inner development.

But here's the more important second part, and that is that the clamor from crossover audiences for YA novels is driven by the *waning* of that *epistēmē* in which subjectivity and the sexual secret formed the mainsprings of disciplinary biopower. For if adult readers are reading contemporary YA fictions, it is not for a nostalgic dip into more satisfying worlds where every girl gets her guy. It can't be. Rather, it is for the way that twenty-first-century fictions for young adults index the profound disruptions in futurity engendered by the dual catastrophes of neoliberalism and anthropogenic climate change. For the turn-of-the-century taxonomies of age and aging sit in reciprocal relation to our models for telling time, for establishing cause and effect, and for thinking of consequences and accumulations. But that itinerary is increasingly disjoined by the apprehension of geological timescales, queer and nonlinear causalities, and the chronic time of toxicity and managed disease. So while it is still the case that these fictions drive toward acquiescence, it is also less and less clear what there is to acquiesce to—at least as that acquiescence is thought to be the wellspring of good character. Indeed, it is *character* and its relation to the foregrounded plot—the problem, the romance, the quest—that is losing salience in favor of setting, that is, of the increasingly visible agencies of the nonhuman surround and of the late capitalist reframing of the child as resource.

Indeed, the novels themselves obsessively thematize this change. John Green's beloved disability narrative *The Fault in Our Stars*[19] makes the most minimal possible gesture toward a world whose health is unquestioned. The novel focuses on three friends who all attend the same cancer support group. In some ways, it is a typical YA novel: boy meets girl, woos girl, beds girl. But the girl in question, our main character, Hazel, has no expectation of marriage because neither she nor her lover has a future to inhabit together. She has not been to school for years because of her illness, and so there are few scenes of anyone trying to fit into an ableist world and no real sense of a normative life expectancy. There is one healthy young person—a supporting character's flaky girlfriend whose two important roles are getting made out with and having her car egged when she dumps her newly blind boyfriend. But the novel's trick ending makes clear the delusory nature of recovery narratives hinged as they are on the solidity of categories like healthy, in remission, cancer-free, not long and really bad. "I miss the future," Hazel says.

But the future that they jokingly imagine is drawn from cheesy science fiction B movies where all of the doctors have robot eyes. Indeed, representation looms large in this novel. The motivating conceit is another novel, which only exists in the diegesis. It's also a disability narrative about a girl with a terminal illness, and it also focuses on small domestic dramas. But it breaks with domestic realism at the very end, when the final sentence hangs unfinished. Hazel is obsessed with this line, and as she endlessly rereads the novel in the hope of starting the story again to find her way to a more satisfying conclusion, she becomes more attached to the possibility of discovering the truth. And so she and her beau use their cancer wish to travel to meet the book's author in Amsterdam. But he won't give her the satisfaction she wants. Increasingly enraged by his refusal, Hazel shouts, "It's impossible not to imagine a future for them. You are the most qualified person to imagine a future for them. Something happened [to them]. . . . I need to know what happens" (192).

Hazel's demand for narrative explanation, for the capacity to imaginatively inhabit a future, even if that future can exist only in imagination, goes unfulfilled. What she comes to instead, by the book's conclusion, is an acquiescence to her father's slightly mystical but emphatically non-human ontology: "All I know of heaven and all I know of death," Hazel says, "is in this park: an elegant universe in ceaseless motion, teeming with ruined ruins and screaming children" (308). This is succor, but of a very cold kind: the universe may be elegant, but it is also profoundly unconcerned for human life, indeed, for any life. In the eye of its vastness, even the familiar things of human existence become estranged. Another dying character in another YA catastrophe puts it like this: "Think of all the toothbrushes."[20] Think of all the things whose material compositions ensure that they will outlast us, becoming deformed by their abundance as much as by the absence of meaningful context.

Karen Thompson Walker's *Age of Miracles* literalizes this view of the universe by making the deformations of time planetary rather than personal. In her novel, the rotation of Earth has started to slow. Time has become unhinged: each day exceeds itself, growing in stutter-stop increments. From the novel's opening in the household of eleven-year-old Julia to its conclusion, the slowing remains unexplained. Julia's story follows the usual YA conventions—she gains and loses friends, reckons with the death of a grandparent, discovers her father's illicit romance, and acquires a young love of her own. But these wheels turn in the background and end abruptly and in tragedy. Her father's love interest moves away; her own dies young. What takes the place of the dramatic interest of these plots is what would have otherwise been the background in any other moment. The slowing kills the birds first, then the whales, as the changed gravity affects echolocation. Ultimately, the stretches of daylight become unbearable as the day grows to encompass weeks. The boyfriend dies of exposure from illicitly meeting Julia in the sunlight. By the end of the book, Julia's family has retreated into their home (now covered in "thick steel sheeting . . . to keep out the radiation"[21]), where they will remain until the oil runs dry or they die of exposure.

There are other moments in other books we could adduce here—the dead love interest in M. T. Anderson's *Feed,* the bare escape in Paolo Bacigalupi's Dickensian *Ship Breaker*—but the point, I think, is clear. YA fiction, which as a genre has much at stake in developmental regularity, has begun instead to record its loss. What, then, of narrative? I turn in the second case study to look at recent films that twine together Anthropocenic conditions and an insurgent *zoē,* the rupture of the narrative line, and the death of the child.

Narrative Causalities

In Terrence Malick's 2011 film *Tree of Life,*[22] the story of a young family in suburban 1950s Texas fractures around a cosmological upwelling, twenty minutes of nebulae, cosmic dust, solar storms, planetary formation, spiraling universes, blood vessels, stream beds, aquifers, conifers, dinosaurs, tidal pools, tsunami waves, mud pits, forest canopy, star fall, jellyfish, meteor strikes, gas geysers, fetuses in utero, and interior shots of beating human hearts. Its tunneling from the macrocosmic life of the cosmos to the fetus in utero takes part in the binding work performed by the child-figure but is also irreducible to that binding. Under the auspices of a religiously inflected vitalist narrative of the sacred life of the child, the film exposes the stuff from which that child is formed. Read in reverse, as the elegiac structure of the film prompts, the biological, ecological, and astrophysical tear through those bindings, exploding from within the fetal image.

Like *Tree of Life,* Lars Van Trier's *Melancholia* (2011)[23] unfolds almost entirely in the visual register. But where Malik's film is split apart by the eruption of planetarity, *Melancholia* narrates that eruption as the terminus of a plot that deploys and then relentlessly unmoors the conventions of realism. After a brief, retrospective modernist prelude, the film begins as if it were a romantic comedy about a wealthy, white family finally marrying off their slightly wacky daughter. But it soon becomes clear that the broad physical comedy of the opening routine—the bride and groom late for their own wedding party because of an impassable road—isn't comedic zaniness but the mania that precedes depression. Once they arrive at the dinner, hours late, the mood and mode have starkly shifted. Now we are in a family melodrama with its cast of mannered characters slowly revealed as monstrous: the drunken, lecherous father; the embittered, overclingy mother; the bad boss; the sneering, violent brother-in-law and his meek, put-upon wife; and the now-dissociative bride who first leaves the party for a hot soak in an upstairs bathroom and then, pulled back downstairs by her scene-averse family, seduces the first man she encounters, dragging him to the center of the broad lawns that surround the estate to assault him in full view of the guests. Predictably, then, scandal spreads, guests leave, the groom packs his suitcases, and the party is over. And so should be the film. But instead of ending, it again switches genres, this time to an illness narrative. The characters who had been roles acquire names and histories: Justine, subject to catatonic depressions; her caregiver sister Claire, wife of wealthy John; their son, Leo. A quiet family drama. And so it goes until what had been a blip in the background, the subject of father–son bonding over a telescope and alarmed maternal research at the family computer, takes over the foreground: the planet Melancholia and its maybe-it-will, maybe-it-won't crash course with Earth. The family story collapses, deflated by the two complex systems both named Melancholia: Justine's neurochemistry and the onrushing planet. And in case we had any doubt about the kind of story we are in now—the apocalyptic kind—Leo's father's suicide makes the terminus of the realist narrative perfectly clear. Through the lens of Leo's telescope, we spend the night watching as Melancholia slides into view—closer and closer until no lens is needed—and then begins to recede. Relief and the return of domestic realism. But by the next morning, John is dead and Melancholia is larger than ever.

Both films traffic in the elegiac, commemorating the social relations that are no longer maintained by the quiescence of the background. As Steven Shaviro writes of *Melancholia,* the worlds these films depict are "tiny, self-enclosed microcosm[s] of Western white bourgeois privilege; and this microcosm is what gets destroyed by the end."[24] I have endeavored to demonstrate, however, that the destruction here is not limited to the world represented on-screen but also and more emphatically enacts a failure of narrative form. In the kaleidoscopic shuffling between generic modes—comedy to melodrama to science fictional apocalypse—the interior lives of the characters become less and less central, their ability to control the resources their wealth provides less and less certain. At one point in the final movement of the movie, Claire takes her son and tries to escape from her home in a golf cart, not fully recognizing that the scale of the impending disaster erases the distinctions of class that made some places safer than others. She returns, bedraggled by rain and hail, with a new acceptance of her entrapment, and it is in the aftermath of this experience that she proposes to Justine a *Titanic*-style garden party: wine and lawn chairs on the veranda stage setting one last performance of classed spectatorship. In this sequence, Claire repeats in miniature the film's own generic staggering, trying first for the heroic survivalist protecting the future through the life of the child, then for the bon vivant welcoming death as the latest droll entertainment. "What do you think of my idea?" she asks Justine. "Do you know what I think of your plan?" Justine replies. "I think it's a piece of shit." Doppelganger of the planet, Justine knows that no narrative is strong enough to reframe the eruption as melodrama. Even the symbolic relation forged between Justine and the planet itself collapses in the face of the strident literalism of the film's end. The planet has the last word.

Here, in the final moments of the film, is young Leo with his mother and his aunt on the grounds of their estate, not in any of its ballrooms or bedrooms but huddled together under a rudimentary lean-to, the barest possible allusion to the protections of the domestic interior, while around them the invading planet engulfs more and more of the sky. No warning of impending doom; this is elegy. So what is it mourning? The mythology of the sky, its bright blue doom revealed as just another alien landscape? The protections of wealth and whiteness? The illusion of home, of human battlements raised against the agency of the nonhuman force? The belated remembrance of that force, which after all subtends all possible human works, *the Anthropocene* a poor name for industrial modernity's triggering of nature's surplus vitality? Or perhaps most simply, it is an elegy for Man, for humanism that is, for the "faith in the unique, self-regulating and intrinsically moral powers of human reason"[25] that insists on the passivity of matter even as it taps its activity as resource? All these, but also the narrative forms to which they gave rise.

Whereas *Tree of Life* thus engages in a form of retrospection that cannot quite hold in or successfully reframe the upwelling of planetarity, *Melancholia* ends with the destruction of all of the narrative forms it employs. Can there be any more persuasive or iconic image of the sudden apprehension of nonhuman vitality than Melancholia burning through the little stick replica of the abandoned mansion beyond? And yet, I want to stop just a moment before the planet consumes the screen image. For what our discussion of the Anthropocene and the biopolitical suggests is that the outside of management isn't the vacuity of total destruction — which is in any case just the volte-face of the human as the redemption of natural life — but the end of those stable relations that allowed for *bios* to capture and contain *zoē* at all. Agamben's image for the "animal separated within the human body itself"[26] under conditions of biopolitics is the coma victim whose livingness is tethered to the machines that maintain it. But planetarity augurs a different emergence of the animal life in the human: an end to the stabilities that enabled judgment and, with it, the stewardship of lively matters, including first and foremost the human *oikos*. In the image of the fort, *Melancholia* gives us an icon for a humbled humanity, no longer steward over Earth but one among many species whose vulnerability can no longer be bolstered behind castlelike walls.

The End, then, and the end of endings.

Acknowledgments

In 2008, when I began this project, I was living in New York City. In the years since, I have traveled from Brooklyn to Bloomington, from Bloomington to Atlanta, from Atlanta to Milwaukee, and from Milwaukee back to Bloomington. I presented pieces of this manuscript at the annual meetings of the Science Fiction Research Association; the Society for Literature, Science, and the Arts; the Modern Language Association; and a score of other conferences, symposia, and workshops. Over the course of these perambulations, I have made more friends and my book has found more interlocutors than I could possibly have hoped and many, many more than I can recount here. But I'm going to try.

This book started as a dissertation at the Graduate Center of the City University of New York, and my first thanks go to my chair, Robert Reid-Pharr, and my committee, Carrie Hintz, Steven Kruger, and Jamie Skye Bianco. My time at the Grad Center was deeply enriched by my experiences as a teaching fellow at Queens College, for which I thank the students of QC, especially Dalia Davoudi, Omari Weekes, Emily Berliner, and Melissa Bobe. The reading group run by Jamie Skye Bianco from 2005 to 2008 was responsible for much of what I do and who I am now. I thank Jamie for those years of conversation and for all the years after; they are still the conversations I hear whenever I sit down to write. I thank as well Robert Diaz, Karen Weingarten, Justin Rogers-Cooper, and Jesse Schwartz for the friendship and the devoted engagement with my first tangled attempts at articulating the ideas in this manuscript. The 2010–11 cohort of Marion L. Brittian Postdoctoral Fellows at Georgia Tech helped me enormously to think through speculative materialisms. I thank, in particular, Jesse Stommel, Tom Lolis, Roger Whitson, Michelle Gibbons, Regina Martin, and Andrew Cooper.

I received crucial support for this book from University of Wisconsin–Milwaukee's Center for 21st Century Studies, where I was a Provost Postdoctoral Fellow. My gratitude goes to the center's 2011–12 Fellows, my fellow postdoc Charlotte Frost, associate directors Mary Mullen and John Blum, and center director Richard Grusin. There are some people who enter one's life as if the place had always been on hold for them. Richard is one of those people for me, and my gratitude for that exceeds even the debt I owe him for the years of support he gave me when things felt most grim. Most recently, this work has been supported by a faculty summer fellowship from Indiana University Bloomington. My colleagues there have already made the long years on the job market more than worth it. Special thanks must go to Jennifer Fleissner, Karma Lochrie, Monique Morgan, Ed Comentale, and Shane Vogel, who pulled me into exciting projects in some cases before I was even on the payroll. Laura Plummer and the women of the Women Faculty Writing Group provided essential writing time, advice, and commiseration.

I am grateful to the following people who have supported me and my work through conversation, invitation, and shared community outside institutional bounds: Everett Hamner, Gerry Canavan, Eric Carl Link, Benjamin Robertson, David Higgins, Alexis Lothian, Aimee Bahng, Hamilton Carroll, Scott Selisker, Steven Shaviro, Peter Paik, Pawel Frelik, Batya Weinbaum, Ritch Calvin, Pete Sands, Veronica Hollinger, Sherryl Vint, Patrick B. Sharp, Lisa Yaszek, James Arnett, Lavelle Porter, Robert Azzarello, Chris Leslie, Katie King, Seo-Young Chu, Karin Sellberg, Peta Hinton, Emma Bianchi, Scott Richmond, Dani Kasprzak, Ali Sperling, Michael O'Rourke, Evan Turner, Heather Latimer, Lynne Huffer, Stacy Alaimo, Myra Hird, Jen Boyle, Cynthia Port, Wan-Chaun Kao, Eileen Joy, Jane Schultz, Megan Musgrave, Jacqui Weeks, Alexis Turner, Emma Young, Charles Carroll, James Paasche, the Occulture, Christopher Breu, Stephen Squibb, Rita Felski, and the New Literary History Post-Critical Seminar crew, Katherine Behar, Stephanie Boluk, and Kathryn Bond Stockton.

All of these people made this life what it is, but I wouldn't be here at all without the following mentors, colleagues, and friends: Jamie Skye Bianco, Tyler Bradway, Dalia Davoudi, Julian Gill-Peterson, Richard

Grusin, Annie McClanahan, Ted Martin, Monique Morgan, Pete Nekola, Laura Lee Roush, Carrie Shanafelt, Jesse Stommel, and Karen Weingarten. A special place goes to Eve Kosofsky Sedgwick, in memoriam.

I am lucky to have so many people to acknowledge and am particularly fortunate to be able to conclude by expressing my love for my family. Scott Sheldon, Barbara de Wilde, Kathy Sheldon, Al Konigsberg, Nancy Varga, Marshall Sheldon, Gloria Sheldon, and my stepsiblings and extended family members have all been a wellspring of support and understanding.

I thank my father, Scott Sheldon, for his delicate work on the book's style and index, for reading with such wit and perspicacity, and for giving me the best (unofficial) tagline for the book imaginable: "When a body that matters meets a body that matters comin' thru the rye." Further thanks go to Holly Monteith for her ace copyediting work and to Steven Bruhm and the anonymous reviewer at the University of Minnesota Press; a huge thank-you goes to my editor, Doug Armato, for finding me, for reading me, and for allowing me to task his patience.

Most of all, I thank Joe Varga. Over our years together, I have become the shy one, less and less able to express in words how much we mean to me. But that's what it's about really: the becoming together, the intimacy and the interval, the habits of sound and rhythm and proximity that make each of us environment for the other.

Notes

Preface

1 *Snowpiercer,* directed by Bong Joon-ho, featuring Chris Evans, Kang-ho Song, and Tilda Swinton (Seoul, Korea: Moho Films, 2014).

2 Margaret Atwood, *MaddAddam* (New York: Random House, 2014); Atwood, *The Year of the Flood* (New York: Random House, 2009); Atwood, *Oryx and Crake* (New York: Random House, 2004).

3 *Children of Men,* directed by Alfonso Cuarón, featuring Clive Owen, Julianna Moore, and Michael Caine (Universal City, Calif.: Universal, 2007).

4 Michel Foucault, *History of Sexuality 1,* trans. Robert Hurley (New York: Vintage, 1978).

5 Michael Wines, "Oklahoma Recognizes Role of Drilling in Earthquakes," *New York Times,* April 21, 2015, A16.

6 Paul J. Crutzen and Eugene F. Stoermer, "The Anthropocene," *International Geosphere-Biosphere Programme Newsletter,* no. 41 (2000).

7 Karen Barad, *Meeting the Universe Halfway: Quantum Physics and the Entanglement of Matter and Meaning* (Durham, N.C.: Duke University Press, 2007); Stacy Alaimo and Susan Hekman, eds., *Material Feminisms* (Bloomington: Indiana University Press, 2007); Timothy Morton, *Ecology without Nature: Rethinking Environmental Aesthetics* (Cambridge, Mass.: Harvard University Press, 2007).

Introduction

1 Kazuo Ishiguro, *Never Let Me Go* (New York: Vintage, 2005), 262–63.

2 I will use "the child" as the grammatical subject throughout this book; however, I do not mean for this to suggest the perspective of any actual child. Instead, I take "the child" as a figuration for analysis.

3 Or the notion that ontogeny repeats phylogeny. Carolyn Steedman, *Strange Dislocations: Childhood and the Idea of Interiority, 1870–1920* (Cambridge, Mass.: Harvard University Press, 1995), 168–69.

4 Foucault, *History of Sexuality 1,* 36.

5   Lee Edelman, *No Future: Queer Theory and the Death Drive* (Durham, N.C.: Duke University Press, 2004).

6   What I mean by "American culture," however, is not the nascence of the author. Instead, I look at discourses that are in some substantive way tagged as American. Thus, while neither Ishiguro nor his novel counts as American, the conjoining of bare life to the state's will to protect its citizens chimes with the indefinite detention camps of the Bush era, itself more discursively American than actually mononational. Much the same claim can be made for Margaret Atwood's *Handmaid's Tale* and MaddAddam trilogy, both of which are set in America. Without fully entering into the extensive debates about periodization and transnational canon formation, my point here is that the scope of what it means for something to be American must be widened in the age of American empire to include those texts that reckon with it as the name of a global social and political *epistēmē*.

7   Donna Haraway, "Manifesto for Cyborgs: Science, Technology, and Socialist Feminism in the 1980s," *Socialist Review* 80 (1985): 65–108.

8   Hannah Arendt, *The Human Condition* (Chicago: University of Chicago Press, 1958), 47.

9   Rosi Braidotti, *The Posthuman* (Cambridge, U.K.: Polity Press, 2013), 3.

10   Donna Haraway, *When Species Meet* (Minneapolis: University of Minnesota Press, 2008), 4.

11   Ibid.

12   Crutzen and Stoermer, "The Anthropocene," 17.

13   Shane Denson, *Postnaturalism: Frankenstein, Film, and the Anthropotechnical Interface* (Bielefeld, Germany: Transcript, 2014), 24.

14   Foucault, *History of Sexuality 1*, 34.

15   Henry James, *The Turn of the Screw: A Norton Critical Edition* (New York: W. W. Norton, 1999).

16   The novel also leaves open the possibility that Miles really does see the ghost of his former groundskeeper, Peter Quint.

17   Sheila Teahan, "'I Caught Him, Yes, I Held Him': The Ghostly Effects of Reading in *The Turn of the Screw*," in *The Turn of the Screw: Case Study in Contemporary Criticism*, 348–65 (Boston: Bedford/St. Martin's, 2004).

18   James, *Turn of the Screw*, 83.

19   Eric Savoy, "Theory *a Tergo* in *The Turn of the Screw*," in *Curiouser: On the Queerness of Children*, ed. Steven Bruhm and Natasha Hurley (Minneapolis: University of Minnesota Press, 2004), 270.

20   Ibid.

21   This claim refers to Sedgwick's essay "Paranoid Reading, Reparative Reading, or, You're So Paranoid You Probably Think This Essay Is about You,"

in *Touching Feeling: Affect, Pedagogy, Performativity,* 123–53 (Durham, N.C.: Duke University Press, 2003).

22 James Kincaid, *Erotic Innocence: The Culture of Child Molesting* (Durham, N.C.: Duke University Press, 1998); Kincaid, *Child-Loving: The Erotic Child and Victorian Culture* (New York: Routledge, 1992). In addition to Kincaid's books, see Judith Levine, *Harmful to Minors: The Perils of Protecting Children from Sex* (New York: Thunder's Mouth Press, 2002), and Roger N. Lancaster, *Sex Panic and the Punitive State* (Berkeley: University of California Press, 2011), for other readings of the sexually vulnerable child.

23 Kincaid, *Child-Loving,* 5.

24 Steven Mintz, *Huck's Raft: A History of American Childhood* (Cambridge, Mass.: Harvard University Press, 2004), 3; Edelman, *No Future,* 21.

25 Kathryn Bond Stockton, *The Queer Child: Or, Growing Sideways in the Twentieth Century* (Durham, N.C.: Duke University Press, 2009), 9. For more on narrative and childhood, including children's literature, see Jacqueline Rose, *The Case of Peter Pan, or the Impossibility of Children's Fiction* (Philadelphia: University of Pennsylvania Press, 1984), and Karen Sánchez-Eppler, *Dependent States: The Child's Part in Nineteenth-Century American Culture* (Chicago: University of Chicago Press, 2005).

26 Viviana Zelizar, *Pricing the Priceless Child: The Changing Social Value of Children* (New York: Basic Books, 1985), 11; Steedman, *Strange Dislocations.*

27 Stockton, *Queer Child,* 13.

28 Bruhm and Hurley, *Curiouser,* xiii.

29 Edelman, *No Future,* 7.

30 Giorgio Agamben, *Means without Ends: Notes on Politics* (Minneapolis: University of Minnesota Press, 2000), 92. Edelman also discusses what he calls the "fascism of the baby's face." Edelman, *No Future,* 75.

31 Michael Taussig, *Defacement: Public Secrecy and the Labor of the Negative* (Stanford, Calif.: Stanford University Press, 1999), 92.

32 Gilles Deleuze and Félix Guattari, *A Thousand Plateaus: Capitalism and Schizophrenia,* trans. Brian Massumi (Minneapolis: University of Minnesota Press, 1987), 180.

33 Emmanuel Levinas, *Alterity and Transcendence,* trans. Michael B. Smith (New York: Columbia University Press, 1999), 140.

34 Jacques Derrida, *The Animal That Therefore I Am,* ed. Marie-Louise Mallet, trans. David Wills (New York: Fordham University Press, 2008). For work on Levinas and environmentalism, see William Edelglass, James Hatley, and Christian Diehm, eds., *Facing Nature: Levinas and Environmental Thought* (Pittsburgh, Pa.: Duquesne University Press, 2012).

35 Deleuze and Guattari, *A Thousand Plateaus,* 188.

36 Claudia Castañeda, *Figurations: Child, Bodies, Worlds* (Durham, N.C.: Duke University Press, 2002), 145.

37 For an explicitly feminist posthumanist take on the face, see Claire Colebrook's chapter "Face Race" in her *Death of the Posthuman: Essays on Extinction,* vol. 1 (Ann Arbor, Mich.: Open Humanities Press, 2014).

38 On the connection between the child and visuality, see Anne Higonnet, *Pictures of Innocence: The History and Crisis of Ideal Childhood* (London: Thames and Hudson, 1998). On the child and cinema, see Vicky Lebeau, *Childhood and Cinema* (London: Reaktion Books, 2008).

39 It is viewable at the Museum of Moving Image's Candidate's Room, http://www.livingroomcandidate.org/commercials/1964/peace-little-girl-daisy.

40 Robert Mann, *Daisy Petals and Mushroom Clouds: LBJ, Barry Goldwater, and the Ad That Changed American Politics* (Baton Rouge: Louisiana University Press, 2011).

41 Ibid., xi.

42 David Higgins, "The Inward Urge: 1960s Science Fiction and Imperialism" (PhD diss., Indiana University, 2011).

43 This line is a misquotation of W. H. Auden's war elegy "September 1, 1939."

44 There is a small point to be made here. The ad is, I think, wise to allow Daisy to remain unmolested by knowledge of the bomb. At the same time, however, the identity the ad sets up between Daisy and the bomb means that her knowledge is no longer her most important quality. The ad, then, encodes the hermeneutic child (who must be sheltered from adult knowledge) while in the act of constructing her successor.

45 *2001: A Space Odyssey,* directed by Stanley Kubrick, written by Arthur C. Clarke, featuring Keir Dullea (Beverly Hills, Calif.: Metro-Goldwyn-Mayer, 1968).

46 Rachel Carson, *Silent Spring* (1962; repr., New York: Mariner Books, 2002).

47 "Interview with Elizabeth Povinelli," by Mat Coleman and Kathryn Yosuff, *Society and Space,* March 6, 2014, http://societyandspace.com/2014/03/06/interview-with-elizabeth-povinelli-with-mat-coleman-and-kathryn-yusoff/.

48 Ishiguro, *Never Let Me Go,* 279.

49 Giorgio Agamben, *Homo Sacer: Sovereign Power and Bare Life* (Stanford, Calif.: Stanford University Press, 1998), 94.

50 Melinda Cooper, *Life as Surplus: Biotechnology and Capitalism in the Neoliberal Era* (Seattle: University of Washington Press, 2008),137–38.

51 Sarah Franklin, *Dolly Mixtures: The Remaking of Genealogy* (Durham, N.C.: Duke University Press, 2007), 27.

52 Donna Haraway, *Modest_Witness@Second_Millennium.FemaleMan©_Meets_OncoMouse™: Feminism and Technoscience* (New York: Routledge, 1997), 134.

53 Eugene Thacker, *After Life* (Chicago: University of Chicago Press, 2010). In addition, see Nikolas Rose, *The Politics of Life-Itself: Biomedicine, Power, and Subjectivity in the 21st Century* (Princeton, N.J.: Princeton University Press, 2007). I greatly admire the work Gil Anidjar does in explaining the structure of the sacred in theories of life-itself. See Anidjar, "The Meaning of Life," *Critical Inquiry* 37, no. 4 (2011): 697–723.

54 Michel Foucault, *The Order of Things: An Archaeology of the Human Sciences* (New York: Vintage, 1970), 387.

55 Ibid., 310.

1. Future

1 COP15 refers to the United Nations's Framework Convention on Climate Change drafted fifteen years earlier and commonly called the "Earth Summit."

2 *Please Help the World,* directed by Mikkel Blaabjerg Poulsen, December 7, 2009, https://www.youtube.com/watch?v=NVGGgncVq-4.

3 Haraway, *Modest Witness@Second Millennium,* 174.

4 Ibid.

5 Unfortunately, this video is no longer hosted by Raise Your Voice. For other videos produced for the occasion, see https://www.youtube.com/playlist ?list=PL26A02117D1F88AC0.

6 See the introduction to this volume for a longer discussion of this advertisement.

7 Haraway, *Modest_Witness@Second_Millennium,* 13.

8 I use the term *popular environmentalism* to distinguish commercial, policy, and activist discourses from literary and academic fields like ecocriticism.

9 Keith Ansell-Pearson, *Philosophy and the Adventure of the Virtual: Bergson and the Time of Life* (New York: Routledge, 2002), 72.

10 Elizabeth Grosz, *The Nick of Time: Politics, Evolution, and the Untimely* (Durham, N.C.: Duke University Press, 2004), 210.

11 Ansell-Pearson, *Philosophy and the Adventure of the Virtual,* 72.

12 Barad, *Meeting the Universe Halfway,* 137.

13 There have been many interesting readings of queer temporality published in the past decade, several explicitly opposed to Edelman's. These include "Queer Temporalities and Postmodern Geographies," a chapter in J. Jack Halberstam's *In a Queer Time and Place,* 1–22 (New York: New York University Press, 2005); Kathryn Bond Stockton's notion of sideways growth in her *The Queer Child*; Heather Love's *Feeling Backward: Loss and the Politics of Queer History* (Cambridge, Mass.: Harvard University Press, 2007); and Elizabeth Freeman's *Time Binds: Queer Temporalities, Queer Histories* (Durham, N.C.: Duke University Press, 2010).

14 See Karen Barad's important essay "Nature's Queer Performativity," *Kvinder, Køn og Forskning,* no. 1–2 (2012): 25–53. I would also be remiss not to mention those books that situate themselves at the intersection of queer theory and ecocriticism. For book-length treatments, see Robert Azzarello, *Queer Environmentality: Ecology, Evolution, and Sexuality in American Literature* (Burlington, Vt.: Ashgate Press, 2012), and Nicole Seymour, *Strange Natures: Futurity, Empathy, and the Queer Ecological Imagination* (Urbana: University of Illinois Press, 2013). For collections, see Noreen Gifney and Myra Hird, eds., *Queering the Non/Human* (Burlington, Vt.: Ashgate Press, 2008), and Catriona Mortimer-Sandilands and Bruce Erickson, eds., *Queer Ecologies: Sex, Nature, Politics, Desire* (Bloomington: Indiana University Press, 2010).

15 Deleuze and Guattari, *A Thousand Plateaus,* 43.

16 Haraway calls that index the "God-tricks." She advocates an ethics based on local knowledge and "standpoint" effects. See her *Simians, Cyborgs, and Women: The Reinvention of Nature* (New York: Routledge, 1991), 189–95.

17 Gilles Deleuze, "Ethology: Spinoza and Us," in *Zone 6: Incorporations,* ed. Jonathan Crary and Sanford Kwinter (New York: Zone Books, 1992), 628.

18 The past few years have seen a number of books published that take on this task. See especially Jeffrey Jerome Cohen, ed., *Prismatic Ecology: Ecotheory beyond Green,* with a foreword by Lawrence Buell (Minneapolis: University of Minnesota Press, 2013).

19 Deleuze, "Ethology," 627.

20 On nonorganic life, see Manuel De Landa, *A Thousand Years of Nonlinear History* (New York: Swerve, 2000).

21 J. G. Ballard, "The Garden of Time," in *The Best Short Stories of J. G. Ballard,* with an introduction by Anthony Burgess, 141–49 (New York: Picador, 2001).

22 Ansell-Pearson, *Philosophy and the Adventure of the Virtual,* 47.

23 *Place* and *space* are pervasive terms in ecocritical writings and register a similar desire for closure. See Aldo Leopold, *A Sand County Almanac and Sketches Here and There* (1949; repr., New York: Oxford University Press, 1987).

24 Ansell-Pearson, *Philosophy and the Adventure of the Virtual,* 50.

25 Brent Bellamy and Irme Szeman name this genre "science faction" in their "Life after People: Science Faction and Ecological Futures," in *Green Planets: Ecology and Science Fiction,* ed. Gerry Canavan, 192–206 (Middletown, Conn.: Wesleyan Press, 2014). For a contemporary update of Carson's fable, see Naomi Oreskes and Erik M. Conway's *The Collapse of Western Civilization: A View from the Future* (New York: Columbia University Press, 2014).

26 Carson, *Silent Spring*, 1.

27 Frederick Buell, *The Future of Environmental Criticism* (Malden, Mass.: Blackwell, 2005), 5, emphasis added.

28 Carson, *Silent Spring*, 168, 169.

29 Arne Naess, "Deep Ecology," in *The Palgrave Environmental Reader*, ed. Daniel G. Payne and Richard S. Newman (New York: Palgrave, 2005), 243; Garrett Hardin, "The Tragedy of the Commons," in Payne and Newman, *Palgrave Environmental*, 38; James Lovelock, *The Revenge of Gaia: Earth's Climate Crisis and the Fate of Humanity* (New York: Basic Books, 2006), 6.

30 E. O. Wilson, "The Environmental Ethic," in Payne and Newman, *Palgrave Environmental*, 272; Murray Bookchin, "Social Ecology," in *The Green Reader: Essays towards a Sustainable Society*, ed. Andrew Dobson (San Francisco: Mercury House, 1991), 60; Winona LaDuke, "The Seventh Generation," in Payne and Newman, *Palgrave Environmental*, 286.

31 Edelman, *No Future*, 28.

32 Ibid., 25.

33 Edelman's work has been greeted with skepticism. For a sense of the debate, see "The Antisocial Thesis in Queer Theory," *PMLA* 121, no. 3 (2006): 819–28.

34 Adam Jasper, "Our Aesthetic Categories: An Interview with Sianne Ngai," *Cabinet* 43 (Fall 2011), http://www.cabinetmagazine.org/issues/43/jasper_ngai.php.

35 Timothy Morton, *Hyperobjects: Philosophy and Ecology after the End of the World* (Minneapolis: University of Minnesota Press, 2013), 134.

36 Al Gore, *An Inconvenient Truth: The Planetary Emergency of Global Warming and What We Can Do about It* (New York: Rodale, 2006), n.p.

37 In *The Future of Life* (New York: Knopf, 2002), E. O. Wilson takes the opposite tack and preemptively addresses the future: "We bequeath to you the synthetic jungles of Hawaii and a scrubland where once thrived the prodigious Amazon forest. . . . Accept our apologies and this audiovisual library that illustrates the wondrous world that used to be" (78).

38 Qtd. in Elizabeth Kolbert, *Field Notes from a Catastrophe: A Front Line Report on Climate Change* (London: Bloomsbury, 2007), 154.

39 Newt Gingrich and Terry L. Maple, *A Contract with the Earth*, with a foreword by E. O. Wilson (Baltimore: Johns Hopkins University Press, 2007), v.

40 Pope Francis, *Laudato Si': On Care for Our Common Home* (Huntington, Ind.: Our Sunday Visitor, 2015).

41 James Hansen, *Storms of My Grandchildren: The Truth about the Coming Climate Change Catastrophe and Our Last Chance to Save Humanity* (London: Bloomsbury Press, 2009), 238–39. He has since retired from NASA to do

legal work on behalf of research groups like Our Children's Trust, http://ourchildrenstrust.org/.

42 Scott Russell Sanders, *A Conservationist Manifesto* (Bloomington: Indiana University Press, 2009), 214.

43 Art Bell and Whitley Strieber, *The Coming Global Superstorm* (New York: Pocket Books, 2000), 236.

44 *After Armageddon,* directed by Stephen Kemp, featuring Rob Hartz, Kathleen Cameron, and James Brown (Arizona: Randy Murray Productions, 2010); *The Last Hours of Humanity: Warming the World to Extinction,* directed by Thom Hartman, October 11, 2013, https://www.youtube.com/watch?v=21D3ByfPTx8; *Six Degrees Could Change the World,* directed by Ron Bowman, featuring Alec Baldwin and Rajendra Pachauri (Washington, D.C.: National Geographic, 2008); *Arctic Death Spiral and the Methane Time Bomb,* https://www.youtube.com/watch?v=m6pFDu7lLV4&nohtml5=False; *Addicted to Plastic: The Rise and Demise of a Modern Miracle,* directed by Ian Connacher (Toronto, Ont.: Cryptic Moth, 2008); *GMO OMG,* directed by Jeremy Seifert, featuring Michael Adam, Cary Fowler, and Don Grimes (Los Angeles, Calif.: Compeller Films, 2013).

45 Brenda Mulford, "We Must Preserve the Earth's Dwindling Resources for My Five Children," *The Onion,* June 28, 2006.

46 I draw much of this description of catastrophe from the writings of chaos theorists. They, however, tend not to use the term, preferring instead to talk about bifurcation points and strange attractors. See Ilya Prigogine and Isabelle Stengers, *Order Out of Chaos: Man's New Dialogue with Nature* (New York: Bantam Books, 1984), 167–70; James Gleick, *Chaos: Making a New Science* (London: Penguin Books, 1987), 139–53; Brian Massumi, *A User's Guide to Capitalism and Schizophrenia: Deviations from Deleuze and Guattari* (Boston: MIT Press, 1992), 58–60.

47 See Jacques Derrida, "On a Newly Arisen Apocalyptic Tone in Philosophy," in *Raising the Tone of Philosophy,* ed. Peter Fenves, 117–73 (Baltimore: The Johns Hopkins University Press, 1993). For a full discussion of apocalypse, see chapter 3.

48 Eve Kosofsky Sedgwick, *Epistemology of the Closet* (Berkeley: University of California Press, 1990).

49 *Southland Tales,* directed by Richard Kelly (Los Angeles, Calif.: Cherry Road Films, 2007).

50 Foucault, *History of Sexuality 1,* 93.

51 Massumi, *A User's Guide to Capitalism and Schizophrenia,* 34.

52 Michel Foucault, *Security, Territory, Population: Lectures at the College De France, 1977—1978,* ed. Michel Senellarf, trans. Graham Burchell (New York: Palgrave, 2007), 79.

53   President George W. Bush, "The National Security Strategy of the USA," address to the nation, September 17, 2002, http://www.state.gov/docu ments/organization/63562.pdf.

54   Brian Massumi, "Potential Politics and the Primacy of Preemption," *Theory and Event* 10, no. 2 (2007): 7.

55   Wilson, *Future of Life*, 39.

56   Hansen, *Revenge of Gaia*, 10.

57   Wilson, *Future of Life*, 132.

58   Jacques Derrida, "No Apocalypse, Not Now (Full Speed Ahead, Seven Missiles, Seven Missives)," *Diacritics* 14, no. 2 (1984): 24.

59   Octavia Butler, "The Evening and the Morning and the Night," *Callaloo* 24, no. 2 (2001): 401–18.

60   Derrida, "No Apocalypse, Not Now," 28.

61   Peter Schwartz and Doug Randall, *An Abrupt Climate Change Scenario and Its Implications for United States National Security*, 3, http://www.climate .org/PDF/clim_change_scenario.pdf.

62   Charles Darwin, *The Origin of Species: A Norton Critical Edition*, ed. Philip Appleman (New York: W. W. Norton, 1985), 149.

63   Darwin elaborates: "Nature, if I may be allowed to personify the natural preservation or survival of the fittest, cares nothing for appearances, except in so far as they are useful to any being" (122). What "usefulness" denotes is determined by the total ecological context, not by a teleological end point.

64   Grosz, *Nick of Time*, 24. Elizabeth Grosz's recent work, from which this quotation is drawn, reevaluates Darwin, Nietzsche, and Bergson from the perspective of temporal mutation. The following quotation might be taken as the work's thesis: "Nietzsche serves . . . as a corrective to contemporary Darwinism, which has sought, beyond the boldness of Darwin's own conjectures, a security that the knowledge of the past and present will preempt and provide us with knowledge of the future, that time is regular, predictable, knowable. What Nietzsche makes clear is that such a knowledge is possible only with the freezing, the arresting of the active dynamism of the will to power, that is, with freezing and thus killing life itself" (111). For a symbiogenetic take on reproduction (as a counterpoint to what I offer here), see Lynn Margulis and Dorian Sagan's *What Is Sex?* (New York: Simon and Schuster, 1997); Myra Hird, *The Origins of Sociable Life: Evolution after Science Studies* (New York: Palgrave, 2009); and Luciana Parisi, *Abstract Sex: Philosophy, Bio-technology, and the Mutations of Desire* (London: Continuum, 2004).

65   Roy Scranton, "Learning How to Die in the Anthropocene," *New York Times*, November 10, 2013, http://opinionator.blogs.nytimes.com/2013/11 /10/learning-how-to-die-in-the-anthropocene/?_r=0. See also Margaret

Atwood, "It's Not Climate Change, It's Everything Change," *Matter,* July 27, 2015, https://medium.com/matter/it-s-not-climate-change-it-s-everything -change-8fd9aa671804.

2. Life

1 Marion Zimmer Bradley, *Darkover Landfall* (New York: Daw Books, 1972).

2 Joanna Russ, *We Who Are About To...* (New York: Dell, 1977).

3 Morton, *Hyperobjects.*

4 See, e.g., Adrienne Rich, "Compulsory Heterosexuality and Lesbian Exis- tence," *Signs* 5, no. 4 (1980): 631–60, and Shulamith Firestone, *The Dialectic of Sex: The Case for Feminist Revolution* (New York: William Morrow, 1970).

5 This temporality recalls the Freudian Oedipal narrative, which Teresa de Lauretis, *Alice Doesn't: Feminism, Semiotics, Cinema* (Bloomington: Indiana University Press, 1984), describes in this way: "The end of the girl's journey, if successful, will bring her to the place where the boy will find her, like Sleeping Beauty, awaiting him, Prince Charming. For the boy has been promised, by the social contract he has entered into at his Oedipal phase, that he will find woman waiting at the end of *his* journey. Thus the itinerary of the female's journey, mapped from the very start on the territory of her own body..., is guided by a compass pointing not to reproduction as the fulfillment of *her* biological destiny, but more exactly to the fulfillment of the promise made to 'the little man'" (133). Roof, "The Ideology of Fair Use: Xeroxing and Reproductive Rights," *Hypatia* 7 (Spring 1992): 63–73, makes a similar point by recourse to laws regarding copyright and legal custody, showing how both privilege male ownership of creative and procreative issue. My argument is intended to highlight the shared complicity, or what de Lauretis calls "seduction" (137), of both men and women in overvaluing individualized responsibility to the future. This might help explain why stories such as Russ's, which reverse the Oedipal metanarrative by assigning active questing to female characters, are only partially successful in avoiding patriarchy. Indeed, I would argue that *We Who Are About To...* is such an upsetting novel because it posits the failure of reversing the Oedipal metanarrative without also rethinking futurity.

6 Joanna Russ, *The Female Man* (Boston: Beacon Press, 1975), 204.

7 Rich, "Compulsory Heterosexuality and Lesbian Existence," 637.

8 See Claire Colebrook, *Sex after Life: Essays on Extinction II* (Ann Arbor Mich.: Open Humanities Press, 2014), for an interesting counterexample.

9 But see Karen Weingarten, *Abortion in the American Imagination before Life and Choice, 1880–1940* (New Brunswick, N.J.: Rutgers University Press, 2014).

10 Samuel R. Delany, *Longer Views: Extended Essay* (Hanover, N.H.: Wesleyan University Press, 1996), 149.

11 Brooks Landon, "Eve at the End of the World: Sexuality and the Reversal of Expectations in Novels by Joanna Russ, Angela Carter, and Thomas Berger," in *Erotic Universe: Sexuality and Fantastic Literature,* ed. Donald Palumbo, 61–73 (Westport, Conn.: Greenwood Press, 1986).

12 Marleen S. Barr, "Reproducing Reproduction, Manipulating Motherhood: Pregnancy and Power," in *Alien to Femininity: Speculative Fiction and Feminist Theory* (Westport, Conn.: Greenwood Press, 1987), 133.

13 Samuel R. Delany, "Shadow and Ash," in *Longer Views,* 148.

14 Marilyn Hacker, "Science Fiction and Feminism: The Work of Joanna Russ," *Chrysalis* 4 (1977): 67–79.

15 Thelma J. Shinn, "Worlds of Words and Swords: Suzette Haden Elgin and Joanna Russ at Work," in *Women Worldwalkers: New Dimensions of Science Fiction and Fantasy,* ed. Jane B. Weedman (Lubbock: Texas Tech University Press, 1985), 211.

16 Barbara Garland, "Joanna Russ," in *Dictionary of Literary Biography,* ed. David Cowart and Thomas L. Wymer (Detroit, Mich.: Gale, 1981), 92.

17 Sherry Ortner, "Is Female to Male as Nature Is to Culture?," *Feminist Studies* 1, no. 2 (1972): 25.

18 In a series of letters and book reviews written between 1979 and 1980 for the *Frontiers* journal, Russ registers the joy of isolating, naming, and describing universal conditions of women's oppression, despite the fact that they turn out to be identical, in her words, to "the establishment of civilization." See esp. Russ, "Review," *Frontiers: A Journal of Women's Studies* 5, no. 3 (1980): 78–79.

19 Robert F. Reid-Pharr, "Tearing the Goat's Flesh: Homosexuality, Abjection, and the Production of a Late Twentieth Century Black Masculinity," *Studies in the Novel* 28, no. 3 (1996): 373.

20 In a compelling, but ultimately unconvincing, reading of this novel, Patrick Murphy argues that the narrator is engaged in a heroic defense of the alien planet's ecology. Murphy, "Suicide, Murder, Culture, and Catastrophe: Joanna Russ's *We Who Are About To . . . ,*" in *State of the Fantastic: Studies in the Theory and Practice of Fantastic Literature and Film: Selected Essays from the Eleventh International Conference on the Fantastic in Arts,* ed. Nicholas Ruddick, 121–31 (Westport, Conn.: Greenwood Press, 1990).

21 In "Exterminating Fetuses: Abortion, Disarmament, and the Sexo-Semiotics of Extraterrestrialism," *Diacritics* 14, no. 2 (1984): 47–59, Zoë Sofia argues that the collapsed future is a mainstay of science fiction. Her reading of male reproductive metaphors as a form of technological determinism against the

"generative energies in non-heterosexuals and others who choose not to re-produce themselves" (58) is clearly close to the argument I am pursuing here.

22 Delany, *Longer Views,* 146, 149.

23 E.g., "We who are about to die salute you."

24 Sarah LeFanu, "The Reader as Subject," in *Feminism and Science Fiction* (Bloomington: Indiana University Press, 1989), 178.

25 Joanna Russ, "The Second Inquisition," in *The Adventures of Alyx* (New York: Pocket Books, 1983).

26 For another take on this dynamic, see Russ's "The Mystery of the Young Gentleman," in *Extra (Ordinary) People,* 63–92 (New York: St. Martin's Press, 1984).

27 Joanna Russ, "Recent Feminist Utopias," in *Future Females: A Critical Anthology,* ed. Marlene S. Barr, 71–86 (Bowling Green, Ohio: Bowling Green State University Popular Press, 1981).

28 This theme continues a long history of child-saving campaigns. See Anthony M. Platt, *The Child Savers: The Invention of Delinquency* (Chicago: University of Chicago Press, 1977).

29 My use of the phrase "sexual" child closely matches Russ's use here. Rather than designating a sexually agential child, I refer to all children who must attend to the installation of proper sexual identity and its expression in gender norms.

30 Kathleen L. Spencer, "Rescuing the Female Child: The Fiction of Joanna Russ," *Science Fiction Studies* 17 (1990): 168.

31 Jeanne Cortiel, *Demand My Writing: Joanna Russ/Feminism/Science Fiction* (Liverpool, U.K.: Liverpool University Press, 1999), 129.

32 Russ, "Recent Feminist Utopias," 80.

33 Russ's later novel *The Two of Them,* with a foreword by Sarah LeFanu (Middletown, Conn.: Wesleyan University Press, 2005), addresses this question. Although I cannot indulge in a full reading of this novel here, suffice it to say that the novel's hero, Irene Waskiewicz, another Trans-Temporal agent, wants to rescue twelve-year-old Zubeydeh and her mother, Zumurrud, from the patriarchal culture of Ka'abah. Her failure to rescue the older woman ultimately shows Irene the limitations of her "enlightened" relationship with her lover and partner, Ernst, who will not let her take the older woman. This suggests that the focus on the younger woman results from the continued reluctance of patriarchal culture to value older women. The dynamic here, though, is more complex than it first appears. Zumurrud doesn't want to leave. In her desire to kidnap Zumurrud, Irene forgets about Dunya, Zumurrud's sister, whom the family keeps locked in a small room inside the family compound and whom the novel explicitly links to

the narrator of Charlotte Perkins Gilman's "The Yellow Wallpaper." All three women suffer, but Irene cannot save them all, even if she could literally take them all off the planet. Instead, she realizes that all four of them need radical structural change rather than any straightforward rescue. In effect, she realizes that there is no outside, no utopia, no place to which she can take them. On the other hand, Russ's authorial intrusion in the novel—she steps into the text to fictionalize a boy child whom Zubeydeh had insisted they rescue—reasserts the priority of *women* over structural roles. The novel is apposite in many ways to Russ's thinking about rescue.

34 Kincaid, *Child-Loving,* 7.

35 Leo Bersani, *The Freudian Body: Psychoanalysis and Art* (New York: Columbia University Press, 1986), 63. On perversity and narrative form, see Paul Morrison, "End Pleasure," *GLQ* 1, no. 1 (1993): 53–63. On children and narrative, see Ellis Hansen, "Knowing Children: Desire and Interpretation in *The Exorcist,*" in Bruhm and Hurley, *Curiouser,* 107–36.

36 Russ, "Recent Feminist Utopias," 83.

37 LeFanu, "Reader as Subject," 178.

38 Kincaid, *Child-Loving,* 90.

39 Here I am thinking of the "rescue thematic" in works like Tipper Gore's *Raising PG Kids in an X-Rated Society* (Nashville, Tenn.: Abingdon Press, 1987) and Christine Hoff Summer's *The War against Boys* (New York: Simon and Schuster, 2000).

40 Jacques Derrida, "Signature, Event, Context," in *Basic Writings,* ed. Barry Stocker (New York: Routledge, 2007), 125. Russ famously denounced "patriarchal theory" in her "Letter to Susan Koppleman," in *To Write Like a Woman: Essays in Feminism and Science Fiction,* 171–77 (Bloomington: Indiana University Press, 1995). Although some of her hostility seems symptomatic of a particular time and place, the letter issues a necessary challenge to the deification of a small lineage of male philosophers. In this case, I think that although Russ's and Derrida's texts engage different conversations, they both aim to counter what Russ calls "the enormous social forces" (173) that keep intact the relationship between presence and salvation.

41 Judith Butler, "Burning Acts: Injurious Speech," in *Performativity and Performance,* ed. Andrew Parker and Eve Kosofsky Sedgwick (New York: Routledge, 1995), 198.

42 Spencer, "Rescuing the Female Child," 173.

43 LeFanu, "Reader as Subject," 174. In an insightful recent essay, Tess Williams, "Castaway: Carnival and Sociobiological Satire in *We Who Are About To . . . ,*" in *On Joanna Russ,* ed. Farah Mendlesohn, 210–25 (Middletown, Conn.: Wesleyan University Press, 2009), regards the novel as an example

of Bakhtinian satire. Although I share many of Williams's critical attitudes, including most importantly her identification of Lori as "a particular site of anti-utopian satire" (215), my reading favors a narrower rubric than "carnival" allows. Rather than reading the novel as "acting to destabilize much of late twentieth-century mainstream Western culture" (210), I focus on its conversation with feminist goals and tactics. I hope that my work, by so locating the novel, has helped to elucidate *why* Russ might want to undermine the "rescued female child" (215) theme.

44 Roland Barthes, *The Pleasure of the Text,* trans. Richard Miller (New York: Noonday Press, 1973), 10.

45 Joanna Russ, "When It Changed," in *The Zanzibar Cat,* 10–21 (New York: Baen Books, 1984).

46 Edelman, *No Future,* 68.

47 Lori is also the name of the first hybrid human–alien child in *Darkover Landfall.*

48 Russ, *We Who Are About To . . . ,* 57.

49 Lauren Berlant, "Live Sex Acts (Parental Advisory: Explicit Material)," in Bruhm and Hurley, *Curiouser,* 61.

50 Russ, *We Who Are About To . . . ,* 95.

51 Something uncomfortable lurks in this too-easy critical killing off of Lori. In fact, Lori's vitality will not be subdued. Even in the moments before her death, she camps, sulks, and arrogantly demands attention. The narrator's description—"I shot her in the back of the head. Did it with the gas gun, shrugging it from my sleeve, practically touching her hair" (95)—makes the act of shooting a species of caress.

52 Spencer, "Rescuing the Female Child," 175.

53 Landon, "Eve at the End of the World," 65.

54 I have not been able to locate the origin of this phrase.

55 This could also reference theater performances. It is compelling to consider *We* as a kind of mixed-media performance. We might see the narrative contained on the pocket voice recorder, which is like television broadcast in its reproducibility, as generated through the performative equivalent of a play performed for an audience of eight. My thanks to Carrie Hintz for this insight.

56 Derrida, "Signature, Event, Context," 118.

57 Ibid.

58 It is true that the narrator relates her decision to print out a transcript of her vocoder diary. The final pages, however, record her actions *after* she prints out the transcript and leaves it under a rock. The novel, in other words, gives us one more false lead in our search for narrative consistency.

3. Planet

1   Cormac McCarthy, *The Road* (New York: Vintage, 2006).

2   Luce Irigaray, *Speculum of the Other Woman* (Ithaca, N.Y.: Cornell University Press, 1985), 243.

3   Mary Wilson Carpenter, "Representing Apocalypse: Sexual Politics and the Violence of Revelation," in *Postmodern Apocalypse: Theory and Cultural Practice at the End,* ed. Richard Dellamora (Philadelphia: University of Pennsylvania Press, 1995), 110.

4   Naomi Morgenstern, "Postapocalyptic Responsibility: Patriarchy at the End of the World in Cormac McCarthy's *The Road,*" *Differences* 25, no. 2 (2014): 37.

5   Martin Heidegger, "Letter on Humanism," in *Basic Writings,* ed. David Farrell Krell (San Francisco: Harper, 1977), 242.

6   Thacker, *In the Dust of This Planet,* 5.

7   Morton, *Hyperobjects,* 106.

8   In a television interview, McCarthy tells Winfrey of his inspiration for the novel. He was in a secluded motel room while traveling with his son, who was nine years old at the time. From his window one night he saw fires burning on a nearby hill. The contrast with his sleeping son's face inspired him to write. "Exclusive Interview with Cormac McCarthy," *The Oprah Winfrey Show,* aired June 6, 2007.

9   William Kennedy, "Left Behind," *The New York Times Book Review,* October 8, 2006, P.1; Bob Hoover, "Nowhere to Hide: Everybody Loses in McCarthy's End Game," *Pittsburgh Post-Gazette,* October 1, 2006, E5; Charles McGrath, "At World's End, Honing a Father/Son Dynamic," *New York Times,* May 27, 2008, E1.

10 For more on geophilosophy and the ungrounded Earth, see Ben Woodard, *On Ungrounded Earth: Towards a New Geophilosophy* (Brooklyn, N.Y.: Punctum Books, 2013).

11 On *oikos* and ecology, see Angela Mitropoulus, "Oikopolitics, and Storms," *The Global South* 3, no. 1 (2009): 66–92.

12 Plato, *Timaeus,* trans. Francis Cornford, ed. Oskar Piest (New York: Macmillan, 1959). In *Raising the Tone of Philosophy,* ed. and trans. Peter Fenves (Baltimore: The Johns Hopkins University Press, 1993), Jacques Derrida remarks on the frequency with which "the Persian and Zoroastrian heritage up to the very numerous Jewish and Christian apocalypses . . . inscribe this or that text of Plato" (136).

13 John Sallis, *Chorology: On Beginning in Plato's Timaeus* (Bloomington: Indiana University Press, 1999), 65.

14 See also Emanuela Bianchi, "Receptacle/*Chōra*: Figuring the Errant Feminine," *Hypatia: Journal of Feminist Theory* 21, no. 4 (2006): 124–46, and Irina Aristarkhova, *Hospitality of the Matrix: Philosophy, Biomedicine, and Culture* (New York: Columbia University Press, 2012).

15 Sallis, *Chorology,* 99.

16 Plato, *Timaeus,* 47. Much as Freud admits his inability to fully understand how girls experience the Oedipus complex, Timaeus admits that he cannot account for the necessity of necessity in his account, saying, "You must not demand the explanation of me" (47).

17 Both Jacques Derrida and Emmanuel Levinas make congruent points. See Derrida, "Chora," in *On the Name,* ed. Thomas Dutoit, trans. David Wood, John P. Leavy Jr., and Ian MacLeod (Stanford, Calif.: Stanford University Press, 1995), and Levinas, *Totality and Infinity: An Essay on Exteriority,* trans. Alphonso Lingis (Pittsburgh, Pa.: Duquesne University Press, 1969).

18 Judith Butler, *Bodies That Matter: On the Discursive Limits of "Sex"* (New York: Routledge, 1993), 41.

19 Emanuela Bianchi names this same quality "the errant feminine." See her "Receptacle/*Chōra.*"

20 Arendt, *Human Condition,* 22.

21 This discussion bears on my reading of *The Children of Men,* which posits a world whose agriculture is fine but whose human women have lost the capacity to conceive. See chapter 5.

22 Arendt coined this term. Her use of it precedes both Foucault's and Agamben's.

23 We should hear in this separation the division that obscures the identity of the *chora* and the *oikos.*

24 Arendt, *Human Condition,* 47.

25 Morton makes a similar point via the term *hyperobject,* which he applies to anything massively extended in time whether or not it is of human manufacture. Morton, *Hyperobjects,* 1.

26 Fredric Jameson, *Archaeologies of the Future: The Desire Called Utopia and Other Science Fictions* (London: Verso, 2005), 199. Jameson fails to attribute this statement, saying only "as someone has observed" (199). That someone is almost certainly Slavoj Žižek, who says it in the 2005 film *Zizek!,* directed by Astra Taylor.

27 McCarthy, *Road,* 23. Calling to mind the 1971 Coca-Cola advertising campaign theme song "I'd Like to Teach the World to Sing/I'd Like to Buy the World a Coke."

28 Arendt, *Human Condition,* 53. Arendt's table references Marx's famous

analysis of commodity fetishism in *Capital, Vol. 1: A Critique of Political Economy,* ed. Fredrich Engels (New York: The Modern Library, 2011), 81.

29 My gratitude to Robert Reid-Pharr for suggesting this phrase to me.

30 Interestingly, Teresa de Lauretis argues for the consonance of narrative expectations and the rhythmic expectations of intercourse. See her *Alice Doesn't.*

31 Frank Kermode, "Endings, Continued," in *Languages of the Unsayable: The Play of Negativity in Literature and Literary Theory,* ed. Sanford Budick and Wolfgang Iser (New York: Columbia University Press, 1989), 91.

32 For another viewpoint on mapping, see Jameson, *Postmodernism,* 413–18.

33 Jameson, *Archaeologies of the Future,* 199.

34 See, e.g., Ron Charles's review of the novel for the *Washington Post.*

35 "Ely" is a pseudonym, a road-name.

36 Jacques Derrida, *Specters of Marx: The State of Debt, the Work of Mourning, and the New International,* trans. Peggy Kamuf, with an introduction by Bernd Magnus and Stephen Cullenberg (New York: Routledge, 1994), 172. Morton uses the expression "strange stranger" to capture the intimacy of the stranger within. See his *Hyperobjects,* 129–30.

37 Derrida, *Specters of Marx,* 173.

38 Giorgio Agamben, *The Coming Community,* trans. Michael Hardt (Minneapolis: University of Minnesota Press, 1993), 105, 1.

39 Derrida, *Raising the Tone of Philosophy,* 121.

40 Jacques Derrida, *Of Grammatology,* trans. Gayatri Spivak (Baltimore: The Johns Hopkins University Press, 1997), 5.

41 Pheng Cheah, "'Mattering': Rev. of *Bodies That Matter: On the Discursive Limits of "Sex"* by Judith Butler and *Volatile Bodies: Toward a Corporeal Feminism* by Elizabeth Grosz," *Diacritics* 26, no. 1 (1996): 134.

42 Jacques Derrida, "Différence," in *Margins of Philosophy,* trans. Alan Bass (Chicago: University of Chicago Press, 1982), 394.

43 Aristarkhova, *Hospitality of the Matrix,* 21.

44 Ibid., 25; Bianchi, "Receptacle/*Chōra,*" 137–38.

4. Birth

1 See chapter 3 for my use of this term. For more on the fold as a philosophical concept, see Deleuze, who uses it to discuss the process of mattering, as in origami pleats or cell mitosis. I adopt it here to indicate the multiplicity of domains and modes of expression that make up the child-figure as well as to intimate the generativity of the child-figure, its ability to iterate folds. See Gilles Deleuze, *The Fold: Leibniz and the Baroque,* trans. and with a foreword by Tom Conley (Minneapolis: University of Minnesota Press,

1992), 86–95; Gilles Deleuze, *Foucault,* trans. Sean Hand, with a foreword by Paul Bove (Minneapolis: University of Minnesota Press, 1988), 101–30; Deleuze and Guattari, *A Thousand Plateaus,* 41–47.

2   Edelman, *No Future,* 86.

3   See my discussion of the face in the introduction.

4   Theodore Roosevelt, "Address to the National Congress of Mothers, March 1905," in *The Yellow Wallpaper,* ed. Dale Bauer (New York: Bedford/St. Martin's, 1998), 204.

5   Alys Eve Weinbaum, *Wayward Reproductions: Genealogies of Race and Nation in Transatlantic Modern Thought* (Durham, N.C.: Duke University Press, 2004), 5.

6   I am indebted to Nicole Shukin's sophisticated analysis of the relations encoded in the notion of stock. See Nicole Shukin, *Animal Capital: Rendering Life in Biopolitical Times* (Minneapolis: University of Minnesota Press, 2009).

7   *The Century of the Child* (New York: Knockerbocker Press, 1912) was the title of an influential 1909 monograph by Ellen Key that advocated for the centrality of the child to a well-functioning society. On biopolitics, see Michael Dillon and Luis Labo-Guerrero's essay "The Biopolitical Imaginary of Species-Being," *Theory, Culture, and Society* 26, no. 1 (2009): 1–23.

8   Eve Kosofsky Sedgwick, *Touching Feeling: Affect, Pedagogy, Performativity* (Durham, N.C.: Duke University Press, 2003), 141.

9   In this connection, see Dorothy Roberts's *Killing the Black Body: Race, Reproduction, and the Meaning of Liberty* (New York: Knopf, 1997) and her excoriating exposure of the structuring exploitation of women of color in reproductive services and of the differential treatment of and access to women's reproductive health services for wealthy white women and women of color. As Roberts makes clear, racial oppression merely changes form under conditions of neoliberalism. See also chapter 5 in this book.

10   My thanks to Annie McClanahan for bringing this point to my attention. Melinda Cooper, *Life as Surplus: Biotechnology and Capitalism in the Neoliberal Era* (Seattle: University of Washington Press, 2008), 60.

11   Somatic capitalism does much of the same work as biocapitalism, as both are about the financialization of biomaterials. I give preference to somatic capitalism (and the key concept of the next chapter, the new enclosures of reproduction) despite the existing concept to emphasize that this is not just a logic of the market but also a transformed relationship to the body. On biocapital, see Michael A. Peters and Priya Venkatesan, "Biocapitalism and the Politics of Life," *Geopolitics, History, and International Relations* 2, no. 2 (2010): 100–122.

12 For a convincing reading of postmodernism in terms of this activation of subindividual capacities, or what he calls the "postbiological," see Colin Milburn, "Nano/Splatter: Disintegrating the Postbiological Body," *New Literary History* 36, no. 2 (2005): 283–311.

13 Stockton, *Queer Child.*

14 Consider for example the profusion-as-destitution caused by red tides.

15 Weinbaum, *Wayward Reproductions,* 2.

16 Foucault, *History of Sexuality 1,* 146.

17 Valerie Hartouni, *Cultural Conceptions: On Reproductive Technologies and the Remaking of Life* (Minneapolis: University of Minnesota Press, 1997), 32.

18 See in particular Rosalind Petchesky, "Fetal Images: The Power of Visual Culture in the Politics of Reproduction," *Feminist Studies* 13, no. 2 (1987): 263–92, and Carol Stabile, "Shooting the Mother: Fetal Photography and the Politics of Disappearance," *Camera Obscura* 28 (January 1992): 179–205.

19 Donna Haraway, "The Promise of Monsters: A Regenerative Politics for Inappropriate/d Others," in *Cultural Studies,* ed. Lawrence Grossberg, Cary Nelson, and Paula A. Treichler (New York: Routledge, 1992), 178.

20 Sarah Franklin, "The Cyborg Embryo: Our Path to Transbiology," *Theory, Culture, and Society* 23, no. 7–8 (2006): 168.

21 Lauren Berlant, "America, 'Fat,' the Fetus," *boundary 2* 21, no. 3 (1994): 147.

22 Margaret Atwood, *In Other Worlds: SF and the Human Imagination* (New York: Doubleday, 2011), 87.

23 Darki Suvin, *Metamorphosis of Science Fiction: On the Poetics and History of a Literary Genre* (New Haven, Conn.: Yale University Press, 1979); Carl Freedman, *Critical Theory and Science Fiction* (Hanover, N.H.: Wesleyan University Press, 2000); Earl Jackson Jr., *Strategies of Deviance: Studies in Gay Male Representation* (Bloomington: Indiana University Press, 1995).

24 Jackson, *Strategies of Deviance,* 102.

25 Sarah LeFanu, *To Write Like a Woman: Feminism and Science Fiction* (Bloomington: Indiana University Press, 1988), 4. Both *feminist* and *science fiction* are contentious terms for Atwood.

26 Heather Latimer, "Popular Culture and Reproductive Politics: *Juno, Knocked-Up,* and the Enduring Legacy of *The Handmaid's Tale,*" *Feminist Theory* 10, no. 2 (2009): 213, 217.

27 That is to say that the choice that Offred's mother and her friends celebrate is turned back by Gilead as a deluded form of subjection to men's sexual needs. What Gilead has restored, the Aunts tell them, is the celebration of life that was denied them by radical feminism.

28 Anne Balsamo, "Public Pregnancies and Cultural Narratives of Surveillance," in *Revisioning, Women, Health, and Healing,* ed. Adele E. Clarke and Virginia L. Olesen (New York: Routledge, 1999), 236.

29 Susan Squier, "Negotiating Boundaries: From Assisted Reproduction to Assisted Replication," in *Playing Dolly: Technocultural Formations, Fantasies, and Fictions of Assisted Reproduction,* ed. E. Ann Kaplan and Susan Squier (New Brunswick, N.J.: Rutgers University Press, 1999), 102, 111.

30 Lynn Margulis and Dorion Sagan, *What Is Sex?* (New York: Nevraumont, 1997), 19.

31 Margaret Atwood, *The Handmaid's Tale* (New York: Anchor Books, 1986).

32 In a excursus on *Handmaid's Tale* in the context of her reading of *Children of Men,* Sarah Trimble calls attention to the context implied by the presence of the colonies and the expulsion of all people of color—"the children of Ham" (83) in the world of Gilead—to those colonies. Trimble argues that this is evidence that the novel primarily encodes fears of the decline of the white race, an explanation also endorsed by Professor Pieixoto, the condescending historian whose lecture about the reconstructed narrative ends the novel. See her "Maternal Back/grounds in *Children of Men*: Notes toward an Arendtian Biopolitics," *Science Fiction Film and Television* 4, no. 2 (2011): 249–70.

33 As Sharon Rose Wilson explains, however, the name Offred offers a range of subversive connotations to astute readers. Most prominently, its encoding of the word *red* connects Offred both to the Red Cap fairy tale tradition and to the color's connection to political dissent. Read slant, Offred resembles the word *offered.* See Wilson, *Margaret Atwood's Fairy-Tale Sexual Politics* (Jackson: University of Mississippi Press, 1993).

34 It is worth noting that the second half of the novel, which concerns an illicit romance between Offred and the household chauffeur Nick, also reveals a sexual underground. Offred is courted by the Commander and eventually taken to a nightclub where sex outside of the Ceremony takes place. This section extends Atwood's critique of gendered relations of power around sex and sexuality.

35 Latimer, "Popular Culture and Reproductive Politics," 213.

36 Arendt, *Human Condition,* 134.

37 Mel Y. Chen, *Animacies: Biopolitics, Racial Mattering, and Queer Affect* (Durham, N.C.: Duke University Press, 2012), 4.

38 Atwood, *Oryx and Crake,* 18.

39 This echoes my discussion of *Never Let Me Go* in the introduction.

40 Which is not to say that these checkpoints are not also fraught with the gendered dimensions of power that accompany surveillance. Jimmy's mother,

who eventually joins the resistance, rants about the disproportionate use of strip-searching by the male guards on the women of the compound (51). In an allusion to Offred's story, Jimmy's mother's accomplice is one of the guards (60).

41 Child sexual slavery is an important theme in the novel. That these various forms of property relationship exist on a continuum rather than occupying their usual polarities of legal–illegal is one of the novel's interventions and deserves further consideration than I give it here.

42 For Gerry Canavan, in his "Hope, but None for Us: Ecological Science Fiction and the End of the World in Margaret Atwood's *Oryx and Crake* and *The Year of the Flood*," *LIT: Literature Interpretation Theory* 23, no. 2 (2012): 138–59, the novel "effectively destabilize[s] the affective coordinates of post-apocalyptic fiction, in which the post-apocalyptic landscape is a horror and the pre-apocalyptic landscape the longed-for object of nostalgia" (141).

43 Atwood, *In Other Worlds,* 128–41.

44 Margaret Atwood, *Payback: Debt and the Shadow Side of Wealth* (Toronto, Ont.: House of Anansi Press, 2008).

45 Atwood, *In Other Worlds,* 129.

46 Atwood, *Oryx and Crake,* 295.

47 Ibid., 206.

48 Barad, "Nature's Queer Performativity," 47.

49 And in case we had any confusion about the biological basis of the fungible relations between sex and violence, the Watson-Crick labs give us the example of a mood-sensing wallpaper whose major commercial flaw is that the embedded energy-sensing algae can't distinguish between lust and rage.

50 Atwood, *In Other Worlds,* 66ff.

51 The full ambivalence of this phrase comes through in its source: Commander Fred, Offred's Commander in Atwood's *Handmaid's Tale,* 211.

52 Margaret Atwood, *Survival: A Thematic Guide to Canadian Literature* (Toronto, Ont.: House of Anansi Press, 2013), 30.

53 Margaret Atwood, *The Blind Assassin* (New York: Anchor Books, 2000), 344.

54 Atwood, *MaddAddam,* 385.

55 Ursula K. Le Guin, "The Carrier Bag Theory of Fiction," in *The Ecocriticism Reader,* ed. Cheryll Glotfelty and Harold Fromm, 149–55 (Athens: University of Georgia Press, 1999).

56 Haraway, *When Species Meet,* 72. See the introduction to this book for a broader discussion of the face.

57 Donna Haraway, "SF: Science Fiction, Speculative Fabulation, String

Figures, So Far," *Ada: Journal of Gender, New Media, and Technology* 3 (2013), http://adanewmedia.org/2013/11/issue3-haraway/.

58 Haraway, *When Species Meet,* 292.

5. Labor

1 Melinda Cooper, *Life as Surplus: Biotechnology and Capitalism in the Neoliberal Era* (Seattle: University of Washington Press, 2008), 11.

2 *Alien,* directed by Ridley Scott, featuring Sigourney Weaver, Tom Skerritt, and John Hurt (Los Angeles, Calif.: Twentieth Century-Fox, 1979).

3 Sarah Trimble, "(White) Rage: Affect, Neoliberalism, and the Family in *28 Days Later* and *28 Weeks Later,*" *Review of Education, Pedagogy, and Cultural Studies* 3, no. 2 (2010): 296.

4 Eugene Thacker, *The Global Genome: Biotechnology, Politics, and Culture* (Boston: MIT Press, 2005), 175.

5 My thanks to Julian Gill-Peterson for suggesting this phrasing.

6 Franklin, *Dolly Mixtures,* 170.

7 An interesting place to look for evidence of this attitude outside of popular media is in the increasing expenditure of investment capital on agricultural land. See the Oakland Institute's 2014 report "Down on the Farm: Wall Street: America's New Farmer," http://www.oaklandinstitute.org/down-on-the-farm. See also Michelle Murphy, "Economization of Life: Calculative Infrastructures of Population and Economy," in *Relational Architectural Ecologies: Architecture, Nature, Subjectivity,* ed. Peg Rawes, 139–55 (New York: Routledge, 2013).

8 For a different sense of what extinction narratives can do, see Stephanie S. Turner, "Open-Ended Stories: Extinction Narratives in Genome Time," *Literature and Medicine* 26, no. 1 (2007): 55–82, and Robert Mitchell, "Sacrifice, Individuation, and the Economics of Genomics," *Literature and Medicine* 26, no. 1 (2007): 126–58.

9 Franklin, *Dolly Mixtures,* 169.

10 While I am not able to give this more than cursory consideration, it is worth noting that this point was made extensively and emphatically by Susan Griffin in *Women and Nature: The Roaring inside Her* (New York: Perennial Books, 1978) and by Carolyn Merchant in *Women, Ecology, and the Scientific Revolution* (San Francisco: Harper and Row, 1980) and forms a core of ecofeminist writings more generally. See Carol J. Adams and Lori Gruen, eds., *Ecofeminism: Feminist Intersections with other Animals and the Earth* (New York: Bloomsbury, 2014).

11 Thacker, *Global Genome,* 201.

12 Ellen Meiksins Wood, *The Origin of Capitalism: A Longer View* (New York: Verso, 2002), 108. See also Ashley Dawson, "Introduction: The New Enclosures," *New Formations* 69 (2010): 8–23. For an account that considers reproduction as labor, see Silvia Federici, *Revolution at Point Zero: Housework, Reproduction, and Feminist Struggle* (Oakland, Calif.: PM Press, 2012).

13 *Children of Men,* directed by Alfonso Cuarón, featuring Clive Owen, Julianne Moore, and Michael Caine (Los Angeles, Calif.: Universal, 2007).

14 *The Possibility of Hope,* directed by Alfonso Cuarón, featuring Slavoj Žižek, Naomi Klein, and James Lovelock (Los Angeles, Calif.: Universal, 2007).

15 A number of feminist theorists have written on the subject of the alien–human hybrid. See esp. Susan Squier, "Interspecies Reproduction: Xenogenic Desire and the Feminist Implications of Hybrids," *Cultural Studies* 12, no. 1 (1998): 360–81; Alina Ferreira, "Primate Tales: Interspecies Pregnancy and Chimerical Beings," *Science Fiction Studies* 35, no. 2 (2008): 223–37; and Sarah Kember, "No Humans Allowed? The Alien in/as Feminist Theory," *Feminist Theory* 12, no. 2 (2011): 183–99.

16 My thanks to Robert Reid-Pharr and Rachel Buff, each of whom made this point to me.

17 Thanks to Shane Vogel for bringing this point to my attention.

18 Alexander G. Weheliye, *Habeas Viscus: Racializing Assemblages, Biopolitics, and Black Feminist Theories of the Human* (Durham, N.C.: Duke University Press, 2014), 2. See also Agamben, *Homo Sacer.*

19 Robin Bernstein makes a related point in her "Tender Angels, Insensate Pickaninnies," in *Racial Innocence: Performing American Childhood from Slavery to Civil Rights,* 30–69 (New York: New York University Press, 2011). Her reading of the reciprocal domination of and detachment from the flesh lacks Weheliye's third term and so is less dynamic.

20 But also as surplus feeling. I am not doing justice here to the fullness of Weheliye's subtle and sustained elaboration of this concept.

21 See Edward E. Baptist's *The Half Has Never Been Told: Slavery and the Making of American Capitalism* (New York: Basic Books, 2014).

22 Dorothy Roberts, *Killing the Black Body: Race, Reproduction, and the Meaning of Liberty* (New York: Vintage, 1997), 9.

23 Weheliye, *Habeas Viscus,* 73.

24 Kara Walker, *A Subtlety, or the Marvelous Sugar Baby,* May 10–July 6, 2014, http://creativetime.org/projects/karawalker/.

25 Audie Cornish, "Artist Kara Walker Draws Us into Bitter History with Something Sweet," National Public Radio, May 16, 2014, http://www.npr.org/2014/05/16/313017716/artist-kara-walker-draws-us-into-bitter-history-with-something-sweet.

26 Jane Bennett, *Vibrant Matter: A Political Ecology of Things* (Durham, N.C.: Duke University Press, 2010), 23.

27 Franklin, *Dolly Mixtures,* 172.

28 On the importance of the background images in the film, see Trimble, "Maternal Back/grounds."

29 Foucault, *Security, Territory, Population,* 73, 349.

30 Ibid., 351.

31 Under conditions of generational enslavement, the state of the child followed that of the mother.

32 Whatever the Human Project might or might not be, the film gives us no reason to suspect that it will not be another player in the global skirmish to control reproduction.

33 Sara Ahmed's reading of *Children of Men* takes up many of the same issues I do, but to very different effect. See her "Happy Futures," in *The Promise of Happiness,* 160–99 (Durham, N.C.: Duke University Press, 2010).

34 On this U.S. Supreme Court ruling, see Paul A. Lombardo, *Three Generations, No Imbeciles: Eugenics, the Supreme Court, and* Buck v. Bell (Baltimore: The Johns Hopkins University Press, 2008).

35 For the full version of this argument, see Karen Weingarten, *Abortion in the American Imagination: Between Life and Choice, 1880–1940* (New Brunswick, N.J.: Rutgers University Press, 2014).

36 Robin Truth Goodman, *Infertilities: Exploring Fictions of Barren Bodies* (Minneapolis: University of Minnesota Press, 2001), 59.

37 Nicholas Francis Cooke, *Satan in Society* (1876; repr., New York: Arno Press, 1974), 155.

38 Elaine Tyler May, *Barren in the Promised Land: Childless Americans and the Pursuit of Happiness* (New York: Basic Books, 1995), 65.

39 Ibid.

40 For more on Sims, see Terri Kapsalis, *Public Privates: Performing Gynecology from Both Ends of the Speculum* (Durham, N.C.: Duke University Press, 1997), and Harriet Washington, *Medical Apartheid: Experimentations on Black Americans from Colonial Times to the Present* (New York: Doubleday, 2006).

41 May, *Barren in the Promised Land,* 65–67.

42 R. H. Foote, "The History of Artificial Insemination: Selected Notes and Notables," *Journal of Animal Science* 80 (2002): 4–5.

43 Cooper, *Life as Surplus,* 134.

44 Sarah Franklin, *Biological Relatives: IVF, Stem Cells, and the Future of Kinship* (Durham, N.C.: Duke University Press, 2013).

45 Ibid., 106.

46 Ibid., 29.

47 Cooper, *Life as Surplus,* 135.

48 Daniel Kevles, "Ananda Chakrabarty Wins a Patent: Biotechnology, Law, and Society, 1972–1980," *Historical Studies in the Physical and Biological Sciences* 25, no. 1 (1994): 111–35. For more on Chakrabarty and relevant patent law, see Sheldon Krimsky, *Biotechnics and Society: The Rise of Industrial Genetics* (Westport, Conn.: Praeger, 1991), 47–49.

49 Ibid., 111–12.

50 Haraway, *Modest_Witness@Second_Millennium,* 78.

51 Ibid., 80.

52 Heather Latimer, "Bioreproductive Futurism: The Pregnant Refugee in Alfonso Cuaron's *Children of Men,*" *Social Text 108* 29, no. 3 (2011): 69. See also her *Reproductive Acts: Sexual Politics in North American Fiction and Film* (Montreal, Quebec: McGill-Queen's University Press, 2013).

53 Latimer, "Bioreproductive Futurism," 69.

54 Haraway, *Modest_Witness@Second_Millennium,* 80.

55 Ronald D. Moore and Carla Robinson, "The Farm," *Battlestar Galactica,* season 2, episode 5, directed by Rod Hardy, aired August 12, 2005 (Los Angeles, Calif.: Universal, 2010).

56 Although beyond the scope of this chapter, it is worth noting that this is not the only simulacrum of a hospital room in contemporary science fiction television used to carry out experiments in fertility. In the episode "Maternity Leave" of the ABC science fiction series *Lost* (that also aired in 2006), the pregnant Claire Littleton is taken against her will as an experimental test subject to find a cure for the infertility that plagues the island where her plane crash-landed. The two sequences bear many structural similarities. Dawn Lambertson, "Maternity Leave," *Lost,* season 2, episode 15, directed by Jack Bender, aired March 1, 2006 (Burbank, Calif.: ABC Studios, 2010).

57 On the long-standing relations between fertility, desire, labor, capital, race, and gender in America, see Hortense J. Spillers, *Black, White, and in Color: Essays on American Literature and Culture* (Chicago: University of Chicago Press, 2003). On the different ways in which white and African American children's innocence has been imagined in American culture, see Bernstein, *Racial Innocence.*

58 The name of the ship seems to allude to the *Alien* sequel *Alien: Resurrection,* and indeed the interior of the ship mimics H. R. Giger's original designs for the film franchise. Not surprisingly, *Alien: Resurrection* is also about inhibitions to technological reproductions. *Alien: Resurrection,* directed by Jean-Pierre Jeunot, featuring Sigourney Weaver and Winona Ryder (Los Angeles, Calif.: Twentieth Century Fox, 1997).

59 Theo is, of course, also the name of the protagonist in *Children of Men.* My thanks to Tyler Bradway for bringing this connection to my attention.

60 In *The Possibility of Hope,* ecologist James Lovelock compares the human species to a disease of the Earth.

61 See Hope Shand, "The New Enclosures: Why Civil Society and Governments Need to Look beyond Life Patenting," *CR: The New Centennial Review* 3, no. 2 (2003): 187–92.

62 Ronald D. Moore, "Daybreak: Part 2 & 3," *Battlestar Galactica,* season 4, episode 20, directed by Michael Rymer, aired March 20, 2009 (Los Angeles, Calif.: Universal, 2010).

Conclusion

1 Arendt, *Human Condition,* 70.

2 Paul J. Crutzen, "Geology of Mankind," *Nature* 415, no. 23 (2002): 23.

3 Karen Barad, "On Touching: The Inhuman That Therefore I Am," *Differences* 25, no. 5 (2012): 207–23.

4 Richard Grusin, introduction to *The Nonhuman Turn* (Minneapolis: University of Minnesota Press, 2015), vii.

5 In the conclusion of his *Molecular Red: Theory for the Anthropocene* (London: Verso, 2015), McKenzie Wark notes the proliferation of alternative names that have sprung up lately—including Donna Haraway's *Cthuthluscene* and Jussi Parrika's *anthrobscene*—and wonders if there isn't something salutatory about humanists reckoning with a scientific term like *Anthropocene.* I recognize that my proposal for alternative names puts me squarely in this camp, but I hope it is clear that my purpose is less to kvetch than to register an important feature of the Anthropocene. For one example, see Jussi Parikka, *The Anthrobscene* (Minneapolis: University of Minnesota Press, 2014).

6 Agamben, *Homo Sacer.*

7 Edelman, *No Future.*

8 Eugene Thacker uses this term in *In the Dust of This Planet,* 8.

9 Ruth Graham, "Against YA," *Slate,* June 5, 2014, http://www.slate.com /articles/arts/books/2014/06/against_ya_adults_should_be_embarras sed_to_read_children_s_books.html.

10 As of August 2015, that is.

11 Jen Doll, "An Adult YA Addict Comes Clean," *Vulture,* October 6, 2013, http://www.vulture.com/2013/10/thirtysomething-teen-on-young-adult -novels.html.

12 Sarah Seltzer, "I Read and Love Both Bridget Jones's Diary and Faulkner's As I Lay Dying—So What?," *xoJane,* June 9, 2014, http://www.xojane

.com/issues/i-read-and-love-both-bridget-joness-diary-and-faulkners-as
-i-lay-dying-so-what.

13 G. Stanley Hall, *Adolescence, Its Relations to Physiology, Anthropology, Sociology, Sex, Crime, Religion and Education* (New York: D. Appleton, 1904).

14 Although we no longer use the racist eugenic language evident here, popular scientific and legal accounts of the judgmentally impaired teen brain still circulate widely.

15 Roberta Trites, *Disturbing the Universe: Power and Repression in Adolescent Literature* (Iowa City: University of Iowa Press, 2000).

16 Ibid., 3.

17 Madeleine L'Engle, *A Wrinkle in Time* (New York: Farrar, Straus, and Giroux, 1962); Lionel Davidson, *Under Plum Lake* (New York: Knopf, 1980); China Miéville, *Un Lun Dun* (New York: Ballantine Books, 2007); Sherman Alexie, *The Absolutely True Diary of a Part Time Indian* (New York: Little, Brown, 2007).

18 Foucault, *History of Sexuality 1.*

19 John Green, *The Fault in Our Stars* (New York: Dalton Books, 2012).

20 Karen Thompson Walker, *The Age of Miracles* (New York: Random House, 2012), 259.

21 Ibid., 268.

22 *Tree of Life,* directed by Terrence Malick, featuring Brad Pitt and Jessica Chastain (Los Angeles, Calif.: Fox Searchlight, 2011).

23 *Melancholia,* directed by Lars Von Trier, featuring Kirsten Dunst and Kiefer Sutherland (Hvidovre, Denmark: Zentropa, 2011).

24 Steven Shaviro, "Melancholia, or the Romantic Anti-Sublime," *Sequence: Serial Studies in Media, Film, and Music,* http://reframe.sussex.ac.uk/sequence/ereading-for-the-end-of-the-world/.

25 Braidotti, *The Posthuman,* 13.

26 Agamben, *Homo Sacer,* 37.

Index

Rebekah Sheldon is assistant professor of English at Indiana University Bloomington.